No Place but UP!

No Place but UP!

Lance S. Fox

Hardcover ISBN 978-1-105-56605-9
Paperback ISBN 978-1-105-68290-2

In recognition of my teammates and friends of Himalayan Experience, Everest Expedition 2009.

For Bailee Marie and Jordan Stevens,
Never give up on your dreams.

The deafening rumble had a crescendo unlike anything I had ever heard. I sprang from my tent to see an explosion of snow and ice as it hurtled downward, swallowing everything in its path. The white cloud began to mushroom as if an atomic bomb had dropped. It was mid-morning, just three days after several of my teammates and I missed being engulfed by one of these enormous blasts.

It was the largest avalanche yet, its fury swept all the way to the edge of base camp. As the roar subsided and the thick plume of ice crystals settled, an even greater commotion began. Our Sherpa began frantically grabbing shovels, ropes, and other rescue gear. The base camp radios crackled to life, alarmed voices dominated the conversations between expedition leaders, would-be rescuers, and base camp doctors.

It was obvious that the inevitable had occurred. Multiple climbers had been on the route; a route now vanished, along with several of the climbers. For now all we could do was keep vigil as the rescue operation commenced. Two injured climbers would be successfully extracted from the frozen rubble, yet a Sherpa would not be so fortunate. The first victim of the climbing season on Everest had been claimed.

In just over a week we would have to head back into the Khumbu Icefall on our final push for the summit. The same precarious ledge of ice and snow responsible for spawning such devastation would still be there waiting for us. It was just a matter of time before the next wave of terror would come crashing down.

Table of Contents

Foreword

To have a dream is one thing, to dream to climb to the summit of Everest is another. To actually fulfill this dream is considerably more difficult, and for most it is perceived as hugely selfish. However for some, they are not only ready to commit to the hardships of climbing, but along the way they also want to help others who are less fortunate than themselves. Lance Fox is one of those special people in the world who has a burning desire to succeed but also has the disposition that enables him to lend a hand to others around him.

After many years, Lance eventually found the time, money, and effort to undertake the practical part of his dream. Along the way he endured considerable personal pain both physically and mentally, won and lost friendships, put his own life in danger, and became a team player amongst a group of strangers who found themselves grouped together to undertake the same challenge. The difference with Lance is that he also wanted to use his veterinary skills to help the local Sherpa people along the way. Through considerable forethought and lobbying, he was able to secure the required equipment and medicine, enabling him to help local Sherpa farmers whilst he traveled to the foot of Mount Everest, an effort that is appreciated by the same people who were to help Lance so much as he climbed up the icy slopes of the same mountain.

This is an insight into the trials and tribulations that Lance endured during his journey to the top of the world, his innermost feelings and observations on a team that bonded together in this most inhospitable environment. The tears and laughter along the way contribute to everyone's personal journey making them each a stronger person and it is this which makes the eventual success a dream come true, rather than a very real nightmare.

Russell Brice

Introduction

Numerous books have been written about Mount Everest. Some are factual, revealing the history of the mountain while others have focused on the climbing drama and tragedies that have accompanied this iconic peak. This book focuses on the emotional, yet overwhelming positive aspects of climbing the Himalayan giant, made possible by the incredible camaraderie of the team of which I was a part. I also share some of the events in my life, which I believe led me to want to travel to such a desolate, hostile place.

This incredible adventure was orchestrated by Himalayan Experience Ltd. and led by mountaineering legend, Russell Brice. How does one adequately thank a person for helping make a dream come true? I owe Russell, as well as the entire Himalayan Experience support staff, a debt of gratitude. Yes, I experienced tough days on the mountain; however, it was the spirit of the climbers, the work ethic of our porters, the preparedness of our doctor, the skills of our guides, the incredible services of the base camp staff, the decision-making of our leader, and most certainly the awesome power of our Sherpa that ensured the success our expedition experienced.

It was the people I met on this voyage and their contribution on the mountain that made all the suffering, both physical and mental, worthwhile. We may have come together as strangers, but we walked away as family. I learned a lesson about the importance of kinship and the unbreakable bond such relationships create.

Why would anyone want to climb Mount Everest—to intentionally place one's self in harm's way? No, I am not a professional mountaineer. I am a veterinarian by trade but most importantly a husband and father. I simply enjoy the solitude, beauty, and challenge that mountains offer. I have not climbed all over the world and in fact did not start climbing until 2006, just three years prior to my Everest ascent.

There are a handful of true mountaineers in the world, and some are outspoken about the masses of rich Westerners who try to climb Everest. Unfortunately, there are those who, driven mainly by their egos, crowd and litter its slopes. Fortunately, not all Westerners on the mountain are self-centered and careless. The people I met and climbed Everest with came with a purpose beyond self-indulgence. We chose to respect its flanks by removing gear, refuse, and even our biological waste.

Although part of a large group, individually, we were unique, climbing to see what we were made of, to fulfill a quest, and most importantly to live life. I admire those who climb all over the world establishing new routes on both climbed and unclimbed peaks. I hope such individuals will respect that I am not one of them, but I am also not a spoiled socialite. I went to Everest not to conquer the mountain but to conquer a dream.

George Leigh Mallory, a renowned British climber in the early twentieth century, was once asked about his vision to try and be the first person to reach Everest's summit. In 1922, he followed that dream and while he didn't top out, he did come within fifteen hundred feet of it. While on tour in the United States to lecture about this incredible adventure, he was asked something along the line of, "Why bother to climb Mount Everest?" Mallory's proposed response was, "Because it is there." Yes, Everest was and will continue to be there to climb, yet to me his answer referred not to the mountain itself. He climbed the mountain because his dream was there.

When you have a vision to do something, whether simple-minded or extraordinary, why deny yourself the opportunity to pursue it? Mallory may not have reached the summit first or so it is believed (he perished on the mountain during a return trip in 1924), but did he really fail? The debate rages within the mountaineering community as to whether he reached the top, his body discovered in 1999 high on the mountain. His death contradicts the concept that success on a mountain is not just about the summit but rather finishing the climb by returning home alive. Despite the tragic ending, I'd like to think he was successful, not because he did or did not reach the summit, but because he chose to actively engage his dream rather than let it idly pass.

Have you ever read the book, *The Little Engine That Could*? If not, I recommend you visit your local library, bookstore, or favorite literary website and get a copy. It might be considered a children's book, but its storyline applies to all ages. Please allow me to indulge.

A shiny, new engine responsible for pulling boxcars of toys to children waiting on the other side of the mountain breaks down. Engine after engine passes by, unwilling to take on the challenge, then the little blue engine comes along. At first, the engine is not certain it can pull those boxcars of toys up and over the steep slopes.

It is not abnormal to have a little self-doubt when faced with a new challenge. Yet like the little blue engine, we often find that the toughest part of any challenge is the willingness to commit. After making the commitment the engine starts to climb the mountain and begins to say, "I think I can. I think I can. I think I can." William Shakespeare once wrote: *To climb steep hills requires a slow pace at first.*

Yes, we need to be realistic about our goals. Yet I believe that when you have a passion for something, if you are willing to make sacrifices and are committed to working hard, anything is possible. You just have to realize it isn't going to happen overnight but rather piece by piece, step by step. Obstacles may even block part of your way. In the face of adversity I am reminded of Sir Winston Churchill's words: *A pessimist sees the difficulty in every opportunity. An optimist sees the opportunity in every difficulty.*

Has Everest changed my life? In certain ways it has, especially how I view life itself and how much more I value the bond of true friendship. I wish I could mention all of my friends in this book because each one has had and will continue to have a valuable role in my life. The list would be a book itself, a lengthy one I am lucky to have. I have also been blessed with a wonderful family, a great career, and good health. I wish I could say I kept a full head of hair too, but bald is beautiful, right?

Before the Everest journey I had not paid a lot of attention to divine intervention or karma. Yet looking back, certain things have happened in my life for a reason. This includes the journey on Everest and what has followed. I lost what I thought was a valued friendship during this adventure yet fortunately gained many new ones. While some things in life are beyond our control, we are solely responsible for how we act, how we react, and ultimately how we feel.

I am not perfect. I have made poor decisions. I have made my share of mistakes. But isn't life about learning from one's mistakes? Isn't it about trying to become better? Despite the challenges I have faced, some of which have been self-inflicted, I have always walked away having learned a valuable lesson. Such lessons in life guide us along a distinct path.

You too may face a challenge at some point while traveling along. It may be small, or it may be significant. It is not the challenge that will define you but rather how you cope with it, and even more importantly what you learn from it. You can either let the challenge keep you down, or you can pick yourself up and become stronger because of it.

My late grandmother Helen Lukasik, who passed away in 2007, just two years shy of reaching one hundred, played a pivotal role in my life. She was not only the picture perfect definition of a wonderful loving grandmother, she was someone I looked up to immensely. She helped take care of my younger brother and me as our father struggled with cancer and our mother worked hard to provide for the family. I give my grandmother credit for teaching me the value of perseverance.

Everyone has bad days, and I am no different. Yet growing up, whenever I seemed down or was feeling a bit too sorry for myself, Grandma Helen would remind me, "Smile and the world smiles with you. Weep and you weep alone." While it is normal to feel a bit sorry for ourselves when times are tough, prolonged self-pity only conjures further negative energy within yourself and for those around you. Look hard enough and you can find the silver lining that resides in all situations. Finding it will help put a smile back on your face.

As a result you will feel better and so will the people closest to you.

I first coined the phrase No Place but UP! back in 2007, early in my climbing career and have since become the proud owner of its trademark with the United States Patent and Trademark Office. The words apply to more than mountaineering however. Give it some thought, when you feel down and are having a bad day or you think the challenge is too great to overcome, remember that there is no place to go but up.

As you read this book, I hope you will be inspired to pursue with passion the "Everest" that resides within you. When you have that spark moment, hold on to it and never let it go. If you truly believe in it, someday it will unfold before you. Try to avoid falling into that group of individuals who someday say, "I wish I would have done that."

I will end this introduction with perhaps the best quote I have heard to date, which reinforces the importance of dreaming. During a visit to an elementary school in 2010, I asked the children why it's so important to dream. With nervous excitement in his voice, a young boy raised his hand and replied, "If you don't have a dream then you don't have a goal.

Chapter One

The Dream Comes Alive

September 16, 1986. It's just after eight o'clock on what appeared to be a sunny and crisp morning. Lying in my hospital bed doing my best to ignore the pain throbbing inside my broken left leg, I tried to eat breakfast. I was also trying to keep my mind from the emotional pain of thinking about my father, Ronald S. Fox, lying in his own hospital bed just two floors away, fighting for his life. For the past eight years he has been in the battle trenches against the cancerous enemy called Hodgkin's lymphoma. Approximately one month ago, pneumonia landed him in intensive care at Marshfield Hospital, about an hour drive from our Central Wisconsin home.

Just four days earlier I was participating in something I loved, Tri-County High School football. A junior at the time, I was blessed with some of my father's running back skills, skills he showed off during his days on the same field located in Plainfield, Wisconsin. The second game of the season would find our team in Bonduel, Wisconsin.

A single play during the second quarter turned out to be the catalyst of an already challenging September. A sweep play to the right, I chose to run the ball wide towards the sidelines instead of cutting up the middle of the field. Two defenders chased me down as I neared the sidelines, my eyes focused on the corner of the end zone. One tackled me high and the other low, just as I planted my left leg to make the final turn for six more points on the board.

Like a thin stick between two strong hands, my lower left leg snapped leaving my foot positioned almost ninety-degrees to the side. The crescendo of pain was incredible. The emergency responders were there within seconds, along with Coach Knuth. He literally had to sit on my chest to keep me from flopping around like a carp on the shore.

With the leg reset and shock beginning to mask reality, the pain miraculously disappeared. I waved at the spectators, some still gasping in horror, as I was loaded into the ambulance. I was taken to the hospital in nearby Shawano, where the attending emergency physician made an obvious diagnosis.

Hours away, my mother Karen was at my father's bedside diligently praying. Due to the extreme circumstances, the doctors arranged for my transport by ambulance to Marshfield, a ride I remember little because of the pain medication and sedatives. I do recall the look on my mother's face when I finally arrived at the hospital. She must have been thinking, "Could it get much worse?" Lucy Ruffalo, my best friend Barry's mother, was there holding vigil with my mother.

When you grow up in small town America, you grow up with an extended family. Similar to Lucy as a second mother, Barry's father Bob has always been my second father. Barry's older sister Bobbi Jo is the closest thing I will ever have to a sister. She has had my back on numerous occasions. Barry and I weren't always angels and "big sis" helped us avoid some major binds. I will be forever grateful to the Ruffalo family for cradling me as one of their own.

Fast-forward a couple of days. My father had been unable to speak for quite some time, due to the endotracheal tube (ET) traveling down his windpipe. Connected to the other end was the artificial respirator forcing air into his lungs, his own body unable to breathe on its own. This particular day would find my father non-responsive after having had yet another invasive procedure to try and heal his failing body, the cancer now riddled throughout. I was taken by wheelchair to see him, the pain in my leg too intense to stand on crutches. Sitting by his bedside, I reached out for his limp hand. I softly whispered, "Dad, I'm here."

His eyes opened as he squeezed my hand. I immediately began to cry, his grip repeatedly clenching as if to say, "It will be okay." Although still in a zombie-like state, he seemed to focus on my leg encased in thick white plaster, propped up like a tray table. I tried to explain why I was in the wheelchair. As he started to drift off into deep sleep once again, with tears slowly rolling down my cheeks I softly said to him, "I love you, Dad." I did not envision at the time that those would be my last words to the man I so admired and looked up to.

As I tried to eat my cereal the next morning, my mother quietly walked into my room. The look on her face spoke volumes. I knew before the words could be formed that my father was gone. His eight-year struggle with cancer was over, and he was finally at peace. With the wheelchair accompanying the discharge orders, the doctors agreed to let my mother take me home early. The ride home felt brutally long. Was this really happening? The bravery my mother displayed through it all reminded me that this in fact was reality in its ugly form. It was time to face the facts, time to grow up.

It doesn't get much flatter than Central Wisconsin. The lack of elevation is countered by the snow and cold of winter, the state's longest season, or so it seems. Who would have known that growing up with those sub-zero temperatures and ample amounts of snow would eventually prepare me for one of the most extreme places on earth? Born in 1970, I was raised for the majority of my youth in or near the oxygen-rich town of Plainfield, barely above sea level.

Growing up with a lack of mountains seems to make such backdrops all that more intriguing. I am not the first flatlander to become "infected with the climbing bug" nor will I be the last. Simply put, mountains have an allure. They dominate the skyline like ladders reaching toward heaven.

Despite the lack of such ladders, I was fortunate to grow up in an environment that allowed me to explore the great outdoors. My parents, in particular my father, instilled in me a deep love for what Mother Nature has to offer. I enjoyed activities such as hunting, fishing, camping, hiking, canoeing, snowshoeing, and cross-country skiing to name just a few. But climb?

When I returned home from Everest in June of 2009 I discovered a photo lying in the bottom of a box in my basement meant to be found. Taken in June of 1972, when I was just two years old, it shows my dad free climbing a rockface on a steep hill. I'd like to think that even though I was not born into a climbing family, a little bit of the "vertical spirit" was seeded in my blood after all.

In any event, throughout my educational years, I worked hard academically as well as athletically. My high school science teacher, Mr. Thomas Whalley, offered me an opportunity that would change my life. His son Richard was one of my closest friends, as well as a classmate. Tom, his wife Judy, and their kids operated a small family dairy near Hancock, Wisconsin. I started helping Richard with chores before we reached high school age, something that increased in frequency as time went on. Years later Mr. Whalley gave me my very first Holstein dairy calf. She would eventually become one of the cows we would milk on the farm. This early exposure to farm life and Mr. Whalley's mentoring helped mold my future career path.

With one phase of education completed, it was on to college in the fall of 1988. After two years of undergraduate studies, I left the University of Wisconsin-LaCrosse in order to help the Whalley family as a full-time farmhand. I had some big shoes to fill because during my second year of college, my dear friend Richard committed suicide.

During my third year of college I lived with Lucy and Bob Ruffalo in Plainfield (my mother had remarried and moved) so that I could drive back and forth from work and home several times per week to nearby UW-Stevens Point in order to finish my pre-veterinary studies. After helping his family, not to mention myself, emerge from losing Richard, I applied for veterinary school at UW-Madison and managed to get accepted for the graduating class of 1995. It was time to start four more years of intense studies.

Veterinary school was a lot like high school, freshmen through seniors, eighty classmates with lockers, books, and tests galore. Yet this time around I would meet my future wife. As a freshman in a small anatomy lab, I would often walk over to the exam table where Katherine studiously worked. I would pretend I knew what I was talking about when it came to naming the veins, arteries, nerves, and muscles in the specimen laying in front of her.

As they say, the rest is history. We married on August 3, 1996, one year after graduation. We practiced veterinary medicine together for several years at the Elkhorn Veterinary Clinic located in Elkhorn, Wisconsin, not far from her childhood home just east of Janesville in the southern part of our state.

November 20, 1997. Fast-forward eleven years to one more of life's challenges. A reminder that life truly is fragile, our son Jordan Stevens Fox decided he wanted to enter the world six weeks early. Katherine was having lunch with a friend and client when her water suddenly broke. That evening I was overjoyed to become a father.

At first everything appeared fine but after a brief cuddle with our newborn son, the doctor and nurses informed us that Jordan was not breathing properly. Despite his five pound and thirteen ounce frame, his early arrival meant his lungs had not fully developed. He was sedated, an ET tube was inserted down his windpipe, and the artificial respirator was turned on. Because he needed to be in a level 4 neonatal intensive care unit, he was transported by ambulance to St. Mary's Hospital in Madison, the city Kathy and I had recently graduated from.

Nearly doubling our debt from veterinary school loans and making only modest salaries as associate veterinarians, we did not have a lot of extra money lying around. With the hospital a couple hours' drive from home, we were lucky enough to secure a ten-dollar-per-night room at the local Ronald McDonald House, ironically just blocks away from our alma mater. This would be our home for the next eleven days.

Jordan was the gentle giant of the ward, and I remember clearly all of the various tubes entering his body, everything from the umbilical catheter, intravenous line, the nasogastric tube (a tube passed through the nose into the stomach), and of course the ET tube. After about twenty-four hours he was able to breathe without the support of the respirator, one less tube protruding from his tiny figure. With nighttime vigils at his side not possible, my wife and I would sit in our charity room trying to keep our minds from thinking constantly of our son's struggle to survive. Reading books was one way of doing this, although the recent years of intense clinical studies had made reading a less than favorable pastime for me.

One day, however, we made a quick stop at the local bookstore to pick up some new literature. It would prove to be a life-altering visit for me. I purchased the National Geographic Society book *Everest, Mountain without Mercy*. The cover had captured my attention, a picture of Mount Everest in the setting sun. It is a story not only about the famous mountain itself but rather centered around the tragic 1996 disaster which claimed the lives of multiple climbers lost high on the mountain's icy slopes during a freak snowstorm. Something about this book not only captivated my senses, it spawned my vision: to stand on top of the world.

From something as simple as a book, my dream became unlocked from within. I remember breezing through the book from cover to cover in record time. Afterwards I quietly told myself that I would someday go to that mountain. I didn't know how, and I didn't know when, but I knew this was my calling. Could I really accomplish such a feat? Other than my childhood family vacations to take in the views at such national parks as Glacier, Yellowstone, and the Grand Tetons, I had never actually climbed anything other than the occasional tree in my childhood front yard. I think I can. I think I can. I think I can....

My father and I enjoying a Wisconsin winter day together.

Chapter Two

Finding the Climber Within

Life continued at a busy pace. We welcomed into the world our daughter, Bailee Marie Fox, born November 15, 1999. Similar to Jordan she too tried to make her entrance into this world six weeks early. Placenta prevea (a condition where the placenta abnormally attaches across the cervix during pregnancy) caused my wife to hemorrhage early one morning. The doctors were able to stop the bleeding and premature contractions, delaying Bailee's arrival for a few weeks.

I needed to visit my physician shortly after her birth. While not life-threatening, I was diagnosed with cold-air induced asthma. The act of climbing was still not on my close-up radar, so I didn't give the diagnosis a second thought, let alone think about the cold weather five miles higher and halfway across the world. I just learned how to cope with the condition in the cold weather of Wisconsin. I was prescribed an oral asthma medication, which has been my savior, taking it only as needed when working or exercising in chilly temperatures. An inhaler stands by on backup in case of emergency situations.

It was definitely a busy year. Relocation accompanied the arrival of our daughter and the diagnosis of asthma. Ten acres of farmland near New London, Wisconsin became home. Evolving into a horse farm, it is located about fifty miles from a much more popular piece of property, Lambeau Field, in Green Bay. Cheesehead pride is evident throughout our state, but its height peaks in Titletown. That same pride would get the best of me halfway across the world, not to mention a bit higher.

Relocation was also accompanied by a change in direction of my veterinary career. By April 2005, I became a Technical Service Veterinarian with Alpharma Animal Health, a global pharmaceutical company based in New Jersey. I was hired to provide global technical sales and support for their products used to promote the health and well being of food-producing animals, specifically in the dairy industry.

As I settled into my new role, I finally started "living the dream," a phrase I occasionally and cheerfully verbalize when climbing. I was barely thirty-six before I actually felt the experience of climbing a mountain. With my friend John McMonagle of Colorado (originally born and raised in Wisconsin too), and his friend Dr. Jeff Des Jardin, I climbed my first two mountains in July of 2006. As part of the Collegiate Peaks of the Colorado Rocky Mountains, Mt. Harvard, and Mt. Columbia are just two of the fifty-four "fourteeners" (peaks 14,000 feet or higher above sea level) found in that beautiful state.

At 14,420 feet (4395m), Mount Harvard is actually the fifth highest peak in the lower forty-eight states. Green to the sport, I remember giving John a hard time about cutting the straps and tags off his backpack before we started our three-day, two-night adventure. He even cut part of his sleeping mattress pad off to save weight. John was more experienced at this than me and as time went on, I too learned just how precious shaving weight would become.

We started at the Harvard-Columbia loop trailhead at approximately 10,000 feet above sea level, working our way up to establish our campsite close to 12,000 feet. Harvard's summit was tantalizingly close from this point, or so it appeared. After an early morning start the next day and just 100 meters to go, we met a man with a golden retriever coming down from their successful summit bid of both peaks. I thought, "If a dog could do it, I sure as heck could too!"

A bit of scrambling led us to Harvard's summit by mid-morning. What a view and sense of accomplishment. It was better than I could have imagined! After a snack, we continued our plan and traversed over to the ridge leading to Columbia's summit.

On top of Mount Harvard after my very first climb.
Photograph by John McMonagle.

Unfortunately we descended hundreds of feet too far to the left, originally trying to avoid the more technical and exposed ridge between the two peaks. Realizing our error, we stopped to regroup. With a few more calories consumed, we started back up towards the 14,077-foot (4291m) summit high above.

I started to fall behind, a sense of sluggishness escalating from within. Then the headache started and finally the nausea, just as I reached the top of my second fourteener. My first official bout with acute mountain sickness or AMS was upon me. Even though we had taken our time gaining elevation on this trip, my body was not happy with the altitude. Considering that several days earlier I had come directly from 740 feet above sea level, I am grateful it had not been worse.

I did not get to spend much time on Columbia's summit, but with each step down its slopes I grew increasingly stronger and less nauseated. At camp I fully appreciated what we had accomplished. I wanted more. Despite the AMS, I felt as though an eventual Everest bid was a realistic goal after all. Still, climbing a fourteener or two in summer is far different than a peak twice as high, covered in snow. I knew I had to get higher, as well as become proficient on ice and snow.

The collection of mountaineering books rapidly filled the shelves at home. Most captured various stories about Everest itself, like the one that sparked my dream. Several more detailed the proper climbing techniques used in mountaineering. Heck, if a book started the dream why not have one or two to help me pursue it?

The summer of 2007 would find me participating in an expedition-skills course at Rainier Mountaineering Incorporated (RMI) in Ashford, Washington. The guides taught us how to use proper crampon technique, roped travel, self-arrest with an ice axe, crevasse rescue, knot tying, and the invaluable technique of the "rest step."

Climbing requires knowing multiple skills, yet the rest step would prove to be one of the most important facets of mountaineering for me. Step, rest the upper leg muscles for a split second by lightly locking the knee joint, step with the other leg, and repeat the process, so on and so on. Giving the leg muscles a temporary pause in the action, allows them to perform for hours on end without prematurely fatiguing–climb for ninety-minutes, rest for fifteen, climb for ninety-minutes, rest for fifteen. The routine is repeated all day long until you reach the top and/or turn around as needed.

A lot of alpine climbing occurs on snow and ice. A natural phenomenon of glaciers is the large cracks in the ice known as crevasses. Crevasses range in size from ones you can easily step over to those that require manmade bridges (such as ladders or boards) to cross. Then there are those you may not actually see from the surface but unknowingly cross via snow bridges.

Snow bridges may or may not hold a person's weight. Therefore on mountains like Rainier, it is necessary to travel in small groups, each member tied into a common rope between them. If a member should break through a snow bridge, the idea is that his or her partners will stop the fall. This is called roped travel unlike fixed-rope climbing. On bigger mountains, like those found in the Himalayas, a rope is anchored into the mountain along the climbing route. Climbers attach themselves to this rope versus each other.

Crampons are the pointy-looking metal things that climbers attach to the bottom of their boots when traveling on or up ice. Think of chains on tires during winter driving. Ice axes come in all shapes and sizes. Regardless of the type of climbing, most look like a cross between an overgrown hammer and an ice pick on steroids. The ice axe is an essential tool for vertical ice climbing, yet it also serves a greater function during alpine climbs. If a climber suddenly slips and begins to slide down an icy slope, the ice axe is used as a braking mechanism. With your body weight as leverage, the axe's sharp point, called a pick, is driven into the ice in order to slow and eventually stop the fall.

After the skills course, our medium-sized group of climbers and guides, led by senior guide Shaun Sears, headed up the flanks of 14,411 foot (4393m) Mount Rainier via the Emmons Glacier, the largest glacier in the lower forty-eight states. Although not the highest point in the United States, Mt. Rainier is the most glaciated peak that offers a vertical climb of over 9,000 feet. In comparison, Everest is close to a 12,000 vertical foot climb from base camp.

My tent mate was Georgina Miranda from California. Like me, Georgina was a novice climber, this being her first alpine style climb too. Georgina and I have stayed in communication since Rainier, her climbing resume expanding to include peaks all over the world. She climbs not just because she enjoys the mountains but for a far greater but less selfish cause. She founded Climb Take Action (www.climbtakeaction.com), an initiative with the goal of empowering women in the Congo. She continues to be an inspiration as she strives to become a member of the 7 Summits club to draw awareness to this campaign.

After two days of climbing, we set up our high camp at approximately 10,000 feet above sea level. We were now positioned for our summit attempt, lingering just over 4,000 feet above us. We awoke just after midnight, ate some instant oatmeal, and roped up as three-person teams, ice axes ready. Stars filled the night sky, and the air was crisp. By dawn we were close to 13,000 feet, and the view was already proving to be spectacular. To stand above the clouds, knowing you got there under your own power is hard to express with words.

Just before dawn, light snow had started to fall. Just after daylight, it started coming down more steadily. The first avalanche check by our guides revealed a very low risk. An hour later, however, revealed a significant increase in risk. While perched on a 45-degree slope with less than 500 vertical feet to go, we were forced to turn around.

The mountain ultimately decides who visits the summit and who doesn't. Today would not be our day. Two days of down climbing with the storm raging above us, we safely returned to RMI headquarters. Turning around was incredibly tough, yet that decision proved to be an invaluable lesson. No summit is worth one's life or even a single body part. Rainier's summit may have eluded me, yet it gave me cause to go even higher.

The expedition course also showed me the importance of teamwork, listening to your guides, and following your gut instinct. Our team had worked well together and had it not been for the weather, all of us would have topped out. I enjoyed learning from Shaun and the other guides, listening to their every word, and watching their every move. Shaun conveyed he had an interest in veterinary medicine so we talked about my career path and where his own might be headed. My comfort with Shaun grew rapidly, so I decided to confide in him as we came off the mountain.

Back on our first day of the course Shaun had us introduce ourselves to the group as well as overview our climbing aspirations. Confidently, I informed the team I someday envisioned an attempt on Mount Everest. This seemed to perk up Shaun's interest or perhaps catch him off guard. Shaun came across as having a great sense of humor as well as a strong, straightforward work ethic. Big wall climbing percolated through his blood. I figured I would broach the Everest subject again in private to get his honest opinion.

Knowing we were well out of danger on the descent I asked Shaun what he thought about my idea of trying to climb Everest, especially if the opportunity came in the near future.

While he suggested I get higher in our atmosphere to see how my body would react, he also let me know he had friends who had reached the top. Although tough physically, his friends shared if a well conditioned body could withstand the extreme altitude, it was the attitude or mental part that was crucial to one's success. He then provided me with some final words of encouragement. Given my strengths over the past few days, he told me if I could get a bit higher, exercise diligently, and remain mentally focused, "Everest was in the bag." It was time to drive my little engine No Place but UP!

Chapter Three

Small Steps Lead to Big Places

Not long before my attempt on Mt. Rainier I struck up a friendship with Jon Hansen, a small business owner in the town where my mother lives. Despite being over ten years my senior, I had heard of him and about his love of climbing. Knowing Jon, my stepfather was kind enough to introduce us one day.

I was immediately drawn to Jon's energy and spirit of adventure. I admitted to him early in our relationship I had an eye on climbing Everest someday. As it turned out, Jon had already committed himself mentally to the same task within the next year or two. Our excitement regarding such a common goal grew, a catalyst for our friendship. Jon took me under his wing, teaching me some of the basics of mountaineering, as well as introducing me to both ice and rock climbing.

The adrenaline rush one feels picking up a frozen waterfall is hard to describe. The arm and leg fatigue is quite another sensation! My first attempts at climbing vertical ice occurred in a gravel-processing pit near Green Bay. The start of winter means the end of the active excavating season. Pumps are used to collect and send the water that pools at the bottom of the excavation process up and over its granite walls. As the mercury dips on the thermometer, the process of creating unique frozen waterfalls commences, some of them reach well over one hundred feet in height.

Maybe it was the idea of carrying the ice climbing tools and digging my crampons into the hard ice. Maybe it was the vertical challenge itself, wrapped in the latest Gore-Tex garments shielding me from the elements. Even though winter is my favorite season and I am glad to have had the opportunity to challenge myself on vertical ice, it is not my passion. The same holds true for vertical rock but with Jon's encouragement I figured I would give that a try too.

Rock climbing at Devil's Lake State Park northwest of Madison offers some of the best granite in the Midwest with climbs of various difficulties, some well over one hundred vertical feet. Similar to the ice climbing near Green Bay, I climbed rock while being top-roped. This means having the rope looped from bottom to top, passing through an anchor before making its way back down to you. One end of the rope is tied onto the climbing harness worn around your waist while your climbing partner, standing firmly at the bottom of the climb, controls the other end.

Known as belaying, your partner feeds the rope through a braking device attached to his or her harness, always keeping both hands on the rope in order to remove the slack as the climber ascends, keeping the rope taught. If the person climbing suddenly pops off the wall, this system is designed to prevent free fall. In essence, you become suspended in midair until you regain your faculties to become one with the wall again. When ready to descend we often yell, "Free ride!" This means your belay partner below uses his or her weight and the braking device to control your rate of descent as you rappel down the side of the rock and/or ice.

It was good to learn how to "read" the rock, to figure out where one should place a finger-hold, a hand-jam, or even just the tips of your shoes. I definitely admire frogs and insects a lot more, as well as individuals who have a passion for big wall climbing. I am in awe of individuals like Shaun Sears who enjoy setting up a hanging platform, like a window washer's setup on the side of a skyscraper, anchored hundreds of feet up on the side of a vertical granite wall in order to rest. Even the coolest Gore-Tex gear does not entice me to pursue that type of sleeping arrangement!

With a couple of fourteeners under my belt, an alpine-style climb on Rainier, and just enough experience with vertical rock and ice, I knew I needed to get higher in our atmosphere. My original plan was to work my way up mountain-by-mountain, step-by-step. I was already planning a trip with RMI to Mexico. Three separate climbs would be involved, all on dormant volcanoes with the largest rising just shy of 19,000 feet above sea level.

I then envisioned myself making an attempt on Mount McKinley or what is often referred to as Denali, which is Athabaskan for "The High One." At 20,320 feet (6194m) it is North America's highest point. Perhaps then I would take off to 22,841-foot (6962m) Aconcagua, South America's highest peak, and finally the Himalayas to take on one of the lower 8000-meter peaks. Jon had successfully climbed Aconcagua after coming close to reaching the top of McKinley. Even though he was forced to turn around on the 8000-meter peak Cho Oyu in the Himalayas, I admired his tenacity and drive to try and get higher in our atmosphere. My thinking at the time had been too shadow Jon, albeit by a few years, with a similar climber résumé before making a bid on Everest.

Early 2008 would change all of that. The last two years not only found me ramping up my climbing skills, I became a fan of New Zealander, Mr. Russell Brice. He is a well-known mountaineer, now based in Chamonix, France. He has climbed all over the world, with fourteen successful 8,000-meter climbs and twice to the top of Everest. He became publicly famous after Himalayan Experience Ltd. (Himex), the company he owns and operates, was filmed for the Discovery Channel's 2006 and 2007 reality television series *Everest: Beyond the Limit*. Jon made his attempt on Cho Oyu with Russell and Himex. He kindly introduced me to Russell via email. I ended up trading multiple emails with Russell to see if it was even feasible for me to be thinking about an Everest attempt so early in my climbing career.

Although he expressed his desire for his clientele to have attempted an 8,000-meter peak prior to Everest, he did not make it compulsory. He felt I was technically competent and knew I would be climbing the Mexico volcanoes in December, just four months prior to the Everest 2009 climbing season. With that in mind and a few more exchanges, Russell formally offered both Jon and me a spot on his expedition to Everest.

With fingers crossed I needed to approach upper management to ask for the time off before I could even think about accepting his offer. There was no time like the present, literally. Russell's offer arrived in my inbox while I was attending a meeting—right alongside those in management I needed to talk to: company president Carol Wrenn, sales leader Jeff Mellinger, and my immediate supervisor Dr. Mark LaVorgna.

Mark thought I was nuts of course, but he and I hit it off from the start of my employment, always trying to find the humor in everything while getting the job done as required. I'm sure at that moment though he debated whether he wanted to take credit for having actually hired me back in 2005. Although surprised, all three were extremely supportive. It turns out I would be the first person in the history of the company granted a prolonged sabbatical from work. Living up to the phrase "it never hurts to ask," I figured I would go for broke with another question so I actually wouldn't go broke!

Climbing Everest can be expensive, and I wasn't going to refinance our home or take out a bank loan to come up with the hefty price tag. One might think asking for almost three months off is bold, but asking for money too might have been considered crazy. I asked Carol if the company might be interested in sponsoring the trip. I informed her I was going to seek enough sponsorship to hopefully cover the cost of the trip. That was February 2008. Fast forward to May.

I was driving west on Interstate 80 in Nebraska, on my way to Colorado for work, as well as a little altitude training on the weekend when my mobile phone rang. I was greeted by Carol's voice on the other end of the line. She informed me the company wanted to be a sponsor! Elated, I enthusiastically thanked her but knew I had to ask another tough question.

With nerves creating a slight oscillation in my voice I inquired, "May I ask how much?" I could only hope she wouldn't be offended, explaining that I simply needed to know in order to seek out the balance of the support from other sponsors. I nearly drove off the road when Carol replied the company wished to sponsor the adventure in its entirety!

I had been part of the company for the past four years. The company in turn was now an integral part of the Everest adventure, a trip that would later be dubbed internally as the Quest for Success. The time off from work and the bulk of the trip's cost was covered. What about the personal time away from family?

At first the news was hard to hear, especially for my wife. Out of fairness to her, however, we only loosely talked about my climbing aspirations to that point. When one hears the word Everest, death and hardship are often conjured. Almost ten years earlier, Kathy and I went to see the IMAX motion picture *Everest.* Originally intended to capture what life is like climbing the tallest mountain in the world, members of the film became part of a heroic rescue operation. The 1996 climbing season on Everest would become the deadliest after a large group of climbers tragically lost their lives high on the mountain during a freak snowstorm.

The disaster was made even more famous by Jon Krakauer's book *Into Thin Air,* which also increased the mountain's association with danger and death. It is fair to say Everest has not gotten overwhelmingly positive publicity beyond the fact that it is the highest point on Earth. I could not blame my family for being concerned about my desire to go to such a place.

Two to three months away is a long absence from family life. I felt guilty about that. I knew I would be putting a lot of responsibility and pressure on Kathy. She would have to juggle her job, the kids, and the house. Jordan and Bailee have learned to assist their mom when I am away for work, yet their ages were a limiting factor. Fortunately great neighbors, Julie and Jamie Dent, Pam and Toby Dent, and Kevin Kalies all offered to be readily available should Kathy need an extra hand with anything.

Russell's safety record was impeccable, having never lost a Westerner. A young Sherpa did perish on one of his expeditions but not because of some unfortunate climbing accident. A hidden medical condition was to blame. Kathy had never rejected my adventurous spirit to date. After talking through it, her fears diminished to a manageable level. At the time of Russell's offer, Bailee was eight and Jordan ten. Being young and inquisitive, they had their own reservations about what I wanted to do.

I have always tried to encourage my children to try new things, to nurture their sense of exploration and wonder. My single greatest hope was that by seeing their dad pursue his dream, they would someday pursue their own. I wanted them to see that nothing comes easy or for free, and that if you work hard, dreams come true. I will never be able to thank them enough for their blessing. With the finances in order and my family's acceptance in hand, I emailed Russell back and accepted his offer. Jon proceeded to do the same. We were now committed to traveling together to try and climb the tallest mountain in the world.

With Nepal looming just over a year away I knew I had to be diligent with my training. I also needed to prepare for my upcoming December climbs in Mexico. The itinerary called for a day climb of 14,639 foot La Malinche (4462m), a two-day climb of 17,159 foot (5230m) Iztaccihuatl (Ixta), and finally an ascent of 18,490 feet (5636m) Pico de Orizaba, all within a nine-day period. Like a steam cooker I felt the pressure build inside. What if my body failed at less than 20,000 feet? How could I possibly try and take on Everest, another 10,000 feet higher than Orizaba?

I have been asked, "How does a guy from Wisconsin train for the highest place on the planet?" The answer might surprise you. Just a few miles from my home stands what I like to refer to as one of the biggest little hills in the state. At approximately 960 feet (an incredible 293 meters!) above sea level, the summit of Mosquito Hill Nature Center would prove that small steps really do lead to big places. Throughout 2008 I fully utilized the hill's ten, up to forty-five degree slopes. I dutifully hiked up and down for hours on end, sometimes without gear, other times fully outfitted.

The winter snow and winds helped to mimic the conditions I might experience on Everest. What was the only missing detail? The altitude, of course, but hey, if you do the math the top of my favorite little hill is only 28,075 feet short of being ranked the highest point on our planet.

I am not a runner, so other than the hill, I used weight training to condition and keep my metabolism ramped up. Other days I would throw my weighted backpack on, jump on the treadmill, and raise its inclination. Toss in a regular bike ride and the aerobic side of conditioning was on pace.

I had to adjust my diet as well, making the commitment to avoid sweets, then the ultimate sacrifice, giving up beer for almost one full year! Big deal you might say? Just behind the agricultural and paper industries, beer production is one of Wisconsin's highest generating revenues. With close to six million people, the average Wisconsinite is reported to consume on average twenty-five liters annually. Okay, not all six million consume beer so the data is skewed heavily towards those that do! Regardless of whether it was a tough decision or not, I was making every commitment necessary in order to stack the odds in my favor for a successful summit the following spring.

Ultimately, the best way to train for climbing is to climb. I have been blessed with a terrific career. I have been to a lot of wonderful places in the world for work. It is not easy being away from family, but traveling has its advantages. Of all the places I visited the Rocky Mountains of Colorado here in the US sit high on my list of special places.

The summer leading up to Everest would find me traveling back to Colorado to work with a couple of my colleagues, Dr. Denny Hausmann and Dr. Mark Branine, both of whom live in that beautiful state. Both have become trusted friends. Denny is a mentor of mine who provided an insightful and positive impact on my career. I give him credit for making the phone call to see if I would be interested in working for Alpharma.

On a personal front, Denny used to tease me that he thought his state tax dollars should go to more important things than rescuing stranded climbers in the Rockies. We have always had a fun loving take-a-jab-at-each-other-type of relationship that has brought me a lot of laughter over the years. I offered to carry some small Catholic medals for him on Everest. Two of the medals were of St. Christopher, the patron saint of travelers. Denny wanted to give them to his grandchildren. I was not familiar with the third medal he handed me. It was St.

Dymphna. I should have known Denny's humor was once again at work. With a smirk on his face he politely informed me St. Dymphna is the patron saint of mental health. With a laugh interjected, I informed him that should I be successful, he would get the medal back for his own use.

Mark, on the other hand, was curious what the vertical life was like so we set some time aside in July of 2008 to attempt a climb of Longs Peak in Rocky Mountain National Park outside of Estes Park, Colorado. I knew this would be a great training exercise for my upcoming climbs in Mexico. It was also nice to know we would have Denny's tax dollars at our disposal should we run into trouble.

At 14,259 feet (4346m) there are several routes to the top, the most popular being the "Keyhole." During our first day in the park we decided to take an acclimatization hike from the parking lot trailhead at around 9,500 feet up to 11,000 feet.

With numerous elk grazing in the pastures around us, we soaked in the views. Just after our turn-around point, a thunderstorm rolled in and decided to drench us in a cold, hard shower of rain and pea-size hail. Both of us were walking on water, and I am not referring to the fact we felt blessed to be in such an amazing part of the world. Rather, the deluge continued and unfortunately both of us ended up with water inside our boots. Still, you have to love and respect Mother Nature no matter what she throws at you.

With our hotel hair dryers posing as makeshift boot dryers, we ate a hearty dinner and hit the sack early. We woke around two o'clock in the morning, in order to hit the trail an hour later. With a ten to eleven hour day ahead this would put us back to the parking lot by midafternoon at the latest. The previous day's acclimatization hike served us well as we made excellent time to the boulder field just in front of the famous keyhole itself. It was a memorable moment. As dawn broke the first rays of light struck the 900-foot tall east rock wall of Longs Peak known as the Diamond. Glowing brilliant orange with a few low lying clouds; it was a Kodak moment for sure.

By seven in the morning we had made it to the base of the keyhole. The weather was less than perfect with a large group of trekkers and climbers scattered about the area. Several tents were pitched within the designated areas of the boulder field. Quite a few people were already turning around at the keyhole itself due to unfavorable conditions on the other side. The upper part of the mountain was shrouded in clouds and mist, the air quite damp and cold for July. Pockets of snow and even the glare of ice could be seen stretching across the route leading to the gulley of boulders which rises at what appeared to be a relatively steep incline towards the summit, just hidden from this vantage point.

It is like another world on the other side of the mountain as you stand at the opening of the keyhole. The route, which until now was clearly marked amidst well-managed switchbacks, was now steep, extremely rocky and poorly defined. At this point, Mark decided he had had enough and was content to have reached 13,000 feet. I was proud of Mark, not only for reaching the keyhole, but also for recognizing his threshold for the day. After a brief discussion Mark encouraged me to continue on to see how far I could get. He waited around for at least an hour watching me zigzag in and out of boulder outcroppings along the shale-laden route.

I finally reached the steepest gulley of the climb, which I mentally labeled the bulls-eye chute. Numerous rocks had bulls-eyes painted on them, showing climbers the way up through the maze. After some minor handholds and careful foot placement circumventing boulder after boulder I came to the area known as the traverse. With roughly three hundred vertical feet to go, this hair-raising three foot wide ledge with an eighteen hundred foot drop to the right is similar to another ledge I hoped to cross in the near future.

Halfway across the world, known as the Cornice Traverse, it's a hair raising ledge leading to a rock wall called the Hillary Step, just under Everest's summit. It is a longer crossing, only a couple feet wide in spots, and has a drop of over a mile on either side. I decided I needed to tackle this traverse as a pre-examination of my nerves for things to come.

The biggest challenge so far had been the thin layer of ice known as verglas that covered the route. Verglas is an almost translucent form of ice that tends to coat every surface without really forming a thick protruding layer. I had battled it during the approach to the chute and could only hope that as the day went on it would start to disappear.

Just before reaching the chute below, I crossed paths with a climber on his way down. I noticed blood trickling down his shin. He had turned around just above where I was now standing, just shy of the summit plateau itself. The early morning weather had the upper slopes of the mountain locked into zero visibility with slippery conditions, the verglas a primary culprit, yet some snow above the traverse was also a contributing factor for his decision to call it a day.

Smart mountaineering means making smart choices, even when the summit is tantalizingly close, just as it had been on Mount Rainier. Today was not his day to summit, and he was not bitter. In fact, as we parted he stated Longs would be here to try another day. It was another great reminder for me to not let summit fever get in the way of making wise decisions on this or any mountain.

Fortunately, by the time I arrived at the traverse the sun was poking through the thick clouds and mist. This, along with rising temperatures combined to help thaw the nasty verglas. Mother Nature was helping with my decision-making skills, well almost. The drop to my right looked intimidating.

I repeatedly reminded myself not to look at the abyss, to focus on where I was placing my hands and feet. My eyes tuned into the rock wall to my left, and to the ledge directly in front of me. Moments later I was safely across, now confronted by the last imposing section leading directly up to the summit plateau.

The final stretch of smooth granite rests at a precarious angle. The sensation of falling backwards is almost nauseating. But with less than 200 vertical feet to go, the top drew me in. With the verglas gone, my level of faith in my hand and footholds increased. Just before nine in the morning I managed to stand on top of my third Colorado fourteener. With an uneventful descent, I met up with Mark back at the parking lot. The mountain wasn't finished with me, however. Before getting in his pickup, I became nauseated with a pounding headache closely behind.

AMS had struck again! I thought to myself that this has to be a joke. Why didn't I come down with it higher up? Perhaps it was a blessing in disguise that it showed up here at the safety of the vehicle and not on the traverse or anywhere else on the route? Would the Mexico climbs mean more AMS? It was difficult to ignore such questions. Maybe I wasn't meant to be a climber. I wasn't willing to throw in the towel just yet.

For the rest of the summer and fall I continued to push myself up and down that biggest little hill back home. Yes, still no beer either! December finally arrived, and I felt like I was in the best shape of my life. It was time to fly to Mexico City to catch up with the RMI team for our volcanoes' excursion. I had been to Mexico for work before, but never to this incredible city. The center square was decorated from top to bottom and lit up with an array of colorful Christmas lights for the upcoming holiday season. There was music playing, large crowds, and even an ice skating rink in the center for the people to enjoy a true taste of winter fun.

That night I got to meet my teammates and guides. I had heard of guide Jon Shea and exchanged an email or two with him prior the trip. Shea has a gifted spirit about him. Energetic, forthright, decisive, and intelligent are just a few of the words I would use to describe him. He gets the job done with serious precision yet knows when to let loose and have fun.

I also had the pleasure of sharing a hotel room and later a tent with Roger Bischoff from Washington state. We hit it off from the start. Roger struck me as a calm, smart guy with an incredible physique. Best to have a guy like him on your side in a bar fight, although I could never picture his kind demeanor ever drawing him into one. With the limited time in the city we would get to know each better during the climbs.

After a wonderful Spanish breakfast the following morning, we loaded up the van and headed to La Malinche. From base camp lodge at 10,000 feet we hiked and scrambled to the summit and back in one day. We arrived back to our sleeping bags just after dark but not before a substantial downpour replaced the need for any type of shower or bath. Similar to the end of my first day on Longs back in July, Mother Nature tested my fortitude. A couple days later we started our climb of Ixta. Just twelve miles from Ixta sits the active volcano Popocatépl, Popo, as it is commonly referred to, and it smoked every day we were there. It was a bit odd climbing so close to a volcano that was anything but dormant! I felt like I was in an episode of *Land of the Lost*.

After a steady day of climbing to our 15,000-foot high camp, Roger and I decided to sleep under the stars. The primitive hut here was for cooking in and barely big enough for a couple people to sleep in. The weather looked promising, so Roger and I felt we could pass on setting up a tent.

We utilized a couple of the pre-constructed rock barriers to lay our sleeping bags and pads behind to help protect us from the mild breeze. A bivy is something we refer to in the mountains as having to survive without adequate shelter or protection. While not a true bivy, we hardly noticed the chilly ambient temperature because the night sky dominated our senses. Thousands of glittering stars danced inside the black chasm as a full moon slowly arched overhead. In the distance, the faint glow of Mexico City lit up the western horizon. It is times like this I want to pinch myself.

Shea was up early getting our "hots" ready. This is what hot water is referred to, which is needed to prepare most mountain meals. As on Rainier, RMI liked to have the guides prepare the water, which in this case came from the glacier just above us. In cases where free flowing water cannot be found to boil, ice is first melted. After a typical breakfast of instant oatmeal and coffee we were climbing again by two in the morning.

Slowly but surely we rest-stepped our way up Ixta, going from rock to rock mixed with ice and finally just ice and snow. We made the summit just as the sun was coming over the eastern horizon. Despite a very steady and cold wind, we gazed towards the horizon to our next goal, the summit of Pico de Orizaba. The mountain was poking through the clouds with its characteristic upper conical shape.

We descended Ixta without incident and made our way to Puebla. Our stay in this beautiful historic city meant a hot shower and something other than instant oatmeal for breakfast. Roger and I walked the streets, stopping often to photograph various images. Our street trek found us buying authentic handmade items for loved ones back home as well as stumbling upon the oldest theater in North America.

That night we met Shea and our teammates, Casey Harrington and Steve Carmo, for a traditional Mexican feast. Casey and Steve are lifelong buddies from the northeast part of the US. That night we spoiled ourselves with a good shot of tequila (okay, maybe a few) and authentic churros, a popular deep-fried Mexican dessert. Perhaps it was the sugar from the churros or the tequila but we decided if all of us made it to the top of Orizaba we would celebrate with churros in hand. Off we went the next day for our third and final climb of the trip.

Pico de Orizaba is North America's third highest point, just behind Mt. McKinley and Mount Logan respectively. Orizaba looks bigger than it is, mainly because it rises abruptly above the relatively flat terrain that surrounds it. La Malinche and Ixta had not only conditioned us for Orizaba, the increasing gain in altitude had trained our bodies to adapt to the thinner air.

A process known as acclimatization, our bodies produce more and more red blood cells the higher we go. More red bloods cells means the body can process the lower oxygen threshold at altitude more efficiently. For example, at the summit of Mount Everest there is approximately 25 to 30 percent of the atmospheric pressure found at sea level. What this means is that for every breath inhaled while on the summit, the body consumes only about a fourth of the oxygen molecules it would get with that same breath at sea level.

It takes the body time to trigger such a response. A popular climbing mantra is "climb high, sleep low." Each time we climb we go just a bit higher. Without proper acclimatization there is an increased risk for AMS, and at extreme altitudes, high altitude pulmonary edema (HAPE) and/or high altitude cerebral edema (HACE).

With HAPE you drown in your own fluids and with HACE, your brain swells; both conditions are fatal, if not recognized and treated. Descending quickly is a crucial therapeutic factor. Although AMS can occur on any mountain, these two fatal conditions are unlikely to occur on slopes such as the Mexico volcanoes. Still, the odds would be in our favor for a successful and safe climb of Orizaba by having the other two summits under our climbing belts.

We drove from Puebla to a climbing hostel not far from the mountain. There we were treated to more authentic Mexican dishes, traditional fire-baked cookies, and one final opportunity to review the gear we would need for the climb. The next day we drove to the Orizaba hut located on the north side of the mountain at roughly 15,000 feet. Though the hut offered excellent shelter it was full of climbers, not to mention an accompanying aroma that would have made the night's rest less appealing. We decided to pitch our tents nearby and enjoy one last night of tranquility with cleaner air.

Another early rise, followed by another steadfast instant oatmeal breakfast by headlamp and it was time to journey up the mountain. I had grown comfortable with the routine, a routine once again greeted by a starlit sky. Rest step by rest step we made our way to the foot of the glacier where we stopped briefly to strap on our crampons. The night wind had a cold bite, but the glow of the glacier helped me to focus on the goal ahead–I mean up.

Steadily we climbed for ninety minutes, rested for five to ten, repeating the process for hours on end. Before we knew it, we were looking down into the dormant crater. We had made the summit of Pico de Orizaba under a beautiful blue sky. In the distance we could see La Maniche and Ixta, along with smoking Popo. Other than a full bottle of soda rocketing down towards us, accidentally dropped by a climber high above, the descent was uneventful and we reached our tents by early afternoon.

We were elated to have successfully climbed all three peaks. Ascending Orizaba without complications eased my concern about the climb on Everest, yet I still didn't know how my body would react above 20,000 feet. I told myself not to dwell on it. For now, I was focusing on the fact that I would leave Mexico with new friendships in tote.

Roger had climbed Denali with RMI, guided by Shea. They had an extremely successful season on "the high one," solidifying their friendship in the process. Beyond his daily job, Roger is an avid photographer and videographer. He created a documentary film about their team and the climb titled *Year of Denali*. After Mexico, Roger invited me to the viewing of his film on the big screen in his boyhood hometown of Maumee, Ohio. Jordan accompanied me on this overnight trip and both of us had a great time. Jordan particularly enjoyed seeing Dad's face on the big screen.

Roger had also put together a short film of our Mexico climbs. It was a pleasant surprise to see it running on a continuous reel prior to the main event. I was happy for Roger as the night was well received by a full audience of family and friends. It was the second big screen showing for him, the first was in Seattle close to where he resides. Roger's film has since aired in Fairbanks, Alaska as part of an annual film festival there.

Shea and I would depart Mexico not just as guide and client but as friends too. During our climbs together, I informed him I was headed to Everest in the spring, just like him. As we shook hands at the airport, I told Shea I would see him in a few months halfway across the world, quietly thinking to myself how great it would be if our reunion occurred on its highest point.

On the summit of Pico de Orizaba with (L to R): Steve Carmo,
Casey Harrington, me, Roger Bischoff, local guide
Fernando Posadas, and Jon Shea.

Chapter Four

Until I See You Again

It was back to my favorite little hill for a few more weeks of intense training. Alongside the conditioning I was able to get my website, www.foxeverest.com up and running. I would use the site as an outlet to send real-time dispatches during the entire expedition.

The communication setup included a satellite phone and personal digital assistant (PDA) linked together using Bluetooth technology in order for me to send blogs directly to the website via satellites. This was also how I received and sent emails to family and friends. I had a small laptop from which I could video chat with my family. This was not always a reliable connection, not to mention an expensive one, so I primarily relied on satellite phone calls and email to stay in touch on almost a daily basis. With solar panels and wires galore I was be able to charge all of my electronic devices using the power of the sun.

The year leading up to the expedition also meant acquiring high-altitude climbing gear. A fair amount of it was shipped in courtesy of the O$_2$ Gear Shop located in Appleton, Wisconsin. Jason Schultz, one of the store's employees and a good friend of mine, was a major contributor in assisting me with these purchases. His advice on certain items, even those he had never sold before, was terrific. After all, how many high-altitude down suits get used in Wisconsin? Todd Loessel, another store employee, assisted me by creating custom foot beds for my boots. There would be a lot of trekking and climbing to do in Nepal so taking care of my feet was top priority.

With just days to go on an empty garage floor I laid out all the gear I proposed to take with me. I cross-referenced Russell's suggested list, checking the items off one by one. Ironically, I was not too concerned with the clothing and technical gear suggested, but the "comfy food" offered while on the mountain was an unknown factor. So alongside the down suit, boots, and ice axe I lined up several large jars of peanut butter and chocolate bars. Recreating Reese's peanut butter cups in my base camp tent would end up being my favorite afternoon indulgence during the expedition.

How many pairs of socks to take? This was just one of many questions I had as my eyes gazed upon the piles of clothes strewn about the floor. How could I get it all to fit in the three expedition duffels? The local newspaper came out to interview me for a story about the trip. The reporter was amazed by the amount of gear that needed to be crammed into the bags. Roll, compress, cinch down, and stuff. Like the rest step technique I repeated the process until all of the gear fit. The duffels were packed to the brim yet each weighed exactly the amount allowed by the airline–in total just over two hundred pounds worth!

Before leaving home I decided I needed to visit my Grandmother Helen's resting place, the Catholic cemetery in Nekoosa, Wisconsin. On my way I stopped at a florist for some fresh flowers. Kneeling at her headstone, I softly spoke to my grandmother. I thanked her for watching over me the last couple of years, not to mention while she was alive. I asked her if she could keep special watch over me on the impending climb. With heartfelt tears, I told her I loved her in the Polish language she taught me many years earlier, "*Ja Cie Kocham.*"

I decided to combine my visit to the cemetery with a visit to my friend Patrick Hoffman, a professor and dairy researcher at the University of Wisconsin extension offices just up the road near Marshfield, the same city where my father spent his last days on this Earth. Because of our common interest in the dairy industry, we had met through work years earlier, developing a friendship along the way. Our relationship had grown to the point where Pat felt comfortable to ask if he could send something along with me to Everest.

Patrick, his wife, and their two children are all black belts in the Korean martial art of Taekwondo. Pat wanted me to carry a small replica of his family's black belt. It was not a selfish request but one that had deeper meaning. The black belt means maturity, persistence, and being unafraid of the dark. In martial arts it can only be earned by persistence, one step at a time. Pat is not a self-centered individual, nor does he embellish on his accomplishments. He was kind enough to share his story with me of how he earned his black belt.

During his black belt test, he tore the medial collateral ligament of his knee, along with a meniscus, and even sustained a partial tear of the anterior collateral ligament. The knee was not only painful, but also very unstable. As he lay on the floor wanting to quit, a voice inside told him, "Don't quit. Just get up and finish this thing." He did just that, persistence and dedication at the forefront of his well-deserved black belt.

When I informed Pat that I was going to climb Everest, his family wanted to send along the replica in hopes it would help support my climb, a commonality between climbing the mountain and his black belt experience. The latter was achieved step by step and now it was my turn. Pat's family thought that maybe by some osmotic process the replica might support me, one step up the mountain at a time. If something bad should happen, maybe it would whisper in my ear, "Just get up and finish this thing." I thanked Pat, letting him know I was both honored and proud to carry the replica.

Everest causes one to think more deeply about everyday life, not just while scaling its flanks but also before and after the climb. I had not been to my dear friend Richard Whalley's gravesite for quite some time, so a visit was long overdue. Similar to my conversation with Grandma Helen I made small talk, informing Richard of where I was headed. I asked him if he wouldn't mind keeping an eye out for me as well.

Similar to my grandmother and father, I knew Richard would be along with me in spirit. A high school graduation picture of Richard, as well as one of Barry, him, and me at the same occasion would be inside my backpack for the entire trip. Barry gave them to me to carry, along with various pictures of his family so they would help watch over me on the trip.

In early March, Kathy and I hosted a winter bonfire for family and friends. It was a farewell party as well. Jon and his family attended and much to my surprise, Kathy surprised Jon and I with a homemade cake in the shape of a mountain, two climbers standing on top. A wonderful toast from her accompanied the sweet treat.

Kathy's mom and dad, along with the rest of my in-laws drove up from southern Wisconsin to throw a few snowballs and send me off to Everest with well wishes. My mother and stepfather, Ira, as well as my brother Ryan and his wife Jenny, along with their boys Benjamin and Nicholas had fun in the snow. I would get to say farewell to Jenny and my nephews in a more private setting during Ben's birthday party the very next day. Yet I knew I would need to see my mother and brother one more time before leaving Wisconsin.

I had mixed emotions as Kathy, Jordan, Bailee, and I drove to my mother's home a couple days prior to my departing for Nepal. Not only would Mom and Ira be there, Ryan was able to be there as well, which I greatly appreciated. It is always nice to spend time with family, and up until that point, I had never had to walk away from family in terms of potential finality. Don't get me wrong. I did not dwell on the possibility of never returning.

It is a fact; however, that when you travel into the unknown, in this case a place not meant for human survival, one has to face the reality this could be your last good-bye. On the upside is the statistical fact that the chance of dying on Everest is dramatically reduced. That is, for every successful summit, the chance of perishing is less than two percent. This is largely due to the use of fixed-rope on the route, better weather forecasting, improved communication equipment, and the advent of commercial guiding. The odds of survival were in my favor. Instead of formal good-byes, I tried to think of my departure as "until I see you again."

Longtime family friend, Lyle Pomplun, was at Mom's too. I was introduced to Lyle through my relationship with the Whalleys years ago. Lyle has become a trusted and close friend, someone I consider family even if we don't share the same DNA. I shook his hand and told him I'd try to stay in touch with an occasional email. Lyle has never been a big email communicator. In fact, I had never actually received one from him to that point. While on the mountain he shocked me with several heartfelt electronic notes.

Even though my brother Ryan is eight years my junior, we have always been close. He is now a respected police officer in the village of Plover, Wisconsin. Days earlier I had asked him if I could carry something in my pack for him. He handed me his challenge coin. At first I teased him about diminishing my chances of success, as it felt like it weighed a ton, despite its small size. Along with the coin he handed over a letter that detailed the coin's history, along with some words of advice for me. This was uncharacteristic for my stoic brother, so I anxiously read it.

It turns out this type of coin is carried by those who serve whether in law enforcement or the armed forces. The legend of the coin's origin dates back to World War I. Air warfare was new at the time. The Army created flying squadrons that consisted of pilots from every walk of life, including students from Ivy League universities.

One such Ivy Leaguer had bronze medals forged bearing the squadron's insignia, which he then handed to his fellow squadron members. They were to be mementos of their service together. One member placed his coin for safekeeping in a leather pouch that he wore around his neck. Not long after, his plane was damaged which forced him to land behind enemy lines. German forces eventually captured him. He was taken to a prisoner of war facility in a German-occupied French village where he was stripped of the personal belongings in his pockets. The leather pouch hanging around his neck was missed.

During a British bombardment of the village, the pilot was able to escape. In order to avoid being captured again he disguised himself by wearing civilian clothes. He came upon a French patrol that was suspicious he was a German saboteur. He was to be executed immediately. The pilot pulled out the coin and lucky for him one of his French captors recognized the squadron insignia. After verification of his identity, the pilot was released back to his squadron. From that point on, every member carried their coin, often challenging each other to produce it at a moment's notice.

Since then the coin has advanced in many ways. The motto on the back of the coin, referred to as the Blauer Maxim by law enforcement, is Detect-Defuse-Defend. This corresponds to recognizing an incoming attack, converting the flinch one might have when threatened into a SPEAR tactic (in law enforcement training SPEAR stands for Spontaneous Protection Enabling Accelerated Response) to stop the attack, using other combative options to gain control, respectively.

The motto on the front of the coin is "Because in your fight, you're point." Point pertains to the first person engaged in a battle, whether the first in a group to deal with the challenge or during a one-on-one confrontation. The confrontation is the fight, yet can be broken down into three fights. The first is you versus you, or the emotional struggle we face during a challenge. If we are confident in our abilities we have won this fight. The second is you versus the physical. When we have trained to our fullest potential, we hope to win the battle. The final fight is you versus the system, or the psychological aspect of any challenge.

Ryan's letter went on to review my three "fights" of the expedition. Even though I would be part of a team on Everest I was "point." I had already won the first fight—despite my short climbing résumé, I did not doubt my abilities. Fight number two was against Everest. While I never viewed the mountain as my enemy, unless Mother Nature turned me back, I would reach its top and make it back home safely. The third fight was with my family. Not a contentious fight, but rather my need to devote most of my thoughts while away on the task at hand. He closed the letter by reminding me I would have angels sitting on my shoulders, Dad on one and Grandma on the other, helping me to achieve my dream.

Although the coin was heavier than I expected, its value far surpassed its weight. I was honored to carry it for my brother. I vowed to keep it in my pack at all times during the expedition, and if I should find the task at hand overwhelming, I would look at the coin to remember to keep on fighting. I would also take along a copy of Ryan's letter for further inspiration. Instead of a customary handshake, my brother would not settle for anything less than a hug. He will never know how much that hug or his letter meant.

With a firm grip, something I have always admired about my stepfather, he took my hand in his own and wished me luck, told me to stay focused, and reminded me to be safe. Even though no one could ever take the place of our father, Ira helped to raise Ryan since he was ten. He has also taken care of my mother and loves her dearly. For that I have been, and always will be, grateful.

Giving my mother one last hug and kiss, at least for the next couple of months, was incredibly difficult. For the past couple of weeks I had been wearing the St. Christopher medal she gave me. This, along with a small metal cylinder containing some of my father's cremated remains, hangs side by side around my neck to date. Like my late grandmother Helen, my mother is a devout Catholic. Mom had the St. Christopher blessed by both a Catholic priest and deacon specifically for the journey to Everest. Mom also gave me the wedding band my dad gave to her so many years ago.

I wear either on my finger or on a necklace, my father's wedding band, a gift my mother gave to me shortly after his death, so this gesture was fitting. I told her I would take care of her ring and that with a bit of luck, it will visit the highest point on our planet, as close to Dad as physically possible.

Before driving away, I promised her I would call as often as I could, both of us realizing there would likely be extended periods without a phone call. I would miss hearing her voice, but I knew we would be in each other's thoughts daily. Similar to Kathy, she put her fears aside and to her credit she maintained her composure, holding back a steady stream of tears.

Before leaving home I told Kathy and the kids I wanted to carry something in my pack from each of them. I wanted to have each of them with me during every step of the journey. My daughter topped my request by making me a beaded necklace that read, "GOOD LUCK AT MT E." She also gave me a small flower pendant to carry.

My son gave me a green marble (he had an extensive marble collection at the time). Kathy handed me a gold horse pendant from one of her necklaces. A request followed suit. She has a deep love and passion for horses so her request, albeit simple, summarized our unified goal, "Carry this pendant to the top and bring it back to me." I told her I would do just that.

I had a small padded pouch, which would hold all of the small items inside my pack. I added to the ever-growing list a couple of small bar coins from my late Grandmother Helen's tavern as well as my wedding ring and my father's wedding ring. I usually wear both unless working out and climbing. I prefer to have them tucked safely away so as not to damage them. This also eliminates the risk of having them cut off or impede the circulation in my fingers should swelling from frostbite occur during cold weather climbs.

Amongst the various daily bills and propaganda in the mail, one day an envelope arrived from my good friend, Dr. Bruce Watt of Canada. Inside the envelope was a note wishing me luck on the trip and a small plastic pendant representing Canada's country flag with its characteristic red maple leaf in the center. He wondered if I might be willing to carry it to the top for him. Back in 1995, months before graduating from veterinary school, I did an externship with Bruce. He helped mold part of my career, so I was honored to carry the pendant for him.

One of the last items given to me to carry in the pouch was an unexpected surprise. It was a five-leaf clover from my close friend and fellow veterinarian, Dr. Julie Gard. She found it growing amongst a patch of clover on a dairy farm not too far from where she lives and works. I have never found a four-leaf clover let alone a five-leaf one, so I figured it would surely bring me extra good luck. I laminated it to protect it from the elements and found a home for it in the pouch.

I decided I needed to round out my collection of memorabilia so I printed a couple small photos of my family. Should I reach it, I did not have the intention of leaving any of the pictures on the summit. I simply wanted to be able to look at my family to see their smiling faces whenever I needed a pick-me-up. I also figured the photos would help me realize the importance of putting one foot forward, steps that would eventually lead me back to them, summit or not. The pouch was now complete.

Yet I still had one more item for my pack, which would help me catapult to the top. I asked my mother, as well as my brother for their permission to take some of Dad's ashes with me to Everest. I was a bit nervous asking them. I had opened his urn twice before, most recently for a small amount of his remains to place inside the necklace cylinder that hangs around my neck.

The first time I opened the urn was when I attended veterinary school. I had retrieved a small amount to place inside a custom-made amethyst necklace I used to wear. The stonecutter had drilled a hole in the crystal's center where I placed the ashes, a stone cap on top sealing the contents within. Replacing the gemstone with the metal cylinder was something I needed to do before Everest to increase the security of dad's ashes at altitude but also so I could give Ryan the original piece. I wanted him to have our dad close to him as well, whenever he wanted.

Because of their willingness, I once again retrieved some of his remains from the urn; placed them in a small plastic container which I tapped tightly closed and labeled "Dad's Ashes." My plan was to have the container in my possession at all times during the adventure. I would be responsible for the remains, and if I made it to the summit, I would release the ashes there.

March 25, 2009. Once again it was time for heartfelt hugs, now for my immediate family. Kathy and the kids drove me to the airport along with my two hundred plus pounds of gear. My family surprised me with a little extra weight to take along.

A couple of years ago Bailee took an interest in playing with Polly Pocket dolls. Sometimes she would get me in the act of dressing these miniature figurines in all kinds of wild fashions. I joked with her one day that I thought the long blond haired girl with full lips and blue mascara was good looking. For some reason I named her Renèe.

I have never lived that one down, occasionally finding Renèe sitting on either my office chair at home or on my bed. Bailee even told her third-grade teacher at the time about my interest in Renèe. Ah the innocence of a young girl's mind.

What a surprise to see Bailee and Kathy pull out Renèe, all dressed up and ready to head to Nepal. She would be my official stowaway inside my carry-on bag. I promised them I would take good care of my blonde traveling companion all the way to base camp. With tickets in hand and the gear already on its way to the plane, I walked my family back to the parking lot.

I asked the kids to help mom out and to do their best in school. We did not share a lot of words. We knew that a lot of uncertainty lay ahead, yet the plan was to once again hold them in early June. I hugged and kissed each one, telling them I loved them. Walking away from my family was one of the most difficult moments in my life. With each step I reminded myself to be brave and to be strong not just for myself but also for them.

Four airports and two calendar days later the plane touched down in Kathmandu (KTM), the capital of Nepal. The last leg of the trip from New Delhi, India into Kathmandu will be one of many fond memories for it was from the plane I first gazed upon the mighty Himalaya Mountains.

The view was breathtaking. The magnitude of this mountain range in terms of its never-ending height, depth, and width is amazing to gaze upon. Even though Everest was not in full view due to cloud cover, I fought back my excitement of finally seeing the Himalayas with my own eyes. As the plane descended, I swallowed deeply and wondered for a moment what I had gotten myself into.

My inspiration as well as greatest gifts of all, Jordan and Bailee.

Chapter Five

No I in Team

A few days prior to leaving, my sponsor created shirts to show its continued support of the climb. On the front of the shirt appeared the slogan Quest for Success with the silhouette of a climber holding a flag embossed with the corporate logo, standing atop a mountain. On the back was a graphic design providing a view of the Everest South Col route, the infamous phrase No Place but UP! appearing at the top. At the bottom of the design was a notice saying "Track Lance Fox's Climb" and my website address. The shirts were shipped to all of the employees of the company around the globe, just as I left for Nepal. When they arrived at everyone's doorstep it was discovered that the print shop accidentally left out the letter "I" in the word climb.

Even though I had never been part of an expedition I had read enough about them and even visited with Everest summiteers to learn that it takes complete team effort to climb to the highest mountain on Earth. Sure, there are climbers who have done it unsupported, whether individually or in very small groups, a mammoth undertaking that I admire greatly. Yet I know my limits. Being a social person who likes to get to know people, expedition life also intrigued me.

From the porters to the base camp staff, guides, and team leader, the power of the climbing Sherpas and the skills of the clientele, an expedition requires a lot of individual contribution to create team chemistry. You cannot be carried up a mountain; only your own physical and mental strength can do that. A harmonious expedition improves both individual and overall team success.

Just like the phrase "there is no 'I' in team," there would be no "I" in climbing Everest. I was anxious to meet my teammates. From all over the world, we would come together as strangers with a common goal. Teamwork would be the key to its success. Henry Ford's words applaud this best: *Coming together is a beginning. Keeping together is progress. Working together is success.*

March 27, 2009. Mountain Experience Pvt Ltd, a sister company to Himex based in KTM, was in charge of all of the logistics while in this bustling city which included our greeting at the airport. Even though the weather back in Wisconsin had a hint of spring in the air, it felt like summer as I stepped off the plane. Kathmandu was basking in a subtropical glow. The sun was out and there was a haze in the air that blocked my view of the surrounding foothills. After a slightly congested drive, I was checking in to the Hotel Tibet, one of several launching pads for Himalayan expeditions.

Even though I was tired from traveling and my internal clock wasn't sure what time it really was (KTM is eleven hours and fifteen minutes ahead of Wisconsin), a warm shower gave me a second wind. My anticipation of meeting Russell revved me up a bit too. For now he was out and about conducting business, so Jon and I decided to take a stroll around the neighborhood. It was hard to believe that I was actually standing in KTM, yet the bustling streets reinforced that I was not having a dream. Motorbikes, rickshaws, people, people, and more people filled the potholed roads.

Hotel Tibet is located in the district of Lazimpat, but it is the local shopping district of Thamel that was too good to be true. Within easy walking distance from the hotel, you can buy just about anything, from clothing to climbing gear and jewelry to souvenirs. I decided I would go back the next day to buy a variety of items for family and friends, storing it all at the Mountain Experience warehouse while away on the expedition. I planned on making it back to Kathmandu in about two months yet figured I might as well take advantage of shopping now since I didn't know if I would be in the mood to barter then.

Before taking a nap back at the hotel, the phone rang. Although I had never spoken to him until now, I immediately recognized the Kiwi voice on the other end of the line. After some small talk to see if I was settled in, Russell extended an invitation to join some members of the team who were already in KTM for a drink downstairs that evening.

With the bags under my eyes slightly recessed, I walked into the outdoor atrium. My tunnel vision locked onto Russell. I have met famous people before, yet it was surreal shaking his hand. Medium in stature with hair like an arctic fox between seasons, Russell is soft-spoken yet direct in his approach. He is a tell-it-like-it-is kind of guy. I got a hint of that through his emails, and I wasn't disappointed by his straightforward mannerisms.

This way of communication is not for everyone, and I have to admit at first I had a difficult time opening up to him. Yet imagine yourself being responsible for the lives of so many people heading to one of the most dangerous places on the planet. There is no time for beating around the bush. Over time my ability to effectively communicate with him would grow, along with my respect and admiration.

After short pleasantries Russell introduced me to the group sitting at the table. I immediately recognized several individuals. Mark Woodward, better known as "Woody," had been part of the Discovery reality program and is one of Russell's premier guides, so it was a pleasure finally meeting him. Like Russell, he is also from New Zealand, has a good sense of humor, and is a serious mountaineer with multiple Everest summits under his belt.

Also sitting at the table was Dr. Monica Piris. As Himex's base camp doctor, she too had been captured on the show, discussing what high altitude can do to the human body or actually treating someone for its potentially life-threatening effects. She is just one of a handful of physicians in the world who specializes in high-altitude medicine. Monica's primary role was to keep the Himex team as healthy as possible during the expedition, but she would also be available to assist with other teams' medical needs as warranted.

After formal introductions we headed across the street for dinner. I sat down next to Christopher Macklin, a young and quick-witted Englishman with a great sense of humor. We clicked right from the get-go. Chris informed me he was a lawyer by trade from London. My Midwest accent pegs me as an American. He proceeded to tell me that his mother was originally from Texas and had lived in several areas of the US before moving to England many years ago.

I also picked up on Chris' fanaticism with sports. It did not matter what the sport, although slightly biased towards rugby and soccer, he seemed to be able to rattle off the names of athletes. When I told him I lived close to Green Bay he dove into American football, listing teams he enjoyed following including my beloved Green Bay Packers. Macklin's energy was infectious. Even though I am eleven years his senior our personalities blended extremely well. Sitting there I knew this was the start of a special friendship.

Our conversation then turned to food and what we might expect to eat for the seventy-plus days. Macklin then rattled off the names and recipes of things I had never heard of, triggered just as the various Chinese dishes were being served at our table. I laughed knowing we'd soon be living on candy bars.

Later in the trip, after consuming copious amounts of carbohydrates in the form of noodles and rice, Macklin's recipes made all of our mouths water, just like Pavlov's dogs. I eventually nicknamed Macklin "Grizz." Not because he was like a grizzly bear searching for new food but because after a while he reminded me of the TV character Grizzly Adams. He chose to ignore his well-groomed looks, not shaving for the entire adventure and, in fact, kept his mop of a beard growing for a while after returning to London.

Even though I wanted to chat with Russell some more, he was busy in conversation at the end of the table for most of the dinner. Forever a gentleman, Russell called me over after the meal to discuss an idea I had emailed him about several months ago. Knowing this trip was the trip of a lifetime, I wanted to give back to the local Sherpa people whom I knew would be contributing to its reality, regardless of whether I made it to the summit or not.

As a veterinarian it came natural to want to promote the well-being of their animals. Since my background and area of expertise has involved working with cattle, the animals I knew I could have the greatest impact on were the yaks. These beautiful creatures are a significant part of the Sherpa's livelihood in the Himalayas. Often used as pack animals, they carry large quantities of goods and gear up the various valleys, weaving through the mountain range. Their wool is used to make clothing and the people also utilize the female yak's (called naks) milk, mainly for making cheese. Interestingly enough, in the lowlands of Nepal yak milk is a growing export market.

In domesticated cattle around the world we routinely deworm them for internal and external parasites. This is not that different than heartworm prevention for your dog. In essence, when you give your pooch a once a month chewable or topical to prevent heartworm disease, you are deworming your dog. Rather than bore you with the details let's just say that all creatures are prone to various parasite infections, especially grazing animals like cattle, which include yaks. Left untreated, such parasites can contribute to poor health. Severe cases can lead to an early death.

Utilizing my industry contacts, I was put in touch with a guy at Intervet/Schering-Plough Animal Health who oversaw one of their cattle deworming products known as Safe Guard. Although the company's name has since changed, ISPAH kindly donated enough oral drench form of the product to treat at least two hundred yaks a couple of times. I shipped the product to Kathmandu weeks prior to my own arrival. Even though the word yak does not appear on the label of very many veterinary products including this one, I decided to take on the sole responsibility of using it on these beautiful animals.

As we wrapped up dinner, Russell informed me the product was safe in storage and would meet us up the valley. He was thinking we might be able to work on some yaks in one or two of the villages near the end of our trek towards Everest base camp. Russell grew up around livestock and was very familiar with what I proposed to do. He was committed to helping out on this project as much as possible, even though getting people safely up Everest was the priority.

Russell has been climbing in the Himalayas since the 1970s with many of those years involved with leading expeditions. He cares deeply for the Sherpa people. To promote their well being, he co-founded Friends of Humanity based in Switzerland (www.friendsofhumanity.ch). My idea of helping the Sherpa by helping their animals was very appealing to Russell. For now all I could do was hope I could pull it off in the middle of such a remote location.

With a full belly it was finally time to meet my hotel mattress. Even though it usually takes my body a couple days to adjust to a major time zone change, the next morning I woke up feeling refreshed. Maybe my body was telling me I better enjoy the relaxation of Kathmandu because in just a couple days the vacation part of this trip would be over.

It was a beautiful day to barter in Thamel along with a visit to the Rum Doodle restaurant. Yeti footprints with the signatures of Everest summiteers fill the walls of this famous establishment. I enjoyed finding the footprints belonging to the late Sir Edmund Hillary and to Reinhold Messner, both climbing legends. Hillary's name is associated with the fact that he was the first Westerner to summit Mount Everest in 1953, alongside Tenzing Norgay. Messner is noted for climbing it without using supplemental oxygen in 1978, the first to do so alongside Peter Habeler.

I couldn't help but ponder how amazing it would be to be able to come back here to have my own footprint on the wall next to such mountaineering legends. After a few slices of surprisingly good pizza it was time to barter.

I managed to acquire some great Nepalese items for my family–several colorful pieces of apparel for my daughter and a handmade chess set for my son (I have made it a point to try and purchase a chess set of local culture for him from the various remote locations I have visited around the world). I did not want to load up too much now, as I knew I would purchase items higher up the valley during the trek to base camp. The necklace I bought for my wife in the jewelry store YAQOOT ended up being a very enlightening purchase.

I conveyed to the owner, Mr. Mansukh Gangadia, that I was looking for a unique piece for my wife. Intrigued, he asked me, "What are you doing in Nepal, brother?" "I came to climb Everest," I cheerfully responded. Reaching into the glass showcase, he didn't act overly surprised by my answer. After all, I was tracing the footsteps of numerous Westerners who had come here to do the same exact thing.

Mansukh proceeded to go through each of the colored stones on the piece, explaining what they were and what they meant. Collectively the stones were said to bring luck to the person wearing them. It was too nice a piece to pass up. Before leaving the shop he proceeded to write me a note, the words forever etched on paper in my scrapbook, as well as engraved in my mind:

To meet and part is the way of life.
To part and meet is the hope of life!
Good luck bro & friend.
See you again.
God bless you.

I decided to carry both the necklace and note with me to base camp, not because I was concerned about leaving such a valuable piece behind in storage but because I figured I could use all the luck I could get. I also decided that if I did, in fact, succeed I would fulfill the words on that note and visit Mansukh before heading back home.

Within the next twenty-four hours most of the Himex team arrived at the hotel except one. Alec Turner from Alaska was having flight problems back home. Jet stream ash from the eruption of Mount Redoubt had grounded air travel. He would catch up with the rest of us at some point on the trek in towards base camp.

Inside the comforts of the hotel's top floor gathering room, Russell held a team meeting so remaining introductions could be made and a few logistics covered. The climbing group consisted of twenty-eight Westerners from all walks of life, a true international team. Instead of just calling out our names, Russell included a little something extra about each one of us.

Despite the initial rough edges, this was the first hint he genuinely cared for and wanted to get to know those who signed on to climb with him.

At this meeting we also met some of the film crew and producers for Discovery's *Everest: Beyond the Limit*. Several months prior to the start of our expedition it was uncertain whether any filming would occur for a third season of the show, a slowing economy and budget cuts heavily weighing in on the debate. In the end it was decided that the show must go on.

Mr. Dick Colthurst, creative director with Tigress Productions, the UK-based company responsible for filming and producing the show, overviewed what we could anticipate from his crew. We would have at least two camera people with us at all times while another film crew would be assigned to International Mountain Guides (IMG). The plan was to capture two different expeditions going up the mountain instead of just Himex, as the prior two seasons had done.

As executive producer of the show, Dick had an ease about him that added to my comfort about having cameras all around. As he wrapped up he said that we should not feel obligated to be filmed. Waivers were passed out so those of us who didn't mind the possibility could sign and return them before checking out of the hotel. I assumed my chance of being filmed was slim as there were a number of superior climbers with interesting stories in the group. I signed the waiver on the spot and handed it back to him.

A final day of sightseeing and one last check of the gear followed. We were allowed to fill a small barrel with the gear we needed for base camp and above. The blue containers reminded me of oil drums back home, only half the size and made of plastic. About four feet tall and two feet in diameter, packing to utilize every square inch of space became an art. All of our barrels would be ferried by helicopter from KTM to a landing strip near the village of Khumjung about a third of the way up the valley towards Everest. Khumjung is home to numerous climbing Sherpas and would be a rest stop for us for a couple of nights on the trek in.

From Khumjung, yaks would be responsible for carrying those barrels the rest of the way to base camp, several days away and about a mile higher in elevation. A porter would be assigned to carry one of our duffels (referred to as a kit bag) with the supplies we needed each night (sleeping bag, warmer clothes, etc.) while trekking up the Khumbu Valley. Each of us in turn would carry a daypack containing water, snacks, rain gear, a few layers of clothing, and of course a camera.

April 1, 2009. The day called for a very early breakfast, so we could board our flights from KTM to Lukla, a small village perched close to 9,400 feet above sea level. This would be the starting point of our trek. I had read about the Lukla Airport, renamed the Tenzing-Hillary Airport in 2008. It historically ranks as one of the most dangerous airports in the world, taking the top spot in 2011.

We broke into smaller groups to accommodate the limited seating on the forty-five minute turbo-prop plane ride. We were given cotton for our ears to dull the noise of the plane's engines. Just minutes into the flight white-capped peaks dominated the skyline. I ignored the roar of the engines and the rattle of the plane's fuselage. We were flying at a fairly low altitude and the peaks on either side of the plane were getting taller and taller.

While not a routine occurrence, several planes have crashed during the approach into Lukla, so at this point thinking about climbing the biggest mountain in the world wasn't exactly the first thing on my mind. Jon was on another plane so I wondered if he, along with our teammates were thinking the same thing.

I looked down at my watch knowing we must be getting close. All of a sudden I saw the mountainside rush past my window. It was as if I could reach out and touch the rock. Rooftops then zipped by. I looked up towards the cockpit, this time my eyes fixated on the runway now in view.

At the white paint marks on the approach end of the runway was a 2,000-foot cliff leading back down into the valley below us and at its far end, a twenty-foot stonewall. Its 1,729-foot length sits at a twelve-degree pitch. Compare this to the relatively flat ground and almost 16,000-foot runway at Denver International Airport, and I knew I was in for a unique landing experience. All the air travel for my job could not have prepared me for this.

The pilot put the plane down right on top of the white paint marks. With no time to waste he was applying reverse thrust to the engines and intense pressure on the brakes. As long as both mechanical devices worked we would stop just short of the wall of stone and gently turn into the compact tarmac area next to the terminal.

Sir Edmund Hillary initiated construction of the airfield back in 1964 in order to make it easier for climbers and trekkers to access the Khumbu without having to walk all the way from Kathmandu as he did in the early 50s. I wasn't thinking about that convenience as the plane's velocity continued to rapidly swallow what remained of the runway. I was focused on the quality of the airplane's brakes.

If I had hair on my head, it would have been standing straight up. That stone wall was getting bigger by the second when all of a sudden the plane eased into a gentle roll and turned onto the tarmac area. With the engines off and the cotton removed from my ears I couldn't help but smile as my feet touched solid ground. I told myself not to think about what the takeoff was going to be like.

It would take a couple of hours for the remaining planes to arrive and for our kit bags to be sorted out amongst all of the gear being ferried in on the flights from KTM. There must have been at least a hundred locals standing just outside the small terminal building, all waiting for a chance to earn money in exchange for ferrying the duffel bags piling up. Before exiting the airport property we stood on top of that now infamous stone wall at the top of the runway to watch several more planes land and takeoff. I was glad my turn was over, at least for now.

We regrouped at a local establishment for breakfast. There we patiently waited to be reunited with our kit bags. I already admitted I am a social person. Whether one on one or in large groups, I enjoy the camaraderie. I consider it a blessing to be able to get to know people. Sitting there in that small lodge with all of my teammates was too good to be true. For most of us, we were stepping into the unknown, and it could not have been more exciting.

My western teammates (L to R). Front row: Shokichi Saito, Eugène Constant, Alec Turner, Jon Hansen, Gilad Stern, Stuart Carder, Zi Qiang Qiu. Second row: Paul Robinson, Antoine Boulanger, Moises Nava, Christopher Macklin, Valerio Massimo, Robby Kojetin, Chris Jones, Kyomi Takiguchi, Takenori Yoshida. Back row: Asbjørn Hjertenes, David Tait, Tommy Rambøl, Thomas Svane Jacobsen, John Black, Chris Dovell, Bruce Parker, Jim Holliday, me, Christophe Vandaele. Not pictured: Megan Delehanty, Billi Bierling, and Ellen Miller.

I would be with these people for the next two months so why delay getting to know them? After all, if I were fortunate enough, I would be clipped into the same fixed-rope to the summit with several of the individuals sitting around me. Creating relationships builds not only friendships but also a necessary level of trust. We were strangers and with the exception of a handful of members, we had never climbed together before.

Trust would be important to develop as our lives could potentially be in each other's hands. However, like many other people I enjoy the solitude of time alone. Everyone needs downtime now and then. The beauty of climbing is that you can get both if you want.

Himex had planned for us to utilize nine full days to reach base camp. Why so long you might ask? The trek alone can be grueling as it encompasses roughly forty miles of up and down terrain with an overall vertical gain of close to one and one-half miles. Physiologically, our bodies were already in the process of acclimatization. Russell designed the trek in to give each of us the best chance of adapting to the ever-growing thinner air with each step we would take.

Our first day was therefore a relatively short one, finding us staying overnight at the Monju Tea House in Phakding. This is where I started to get to know my teammate, Jim Holliday from Pittsburgh, Pennsylvania. I was standing outside of the tea house as the sun started to set behind the mountains. A voice from behind called out, "That's a funny looking hat you have there." I whirled around to see Jim wearing the same hat!

Ironically we had purchased them at our local Recreational Equipment Inc. stores back home. Their long tassels and big ear flaps did not necessarily make them glamorous fashion statements but did a great job of keeping the heat in. We had a good laugh about trying to outdo each other on the fashion runway in Phakding.

Although Jim is the same height as me, he appeared much bigger. No, not overweight but rather big boned. Oh yeah, and big feet too! I teased him that he was probably a tremendous swimmer with those flippers he was toting around. He argued that he was terrible in the water but agreed he had big feet. For now I dubbed him "Big Jim," a name everyone else seemed to adopt as well. Aside from the fifteen-year age difference, Big Jim and I learned quickly that we shared a lot in common.

He lost his mother several years ago and had come on this trip to honor her by hopefully leaving a small picture of her at the top of the world. Our family lineage was similar, Polish on the maternal side and mostly English on the paternal side. We were also able to communicate using a few Polish words and broken phrases. Our pace on the trek seemed to complement each other, so it was enjoyable to learn more about each other walking side by side. Another lifelong relationship was in full swing.

By day three we arrived at the village of Namche Bazaar perched just over 11,000 feet. It is a bustling mountain community that has been blessed by the tourism industry. Running water, electricity, satellite Internet, and even television are just some of the luxuries found here. The village is horseshoe-shaped set into the side of a very large ridge with multiple terraces rising along the hillside. As you can imagine, a beautiful backdrop with snow-capped peaks surrounds it.

The terraces intrigued me. Some are used to shelter yaks while most are designed to grow potatoes, a staple crop for the Sherpa people that is hand-planted every spring. And to think, in less than sixty days from now these terraces would be green with life. The walls of the numerous buildings here are made of hand-carved riverbed stone carried up from the valley below. From dawn to dusk Sherpa men chisel away at the rocks, each creating just a few per day. I learned the average Sherpa earns on average 250 to 2,500 US dollars annually, yet they appeared to be very grateful for what little they have. I also admired their work ethic and willingness to give you the shirt off their back.

As part of our continued altitude adjustment, Russell had us staying in Namche for two nights. Multiple gear stores lined the cobblestone-like paths, which allowed us to purchase last minute items. I happened to score a pair of nice Mammut down tent booties at one store. I saw that several of our climbing guides were wearing hand-carved stone or yak bone necklaces. They are said to bring good luck, so I visited the shop adjacent to the coffee shop to see if I could find one. I immediately found two made of yak bone along with some traditional *lung ta* (Tibetan for wind horse) prayer flags.

A traditional *lung ta* is made of five distinct colored flags tied together on a string, each color symbolizing the key elements of life in a specific order from left to right. Blue symbolizes sky or space, white is for air or wind, red is for fire, green for water, and yellow represents earth. Written on each of the flags are prayers, mantras, and symbols. It is believed that when the wind blows through the prayers and mantras, it will bring compassion and good will into all pervading space, to benefit all who walk within it. We would pass many flags on the trek as well as up the mountain.

The shop owner was extremely nice, as well as inquisitive. After he learned I was there to attempt to climb Sagarmatha, the Nepali name for Everest, he presented me with a silk *khata*, often referred to as a prayer scarf. The Dalai Lama offers them to diplomats to symbolize purity of intention at the start of a relationship. I told him how honored I felt, and that if I were lucky enough to make it to the top I would visit his shop again on the trek out to Lukla. He then helped adjust the length of one my necklaces before placing it around my neck. My intent was to wear it for the remainder of the trip then give it to my son when I got home.

I also planned to carry a roll of prayer flags up with me to honor Sagarmatha, should she be kind enough to grant me access to her summit. Sagarmatha means "goddess of the sky." Loosely translated, *sagar* means sky and *matha* means forehead. The people of Nepal believe that when you stand on the summit of Mount Everest you stand with your head above the clouds. It is a word that reminds me of a famous phrase; *carpe diem* or seize the day. Hopefully sometime next month I would be able to do both, but about 18,000 feet higher.

Until Namche I had never had my head professionally shaved. Yes, I can grow hair around the sides of my head just no longer on top. Does Friar Tuck ring a bell? I have shaved my own head since first breaking out the blade around 2002 when reality finally set in that it was either a clean-shaven head or the monk look for the rest of my life.

I decided I wasn't going to let my facial whiskers or the friar look prevail as I climbed the tallest mountain in the world. I couldn't resist visiting the local barbershop that I passed by on the walk into the village. Seeing that straight blade made me a bit anxious—the barber only nicked me once. He even massaged my scalp when he was done shaving. One of the phrases I like to use is that you never see expensive marble sitting atop cheap wood furniture. The barber brought out the shine in my marble.

During the process of changing my shirt back at the lodge later in the day, I accidentally snagged the necklace Bailee had made for me. Beads went flying all over the room. My heart sank as I tried to find each one so I could put it back together.

The cord was beyond repair so once again I headed back down the steep set of steps leading to the shops below.

I went straight to the shop where I purchased the yak bone necklaces. My *khata* friend carefully restrung the beads on an adjustable cord. Before placing it around my neck I noticed the "D" in the word GOOD was backwards. With a smile and a quick adjustment the necklace was back around my neck.

I reminded the shop owner I would stop back on the trek out to purchase a yak bell or two from him. They are similar to cow bells, something I remember from my youth so I thought it would be great to take home a native sound from this country. I thought that perhaps the sound of the yak bell would facilitate memories of being in such a beautiful place.

Knowing we would eventually be religiously consuming mainly instant coffee and/or tea in the morning, several of us decided to have a real coffee our final morning before heading up over the large ridge above us. On the other side was the village of Khumjung, home of Phurba Tashi Sherpa, our lead sirdar or head Sherpa of the expedition. Prior to 2009, Phurba had stood on top of Mount Everest well over a dozen times. He is a trusted friend and extremely valuable part of Russell's expeditions. I was anxious to meet this Everest icon.

As we passed the entry arch into the village, we walked past history. Immediately to our right was the first high school the late Sir Edmund Hillary helped build. Hillary helped create the Himalayan Trust, a foundation designed to help the people of Nepal, primarily those within the Khumbu, by constructing schools and hospitals. I not only admired his will to get to the top of the world but also his tenacity to help the people that influenced his life. I would later learn that Russell himself helped Hillary build a school in Nepal, the early start of his humanitarian days.

We stayed at Phurba's Tashi Friendship Lodge for the next two nights. Although Phurba was not there upon our arrival his immediate family was, including his three young boys (two of whom are identical twins) and one of his daughters. It took them a while to warm up to us yet the Nerf football I brought along seemed to break the ice. Unfortunately, as Westerners not yet used to the thin air, we were no match for them. Growing up at just under 13,000 feet meant they could run circles around us even though they appeared to be just walking. Our game of keep away was more like a game of keep the breath away. Yet it was so much fun to see the smiles on their faces and to hear them laugh.

Eventually Phurba arrived and it was an honor to finally shake his hand. He is tall with a strong build for a Sherpa. It was obvious he was powerful by design. Friendly and charismatic, he is well respected by his peers. I looked forward to learning more about him, especially when it came time to administer the cattle dewormer to some of his family's yaks that would be used to porter our gear to base camp. Due to some logistical issues, the product ended up bypassing Khumjung, heading a bit further up the valley.

There was still plenty of time to do that work, so our full rest day at Khumjung found several of us heading up the hill to the Everest View Hotel. The name of this establishment says it all as its location was picked so that patrons could enjoy the view of the tallest mountain in the world, still miles away. I had been waiting twelve years to see it with my own eyes, so the anticipation was burning inside.

The day started with partly sunny skies. The holy peak Ama Dablam came into view first, high above the Tengboche Monastery in the far distance. At 22,359 (6812m) it looked huge, so I could only imagine how big Everest would appear. Then Nuptse, the peak south of Everest, appeared. My heartbeat started to pick up. When Lhotse, the fourth highest peak in the world and the one intimately connected to Everest's southeastern flank started to peak from behind the clouds, it was almost too hard to take. The thick grey mass inched away minute by minute. Then, as if my patience had not been tested enough the winds shifted which caused the curtain of clouds to tightly close. Today would not be the day my eyes would gaze upon Everest.

The next morning we again woke to partly sunny skies. Prior to departing the Friendship Lodge, Phurba's father paid us a visit. A holy lama, he offered each of us a silk *khata* that he had blessed for our safe journey on Everest. Even though I had already received a *khata* from the shop owner in Namche, I knew this one would remain inside my backpack while on the mountain.

Phurba's entire family then came outside to bid each of us farewell with a nod and the customary word *namaste*. *Namaste* is used as a greeting and a farewell, a verbal form of exchanging goodwill. For argument's sake it is simply a great word. Countless more would be exchanged with the numerous porters, Sherpas, climbers, and trekkers I would encounter along the way.

Our next goal was the village of Tengboche. At just under 13,000 feet, it is home to one of the highest and oldest Buddhist monasteries in the world. Since we did not get to see Sagarmatha from the Everest View Hotel, we sought views from Tengboche that we had been told were typically outstanding. As fate would have it, however, when we arrived in the village the clouds once again enveloped the giant rock in the distance. The mountain was once again teasing me, as if playing the longest game of peek-a-boo I had ever played. Before retiring for the day, most of us went into the local bakery for a sweet treat, much needed carbohydrates to replenish the energy we had lost during the up and down trek from Khumjung.

Similar to my introduction to Big Jim back in Phakding, I thoroughly enjoyed getting to know my other teammates one by one during the trek. Today would be no different. Moises Nava from Mexico and Stuart Carder from England were two other gents with which I seemed to hit it off. Stuart is barely my senior and we clicked, feeding off of each other's one-liners. I decided Stuey was a fitting nickname, something I'm sure he had heard before. The conversation within the bakery continued with many laughs.

It was Moises' turn next. We began to tease him that pronouncing his name (the first syllable pronounced *moy* like *soy*) proved awkward for our Western tongues. Moses (as in the biblical reference) sounded better to us. He had heard it before and didn't mind. We couldn't help but turn our focus away from the teasing every once in a while to stare out the windows. We were holding out hope that we might still catch a glimpse of Everest before the sun set, but the clouds didn't look like they were going to relax their grip on the mountain.

Remember the story of how Moses parted the Red Sea? Whether it was just ironic timing or divine intervention, what happened next was amazing. When Moises stepped out of the bakery the clouds began to part. Like a mindboggling magic trick, Everest suddenly appeared before our eyes. I admit I could not hold back the tears. After twelve years of seeing it only in film and on paper, the most captivating mountain in the world greeted us with a smile, piercing the sky above with tremendous authority.

Giddy as schoolchildren ill-defines how we began to act. What a sight with its characteristic plume of snow flowing from the summit, another three vertical miles above us. That iconic streak of blowing snow reminded me of a long trail of chimney smoke suspended in the air on a cold winter day back home.

We playfully thanked Moises for parting the clouds. I took numerous photos of the mountain and the others, the smile on their faces rapidly spreading throughout the team like a virus. We knew we had a lot of ground to cover between Tengboche and the summit, yet being able to see it for the first time was not only magical, it was inspirational. It would take time, hard work, physical and mental fitness, luck, and of course good weather before we could reach the top.

Every spring, historically towards the end of May to early June, there's a small window of opportunity that allows climbers to sneak up to the summit. It is during this brief period of time the jet stream winds that normally pummel the summit on a relatively constant basis, fade and shift to the north. This period of calm usually only lasts for a couple weeks at most.

Modern weather forecasting has increased the predictability of this jet stream pattern. Being able to do so allows climbers to more accurately time the weeklong voyage from base camp to summit and back. There are no guarantees that the winds will always cooperate, whether completely shifting away or perhaps returning prematurely. For now all we could do was hope the historical pattern would continue for us this spring.

During our two-night stay in Tengboche, some of us went into the monastery to observe the Buddhist monks' chants and prayers. It was an incredible experience to witness their beliefs. As we exited the building, we walked around its perimeter in a clockwise fashion, spinning the numerous prayer wheels attached to its walls. In fact, we had been spinning hundreds of such wheels along the entire trekking route.

Spinning a wheel is analogous to seeking a blessing from Buddha, so why not collect as many as possible? Similar to the wheels, numerous hand-carved stone prayer tablets lined the route as well. They're there to bless the immediate area and passersby, so long as they are passed to the left or in a clockwise fashion. We learned this on the first day of the trek, and I was not about to pass on the right. I felt a connection to the local customs and wanted to absorb as much good karma as possible.

The Tibetans refer to Everest as Chomolungma, which means "goddess mother of the world." The day we left Tengboche the skies were clear. Chomolungma stood in the distance as if saying, "I'll be waiting for you." As we descended the valley below, we were told that the mountain would be out of view until our final day of trekking. After a couple of nights in the village of Dingboche at the base of Ama Dablam, we eventually made our way to Himex's interim base camp near the foot of Mount Lobuche, one of several trekking peaks in the Khumbu Valley.

As we gained the ridge leading down into camp, we passed numerous *chortans*. These hand-constructed stone pillars honor those who died climbing Mount Everest, a tally well over two hundred to date. Among the memorials was Scott Fischer's, a premiere American mountain guide who died during the 1996 tragedy. It is humbling to pass such monuments knowing you are heading to the same place where these people lost their lives. They are a solemn reminder that the mountain ultimately holds the key to success or finality.

At just under 16,000 feet (approximately 1,500 feet higher than the highest point in the US), Lobuche base camp was a three to four hour walk from Everest base camp, yet the ever-thinning air meant those few hours would feel like we were walking on the moon. To be honest, it was actually nice to be in a tent for a change. It was time to get used to the fact that the thin nylon membranes would represent our shelter from the environment for at least the next month and a half.

Russell was planning for us to climb to the top of Lobuche, another 4,000 feet above us, as part of the conditioning and acclimatization process before even stepping foot on Everest itself. At 20,080 feet, its summit is just two hundred and forty feet shy of Mt. McKinley's summit. Looking up at the route took away any notion it was going to be an easy trekking peak. Soon we would be back to try and reach the summit, not just once but twice.

Chapter Six

Home Away From Home

April 9, 2009. After trekking nearly thirty-eight miles with a vertical gain of one and a half miles, our team finally reached Himex Everest base camp, perched on the outer edges of the Khumbu Glacier. My arrival into our home away from home was less than glorious. Ten minutes and within visual range of our tents I started to feel nauseous. Moments later an incredible wave of fatigue hit me. Vomiting ensued making the inning a perfect three and out. AMS was once again paying me a visit, this time with vengeance.

I was trekking with Big Jim and Stuey at the time. Sick physically, my pride hurt as well, it was embarrassing to come so far, only to have this unpredictable condition take away an almost picture perfect trek in from Lukla. Stuey and Jim could not have been more compassionate. Stuey grabbed my backpack and Jim put his arm around my shoulder to help support me. We slowly walked the last few hundred meters into camp.

The thought of Stuey carrying my pack was more than I could bear, so after a bit of pathetic pleading he reluctantly handed it back to me. My pride may have been bent, but it was not completely broken. I wanted to finish the last few meters under my own power.

I admit I also didn't want Russell to see my incredibly weakened state. He greeted us with a smile as we entered the miniature tent city. It was all I could do to muster up the same, and then proceed directly to the elevated three-tiered tent platforms to find a tent. Grizz had gotten to camp well ahead of us and kindly reserved me a tent near his own. Both Stuey and

Grizz's tents were right above me, and Big Jim's a couple spots from them. I appreciated having a private place to lie down, my nausea now in full swing.

For forty-eight hours I battled the condition. I wasn't alone as several other members, including Jon, were fighting it as well. Like him, they appeared worse than me, so I could only imagine how they must have been feeling inside. Have you ever had a hangover? I have had a hangover or two in my life. AMS feels like that but magnified in intensity. Those first two days in base camp crept by. I had a difficult time keeping food down. I started to doubt whether I'd be able to climb Everest and I hadn't even put on a crampon yet!

I lost almost eight pounds of bodyweight because of the AMS, a fraction of what was to come. It turns out the early bout of illness would be a blessing in disguise. Aside from an occasional round of loose bowels, my initial recovery seemed to strengthen me. I never got AMS or even a hint of its symptoms again. At various times, Dr. Piris had her hands full trying to heal those of us stricken by the altitude. I had a couple minor respiratory problems later on due to my cold-air induced asthma, but she helped me out each time. I will be forever grateful. Others would be less fortunate.

Jon was one of those that seemed to draw the short straw. During the trek up the hill to Tengboche he broke with diarrhea. Shortly after that he developed a nagging cough and persistent headache. During my recovery Dr. Piris had me sleep in Jon's tent one night to make sure everything was okay while he breathed the bottle oxygen she prescribed. Needless to say, we looked like a pair of soiled field workers, not athletes ready to take on a big mountain. It would take days before either one of us could really enjoy our surroundings.

Traditional base camp sat another twenty to thirty minutes walk farther up the glacier from Himex base camp. Our camp was deliberately set up away from the common trail along the glacier used to reach traditional base camp. Russell felt it best to limit the amount of foot traffic into our camp in order to reduce the risk of contracting communicable diseases from the various climbers, porters, and trekkers passing by.

Himex base camp was indeed a miniature city. All the paid climbers were given their own tent. The same rule applied to the guides and Dr. Piris. The camp also included a cook tent, three large dining tents, and two restroom tents each containing a shower area. Several long Sherpa tents had been erected along with a couple storage tents, and lastly a communal structure referred to as the white pod. The pod reminded me of an astronomy tower minus the telescope protruding from within. The brilliant white nylon dome structure, complete with a foyer entrance constructed of plywood, was the centerpiece of camp.

The envy of other expeditions, it would eventually be nicknamed the Tiger Dome because of the tiger-shaped rug that donned the center of the floor inside. It also housed a flat-screen television and DVD player, an espresso machine, a stereo with surround-sound speakers, lounge chairs, coffee tables, a charging station for iPods and laptops, and last but not least, a bar with stools!

Why such luxuries you might ask? Not only did Russell want to offer us some of the comforts from back home but this structure was designed to unite us under one common roof to build team spirit. Even though I enjoyed the sanctuary of my individual tent, the white pod allowed all of us to get to know one another, to build trust, and ultimately the camaraderie we would need in order to work together on the mountain.

Teamwork included our base camp staff. I cannot say enough wonderful things about this group of men. When we found ourselves in base camp in-between climbs, the staff would come to our individual tents starting around seven in the morning as part of a formal wakeup call. They would offer us a choice of tea and present us with a warm moistened cloth to wipe our faces. Room service in the Himalayas!

Breakfast was usually served around eight o'clock. It was customarily announced by one of the staff members beating a pot or pan. That same dinner bell would ring out prior to lunch and dinner, usually at half past noon and around six in the evening, respectively.

The cook tent actually contained a fully operational gas stove. On a regular basis porters would deliver fresh gas tanks, toting away the empty ones on their way back down the valley. Tashi, our head cook, used the stove to prepare many scrumptious meals. It was also used to bake numerous treats, including rolls and cakes. In fact, Russell had hired for our expedition a young Kiwi chef by the name of Haydn Fisher. Haydn's primary responsibility was to teach Tashi and the cook staff how to make desserts, something they did not have a lot of experience with.

I can testify that they listened to Haydn well because the cakes were absolutely amazing. This Kiwi also has a terrific sense of humor and a zest for life. I admired that and would frequently join South African Robby Kojetin in provoking Haydn to impersonate Arnold Schwarzenegger's character from the movie *Predator*. He did it perfectly every time; yelling out, "Get out! Get to the chopper!"

Downtime in base camp was fairly uneventful yet habitual. It was during the seven o'clock greetings from the base camp staff that I started to befriend Mingma, a young Sherpa boy who spoke very little English. He was always busy working around base camp, rarely pausing for a rest. I admired his work ethic as well as the fact that he always seemed to have a smile on his face.

After "tea in bed" I would usually do a quick check of email using my PDA to satellite phone connection. I would then get dressed and head to the dining tents to have a hot cup of coffee with my teammates. At this point the sun would start to rise above the west shoulder of Everest, greeting our camp with very welcomed warmth. Slowly but surely camp would come to life.

Beyond washing clothes, some days my British teammates and I would take turns teaching each other how to throw the Nerf football, rugby and American style. Sometimes Mingma would take a short break and toss it around with us. At one point the film crew decided to capture Grizz and me testing our throwing and catching abilities utilizing our newfound skills. Let's just say I'm glad they didn't show that footage on the television program.

Fresh snowfall meant clearing the camp trails and assisting with snow removal from atop the tents. It also meant terrific snowball fights. We would often challenge each other to target certain items, including each other. Robby Kojetin and John Black, both from South Africa, would often retreat to one of their tents soon after breakfast to send blogs to the Internet.

One morning some of the guides challenged me to throw a snowball at their tent to see just how close I could hit one of my South African pals. I had played baseball for a few years during my youth, yet my accuracy with a snowball wasn't always spot on. That particular morning the arm was loose and limber. At about thirty yards away I wound my arm up like a small catapult.

I don't know if it registered at first who might have thrown it, the fact that I had my head down while the guides around me were laughing, not to mention pointing fingers in my direction tipped him off. The ball of compressed ice crystals had found its mark, piercing through John's open tent door. Robby was perched just inside the door.

With particles of snow all over his side, Robby turned to give me a look; a glare that indicated verbal payback would soon be his revenge. Luckily he was smiling. Robby is a quick-witted as well as sharp-tongued lad. Whether it was his one-liners or the games he helped create for our amusement within the Tiger Dome, his uplifting presence on this expedition was second to none.

Base camp life gave each of us a unique opportunity to learn more about one another, snowballs or not. I had yet to get to know my Norwegian teammates, Tommy Rambøl, Thomas Svane Jacobsen, and Asbjørn Hjertenes. Through the first couple of weeks of the trip they had been very reserved, typically keeping to themselves. I admired their focus and dedication to the task at hand.

One night, however, my perception of their need to remain reserved was shattered. We were sitting in the dining tent for dinner, well after dark. As usual, Thomas and Tommy had little to say during the meal. For no apparent reason the lights went out in the tent. After a few seconds of muttering the tent fell completely silent. What lit the tent up next was not the light from the restored battery but our extreme laughter. As if written for a late-night talk show, Thomas suddenly yelled out, "Tommy, get your hand off my leg!"

From that moment on I knew it would be okay to tease these guys a bit. It was probably one of, if not the best one-liner during the course of the expedition. Robby's line however, caught on film for the Discovery show, is a close rival. While sitting in his tent alongside Grizz high on the South Col at 26,000 feet, winds threatening to relocate the tent along with them, the words poignantly rolled off his quick-witted tongue, "Well, I don't foresee a bright future for the postcard industry from here."

The dining tent is where I re-nicknamed Jim Holliday "Big Hot Gouda." I added Gouda because I came from the number one state for cheese production in the US and Jim wanted to be an honorary Cheesehead. The word "Hot" originated from the fact that Jim put hot sauce on just about everything he ate. Years earlier he started losing his sensation of taste so hot sauce at least provided him with some sort of flavor to his food.

One morning I slipped into Big Hot Gouda's favorite dining tent where he would customarily sit in the back corner during every meal. With a black marker I labeled one of the hot sauce containers "Big Hot Gouda's—Do Not Touch." He would often be in the dining tent hours ahead of schedule, reading his book. We teased him that the only reason he got there so early was not only because he wanted to protect the contents of the hot sauce container, but that there was only one portable heater inside, and it just so happened to be in his corner.

April 12, 2009. Our Sherpas conducted a Puja ceremony today. At the highest point of our miniature city they constructed a rock altar. In the center rose a thin pole. Fixed to the top of the pole were several long prayer flags stretching out in three distinct directions. I had read about this religious tradition and had witnessed it on numerous television documentaries, including the series we were now being filmed for. The Sherpas believe gods and goddesses live on top of the mountains. The Puja ceremony was a requirement before any climb could occur, in order to ask for our safe passage up the mountain. With the smoke and smell of juniper incense blowing in the winds, along with the prayer flags, the Sherpas chanted and prayed to Sagarmatha.

With our ice axes blessed at the Puja altar, the Sherpas ended the ceremony by rubbing blessed flour on our faces. We were eventually given blessed barley and grain to place inside our packs. Phurba distributed pieces of yarn that had also been blessed and tied with a special knot in the center by a nearby holy lama. I decided to wear the yarn around my neck for the remainder of the trip. What was one more thing tied around it at this point? Seriously, it was an honor receiving both items as well as being a part of the Puja. I felt even more connected to the Sherpa way of thinking.

Jim Holliday and I showing off our Sherpa hats at the Puja altar.
Photograph by Moises Nava.

Chapter 7
Test Time on Lobuche

For the past couple of weeks, a group of Sherpas known as the Icefall Doctors had been establishing the route up through the Khumbu Icefall. Perched just above base camp this is one of, if not the most dangerous part of the climbing route. When a glacier forms on a mountain, gravity pulls it downward through the path of least resistance. Here this meant the valley between Everest's west shoulder and Nuptse, a 25,791-foot (7861m) peak. As the flowing ice and debris approaches rising temperatures in the lower elevations, the same gravitational pull breaks it apart into what is referred to as an icefall.

There are three distinct risks within the icefall. The large ice blocks, which form as a glacier breaks apart, are known as seracs. Some are the size of multiple story office buildings and without a moment's notice can collapse. In 2006, three Sherpas were crushed to death when the serac they were standing under did just that.

Then there are the large gaping cracks between the seracs that are referred to as crevasses. Tiny ones are jumped over. The bottom can be visible or often they appear bottomless, hundreds of feet deep and can even widen to incredible diameters. Snow bridges will form across the narrow ones. While their stability is not always guaranteed, these bridges are used to quickly yet gently walk across to other side.

When the crevasses are too wide to jump or allow for snow to form a bridge, the icefall doctors would construct manmade bridges using ten-foot aluminum ladder sections. The really wide ones call for multiple sections lashed together with rope. A safety-line, which you clip into, accompanies these ladder crossings, so if you do fall off the swaying bridge, the rope suspends you in midair, at least in theory.

Prior to this trip I had been practicing walking across such ladders back home using my twenty-foot aluminum extension ladder stretched across large snowdrifts. With my big mountaineering boots and crampons strapped on I would get the feel of how to place my feet on the rungs. Luckily for me, I have good size feet, so I am able to place them with my crampons touching the rung in front of my toes as well as the one at the heel. I did not set up a safety-line as I wanted to test my balancing skills. Needless to say I fell into my miniature crevasse numerous times. There was no way I was going to avoid using the safety-lines in the icefall!

The west shoulder of Everest towers over one side of the icefall, which spawns the third risk: avalanches. Suspended on the shoulder are several large ice shelves precariously hanging above the icefall, just waiting to release tons of snow and ice down on the route below. No one knew when one of these massive waves of destruction might come crashing down. It was just a matter of time.

Given Russell's concern for everyone's safety he devised a unique plan for our continued acclimatization and training while keeping us out of the dreaded icefall. Due to our large size, we would divide into three separate climbing teams. We would then make the three-hour trek back down the valley to climb Lobuche East, the teams separated by a day.

The teams remaining behind at Everest base camp would take advantage of the rope and ladder training area the guides had established in a safe section of the icefall closer to base camp. It would be nice to practice on the real-life range set up by our guides. We would also get to brush up on our fixed-rope travel skills, crampon techniques, and rappelling abilities.

April 17, 2009. The first team headed down to Lobuche base camp for the night to prepare for the next day's climb. The second team followed a day later and finally, the third and final team, which I was a part of, set out on the five-mile trek back down to Lobuche on April 19. Although Lobuche base camp had enough tents for all of us, it did not have as big a setup for the base camp staff. In order to accommodate the large number of meals needed, a staggered calendar program worked best. This would also give the guides a chance to better assist as well as evaluate each climber's individual performance.

After a good night's rest, a hot breakfast, and final gear check, our team set off through the initial rocky moraine just above camp. The first day's goal was about 1,500 feet higher, our tents set up on a fairly flat granite rock plateau. From there it was another 2,500 vertical feet to the summit. I felt pretty good the morning of April 20 and set off on the comfortable pace set by our lead guide for the day, Shinji Tamura. Only fifteen minutes out of camp we reached a place that required us to strap our crampons on our boots.

Our team started to stretch out a bit. One of the biggest challenges for me was to learn to not take off too fast after a break or short rest. About two-thirds of the way up, my Japanese teammates passed me. Close to sixty years of age, both Shokichi Saito and Takenori Yoshida were forces to be reckoned with. I admired their strength, focus, and determination.

Saito in particular had a terrific sense of humor. Did I mention both of them had already stood on top of Everest via its northern route through Tibet? My third Japanese teammate, Kyomi Takiguchi, was somewhere below us with Himex guide Hiroyuki Kuraoka (aka "Hiro"). At over sixty years of age, she was not the fastest or strongest on the team, yet she put one foot in front of the other and never complained. For me, she was a poster child of No Place but UP!

Just ahead of the Japanese men were Billi Bierling and Ellen Miller, the first to summit Lobuche that day. Both were extremely fit, barely breaking a sweat during the climb. Billi is a journalist and athlete living in Kathmandu yet originates from Germany. She was here to climb Everest after having spent years interviewing climbers who had done so. She now wanted to see what the climb was like firsthand.

Ellen is from Vail, Colorado and is the first (and only at the time of writing this book) American woman to summit Everest from both the north and south sides. She was here to attempt Lhotse, the fourth highest mountain in the world and

Everest's southern neighbor. Ellen has spent years climbing and trekking in Nepal. What is even more impressive about her is that one year earlier she had a total hip replacement performed. Her climb on Lhotse was a fiftieth birthday gift to herself. To put it mildly, Ellen is an inspiration to many including myself.

As Billi and Ellen made their way down from the summit, Shinji, Saito, Takenori, and I approached the top. I thought I was daydreaming because with just ten meters to go Saito got down on his belly and literally swam to the top, laughing all the way. I really enjoyed his lightheartedness and sense of joy about all things.

Trailing a few minutes behind, I finally joined them at the summit. Required when arriving into camps and various checkpoints like the summit, everyone reports in to Russell. The tragedies that have occurred on Everest due to lack of communication warranted each of us having our own handheld radio. To add to this improved level of communication, Russell was even watching us on the final summit ridge through a telescope while perched comfortably back at Everest base camp, five miles away.

The views from the summit were stunning as the weather was unbelievable. We had blue skies with minimal clouds and a temperature comfortable enough to wear a thin pair of gloves and just one layer of clothing. My Japanese colleagues and I stayed on top for a while to take photos, each of us transfixed on Sagarmatha in the distance high above our home away from home.

It looked big, towering above nearby Nuptse and the west shoulder, both of which appear large when standing at base camp. Lhotse appeared to even be dwarfed by Everest. Makalu and Cho Oyu, two other 8,000-meter peaks were clearly visible in the distance as well. Even though the five-mile trek between Everest and Lobuche was something I was less than enthusiastic about, the fact that we had such incredible views and were avoiding excessive trips through the Khumbu Icefall made climbing on Lobuche appealing.

I wish I could say the first descent of Lobuche was uneventful. No one got hurt. But just below the summit there was a small crevasse we had to jump over. Throughout the journey so far I kept my digital camera in a small pouch that I then attached to one of the gear loops on the side of my pack's waist belt. The pouch had both zipper and Velcro closures to secure the camera in place. Occasionally I would simply close the pouch with just the Velcro flap. This proved to be a poor decision because after another forty-five minutes of descending, I reached for the camera to take a photo of some of my colleagues coming up the route. The camera was gone! I had a backup camera at Everest base camp but had not backed up all of the pictures on the camera that was surely now at the bottom of Lobuche somewhere. I was mad at myself to put it mildly.

Hiro was still ascending with Kyomi, so I asked him if he would look for my camera on his way up to the summit. I knew it was a long shot given the pitch on most of the upper route, yet he gladly accepted the task. Before continuing on with my descent I told him I would owe him whatever he wanted if he found it.

Just as I approached our tents on the granite moraine my radio came to life. It was Hiro on the other end. He found my camera! Apparently it slipped out of the camera pouch just as I jumped the crevasse near the summit. It was lying close to the trail just a few feet away from falling in. So what did I owe him for finding the treasure? Five beers once back at Everest base camp. We joked about it over the radio and of course I could not thank him enough. I was lucky once again.

With the rest of the descent uneventful and a rest at the bottom, we eventually made the three-hour trek back up to Everest base camp. Some of us stopped at Gorak Shep, the tiny village within an hour's walk of camp to have a Coke and even utilize the satellite Internet service. Even though the climb went well, I still felt a bit off and the trek back aggravated me. I have to admit I did not overly enjoy that particular stretch of the trekking route.

A lot of up and down rocky terrain and being tired from the climb did not help my attitude. Despite feeling a bit grumpy about the walk I was glad to finally be back at base camp and my tent. I was overdue for a shower, so knowing a good cleansing was waiting for me picked my mood up a bit too.

At the start of the trip the shower units failed to work adequately, despite Stuey's best efforts as a plumber to fix them. Luckily there was a small hand-held pump sprayer that the base camp staff filled with hot water when asked. Russell requested that we limit our showers to once every seven to ten days at most.

We respected that request because all of the base camp water used not only for showers but also for cooking and drinking came from a small, nearby glacial pool. The base camp staff would haul it in large containers on a daily basis. The water was then boiled in the kitchen tent to make it safe for use.

Showers meant a lot of work as well as cost, hence the reason for limited use. Good thing I brought plenty of wet wipes! Still, we were lucky to have the ability to shower even if just once per week. During the early years of climbing Everest this luxury did not exist and in fact some expeditions today still do not offer such amenities. Imagine going for two to three months at a time without a shower. Whew, I mean wow!

It was once again great to have a few days off in order to build our strength back up for the second round on Lobuche. Russ took advantage of this time to visit with each of us individually to review our progress to date. With the sun shining I sat down outside the Tiger Dome with him, the film crew capturing our exchange.

His directness did not wane because the first words out of his mouth were, "Lance, I am not concerned about your climbing skills. Just harness your energy to maintain a steady pace." He elaborated slightly on how to use my enthusiasm to pace myself. His observation was spot on as I continued the bad habit of starting out too fast. He reinforced that a steady pace from the start would get me to the top with plenty of energy left to get down safely. He caught me off guard when he abruptly changed the subject, his mind now clearly focused on Jon Hansen.

Although we never climbed any mountains together before Everest, traveling together to the other side of the world with Jon seemed fitting. We had labeled our trip the "Cheezehead" expedition (the letter 'z' was intentional). Jon created a terrific logo representing our Wisconsin pride. I, in turn, had my local embroidery shop create patches and flags with the logo so we could proudly display it on our gear, and with a bit of luck, on top of the world. Riddled with patches, the logo complimented my sponsor's patches, not to mention the stars and stripes of the US flag.

The separate punches of diarrhea and AMS seemed to hinder Jon's recovery. Just minutes into the Lobuche climb above camp, Jon started to falter. He informed me he wasn't going to be able to keep the pace the majority of us were on.

So he settled in just behind Dr. Piris who aside from being a physician is also a fit climber. She had come along to enjoy the climb, as well as be readily available should anyone need medical attention. As they approached the summit ridge, Jon decided not to finish the final fifty vertical meters or so to the summit.

One thing about Russell is that he does not miss a thing. Whether it's a piece of paper lying within the rocks around base camp or the performance of his climbers on a peak five miles away, he was aware of everything. Lobuche was not only part of our acclimatization and training program, but it also served as a test. It wasn't like the climbing roster in the Tiger Dome was stamped "EXAM" in big red letters, yet our performance was definitely being evaluated.

Russell and the guides were already starting to construct the Everest summit teams, still weeks away from being announced. The goal was to match climbers with similar speeds. They didn't want us to be stretched out all over the route just in case problems arose. At least two teams would be necessary because of the size of our expedition.

Russ had taken into account that Jon and I had hoped to climb together. The first thing he asked me was if I felt comfortable being separated from Jon. Despite his acclimatization problems, Russ then conveyed that he and the guides had concerns about Jon's attitude. They had picked up on his increasing level of tension. Russ and I both agreed there was still time for Jon's body to respond favorably to the altitude. I thought that if it did, maybe his mood would change and we could still end up high on the mountain together.

I let Russell know I felt comfortable climbing with everyone on the team and would do as he instructed. Although not a dictatorship, the expedition was not necessarily a democracy either. What if soldiers did not follow the orders of their superiors? What if employees did not follow the guidelines set by upper management? What if students disobeyed their teacher's instructions?

Just like everyone else on the expedition, I was here to climb a mountain. I also wanted to follow Russell's guidance. After all, making tough decisions is what all of us were paying him to do. I considered it a blessing to be teamed up with any of my newfound friends. Yes, I was disappointed that Jon and I were going to be initially separated, yet we still had another climb on Lobuche so I held out hope.

Before our trip together started, Jon made it a point to bring up the possibility that one of us may not perform as well as the other, perhaps not even being able to continue up the mountain. After all, he was a much more experienced climber than I and, as previously mentioned, had a better idea of what climbing on an expedition was like. We agreed that we needed to be prepared for that scenario. As I sat there talking to Russell I couldn't help but think back to that conversation.

Even though teamwork is vital for the success of any expedition, it is a member's individual performance that has the greatest influence over his or her own personal success on the mountain. Genetics does play a big part in determining how well the body adapts to altitude. Russell would remind us from time to time that as individuals, we were solely responsible for how we moved and how we breathed. He also reinforced the need to remain in control of our emotions.

Months after the trip, the Discovery program highlighted an interview with Jon where he had stopped short of Lobuche's summit. It was clear he was concerned with his performance, not to mention perhaps a bit envious of not being a part of us performing stronger, referring to us as the "*gran turismo.*" He also reported that he had nothing to prove by reaching the summit, content acclimatizing right where he was. This was one of the things Russell and the guides had been watching for during our first-round exam, commitment.

There were several members who had come to Everest in hopes of climbing to the summit together. Tommy Rambøl,

Thomas Svane Jacobsen, and Asbjørn Hjertenes from Norway were an obvious threesome. Robby Kojetin and John Black from South Africa were not only good friends but climbing partners as well, alongside their fellow countryman and friend Gilad Stern. Chris Dovell of England and Chris Jones of Ireland had paired up as well.

Robby and John were performing differently too and as a result ended up on separate teams up the mountain. Asbjørn's body had a difficult time adjusting to the altitude. Sadly, this would cause him to leave the expedition early while Thomas and Tommy continued on.

Paul Robinson and Bruce Parker, both from the US, had some climbing history together. They had reached the summit of Cho Oyu with Russell and Himex. Although Bruce was a slightly stronger climber, their respective paces allowed them to remain on the same team. The same was true of Dovell and Jones.

Before my review with Russell ended, I emphasized that I thought Jon was strong enough to get this thing done, but that I was concerned he was beating himself up mentally. I had not asked Jon why he stopped so close to the summit of Lobuche. Russell agreed and wanted to give everyone a fair chance at the summit, adjusting the acclimatization program for those who needed it. Aside from part of that exchange airing on the show, Russell detailed a bit further his concern of the mental barriers Jon seemed to battle. Yet true to his word, he offered up that if Jon could work through those barriers, he would be able to reach the top.

As it turns out, Jon elected not to make a second attempt on Lobuche like the rest of us. Instead he used that time to rest and recover at Everest base camp. This allowed him to muster up the strength needed to climb with his team up through the icefall a couple days behind the team I was on. The plan was for all of us to climb to Camp III over several days, and then return to base camp to wait for our summit window to open up.

Unfortunately the climb to Camp I, a height nearly identical to Lobuche's summit, would prove too much for Jon. He decided he could not go any higher. After I arrived into Camp III, I heard some chatter on the radio between the guides and Russell that Jon elected to turn around. It left me with an empty feeling in my stomach.

Two days later I arrived at base camp to find Jon waiting for me at the Puja altar. I was happy to see him yet at the same time sad that he was heading home. He had a wonderful smile on his face. One of the things I admired most about Jon was his level of enthusiasm and zest for life. The mountain unfortunately stripped some of that away from him, and it was hard to watch.

I knew his decision to leave the expedition early could not have been an easy one to make. Yet, had he continued to push himself too far, worse things could have happened. I respected his choice to return safely home to his family. While the camera rolled, we embraced and shared a few tears. Jon whispered in my ear to be strong but climb safe, to remember my family back home waiting for me. My friend then quietly turned around and walked out of camp.

Sharing one last smile with Jon Hansen before his departure from base camp. Photograph by Moises Nava.

I emailed Jon about a week later to verify he had gotten home okay. Jon had never been big about email during the time

I got to know him, yet he did respond to let me know he had safely returned to Wisconsin and to thank me. One of the few perks of flying a lot for business is my frequent flyer account. I used some of the miles to bump both Jon and I into first class for the round-trip flights, so it was nice to know the airline allowed him to keep that ticket given the change in dates. I knew it was a small consolation prize given the premature and disappointing end to his trip, but I hoped it made the twenty-four hour venture back home a bit more tolerable.

On the flip side of the perseverance coin was my teammate Megan Delehanty from California. She contracted a respiratory ailment early in the trip that resulted in a harsh cough. The coughing spells strained her back muscles, causing her constant pain. As a result she fell behind the rest of us, her body needing longer to adjust to the altitude. Instead of walking back and forth between respective base camps, Russell had her stay at Lobuche to try and recover in the thicker air.

The body tends to heal quicker at lower elevations. Breathing is of course easier, but sleeping more soundly is a bonus as well. I admired Megan's tenacity and willingness to be separated from the rest of us. A couple of years earlier she attempted Everest from the north side, only to be turned around high on the mountain after concerns over a dwindling oxygen supply. Her perseverance and ability to push through the discomfort would later prove invaluable.

April 23, 2009. It was time for round two on Lobuche that also resulted in a change to the climbing team rosters. I was steadily improving and as a result, Russell bumped me up to the middle team. The plan was to climb from Lobuche base camp all the way to the summit in one push, sleeping on the summit ridge for one night in order to advance the acclimatization process.

Big Jim ended up on the same team, so we decided to be tent mates. I was fortunate again to have Shinji as our team's lead guide. I had grown comfortable with his style and pace. Getting stronger also allowed me to apply Russell's earlier advice. I paced myself, staying step for step with Shinji up the entire mountain. When he rested I rested, when he climbed I climbed. The rhythm felt great.

The iPod tunes jamming in my ear (I left one ear open to listen to my two-way radio) had something to do with the comfortable pace too I'm sure. As we gained the summit ridge, Shinji decided to stop to make sure everything was in order with the setup of our tents. I wanted to continue on to the summit, now less than twenty minutes away, so Shinji gave me his permission. On another picture perfect afternoon I topped out on the summit of Lobuche for a second time.

Ellen worked her way up to join me, soon after Billi complimented our trifecta. Billi then decided to radio Big Boss (Russell's nickname given to him by the Sherpas years earlier) to inform him that "Team Didi" had arrived on top. I wasn't quite sure what a "*didi*" was at first, but it was obvious that Ellen and Billi reveled in the self-proclaimed title for our group. I found out later that *didi* in Nepali translates to sister. No wonder Big Boss teased the ladies a bit over the radio about my membership into such a group.

Aside from the bantering on the radio, I will never forget my time with Ellen on Lobuche's summit. She paid me a nice compliment while we stood there taking in the amazing views of the Himalayas all around us. "You are going to make it," she said. I asked her what she meant. After our first trip up Lobuche we had talked about my abbreviated climbing career and that Lobuche had been the highest point I had ever reached. She proceeded to elaborate under the blue sky.

She had been climbing enough in the Himalayas to sense which individuals had what it took to reach the top of Everest. Remember, she climbed to the summit not just once but twice, so I knew she had great insight. I gave her a big hug and thanked her. It certainly was a boost to my confidence, yet I also realized I had a long way to go, literally.

It was time to descend from the summit one last time. I made sure my camera was securely stowed away in my pack before jumping the now infamous crevasse just below the top. I thought to myself that another five beers to Hiro might just break my bank account. As I neared the tent platform I could see Christophe Vandaele, our Flemish-American teammate from New York City coming up the route just below the ridge.

Like Big Jim, I had gotten to know Christophe during the trek in as well as during our downtime in base camp. Christophe epitomizes the story of going from rags to riches. Born in Belgium, he came to the US with very little money in his pockets. While it took time, he eventually became a self-made entrepreneur and is now a dual citizen of both countries. He is also a gifted triathlon competitor.

During the initial trek into base camp, Christophe succumbed to AMS too. His condition waxed and waned to a greater degree however. Each time he tried to climb higher than the previous time, the altitude seemed to hit him with greater vengeance. Yet similar to Megan he put his best foot forward trying to overcome the odds against him, the sign of a true competitor.

When Christophe arrived at the tent platform the altitude once again zapped him of his strength. I am sure that at sea level he could out swim, out run, and out bike most of us. At altitude it was quite the opposite. His body's response made me appreciate all the more the role genetics must indeed play in the sport of climbing. All of us admired Christophe's desire to keep trying. Giving in without trying and trying again was simply not an option for him.

As Big Jim arrived at the ridge we threw our gear into the end tent on the upper row, mainly for the unobstructed view of Sagarmatha. Billi and Ellen ended up in the tent right across from us. They gazed over at us with puppy dog eyes as we munched on some Pringles potato chips we had carried up in our packs. Given their solemn looks how could we not share?

The tents were close enough to allow us to toss over one of our extra containers. We wanted to know what they were willing to toss back in exchange. They started to laugh as Ellen held up a pair of men's boxers! She found it tucked inside her Himex sleeping bag, which of course had been used the night before by someone on the first team.

Ellen got on the radio to Russell to see if anyone wanted to claim them. The laughing coming from the ladies' tent was infectious. Russell was in a good mood and joined in on the revelry over the radio. No one wanted to claim the mysterious boxers.

As the sun began to set in the west we peered out our tent door to capture some incredible images of Sagarmatha basking in the fading light. I enjoyed Big Jim's company in the tent that night, once again seizing the opportunity to tease him about his enormous flippers. We decided to skip breakfast the next morning. Instead we put on our harnesses and crampons to start the two-hour descent just after sunrise, hoping to grab a bite to eat down at our Lobuche base camp dining tent.

I wish I could say I was two for two in terms of smooth descents, aside from the camera debacle the first time down Lobuche's flanks. Even though it had only been a week since we were last here, the rising spring temperatures had caused the ice and snow to retreat further up the mountain. Therefore we needed to remove our crampons hundreds of feet higher above the moraine compared to the first climb. This left a large section of moderately angled smooth granite rock to negotiate before reaching the relatively flat moraine itself.

The runoff from above accentuated the slippery feel to the rock. With just under two hundred feet to go I lost my footing, fell backwards and started to slide. As I began to accelerate downwards all I could think about was tumbling out of control and breaking a leg or worse. I tried to get a finger hold on the tiny cracks in the granite but they passed by too quickly.

With another hundred feet of acceleration to go, I caught a glimpse of a large indentation in the rock just ahead. I was able to jam a boot in the dimple and reach back with my hand, which slowed my fall enough to where I knew I would be intact at the bottom. Moments later I came to a sudden stop. The only harm was my pride, a wet bottom, and a few scuffs on my backpack. I got lucky.

After regaining my composure, I slowly made my way back down the rock-filled valley just below the moraine. I was glad to be back in the safety of our dining tent. After a quick brunch and a few exhausting hours of trekking, we arrived back in Everest base camp. The second round-trip only took just over forty-eight hours to complete.

A couple days later, we were all back in our home away from home. Even Megan rounded out base camp as she, too, successfully reached the summit with the third Lobuche team and was now with the rest of us. Russell decided to host a celebration for our acclimatization efforts, a sort of pre-Everest climbing party in the Tiger Dome. It was a great way to blow off some steam. We were getting stronger and now even more anxious to see what climbing on Everest was really like.

Chapter Eight

A Happy Yak Is a Healthy Yak

As the end of April approached, my plans to work with the Sherpa people and their yaks had not come together. I was concerned that if it didn't happen before we headed up Everest I might never get the chance. During my second climb of Lobuche I came across the dewormer in the camp's storage tent.

Fortunately Phurba was present overseeing the setup of our summit ridge tents at the time. I asked if he could arrange for at least one of the containers and a dosing applicator to be portered up to Everest base camp.

After climbing Lobuche I hadn't seen as many yaks on the trail to traditional base camp. One morning in Himex base camp, however, Russell surprised me with news that a yak train would soon be arriving to our camp. It was show time! Phurba went to the storage tent to retrieve the container and applicator. I immediately proceeded to put the dosing applicator together. I patiently waited for the sound of a yak bell to pierce the morning air.

I admit I felt a bit nervous about working on the yaks. For years I had comfortably worked on domesticated cattle, yet keep in mind, the majority of them had been properly restrained in order to keep not only myself but also them safe during routine procedures like deworming. Using cattle chutes or pens would obviously not be the case here in the middle of the Himalayas. For the past few weeks I had been observing these beautiful animals as we trekked up the valley.

The traditional yak is short in stature with prominent curled horns and a long, shaggy coat. There are black ones, brown ones, blonde ones, and shades in between. I also had observed a large number that appeared to be crossbreeds, a mix of traditional yak and what I grew up around, the black and white domesticated Holstein. As you might guess the crossbreeds have a mottled black and white appearance. They are slightly smaller in stature with a coat not quite as shaggy.

Traditional male yaks can easily weigh between 700 to 1,000 pounds with female naks weighing in a few hundred pounds lighter on average. I noticed that when they encountered people on the trail it was not the yaks that moved out of the way. However the crossbreeds seemed a little more docile, perhaps weighing one-half to two-thirds as much.

During one of my rest days, back between Lobuche climbs, I had approached one of the yaks to see how it would react to my presence. I also wanted to get a few photos. I asked Phurba if he would mind holding the animal while I had my picture taken with it. Although I had met Phurba back in Khumjung I had not said I was the animal doctor who planned on working on the yaks. I'm sure he thought I was just another crazy Westerner here to climb a big mountain. Still, he kindly agreed.

In case you don't know, cattle veterinarians sometimes spend a respectable amount of time with their arm up the backside of female cows. We do this to manually palpate the reproductive tract to determine the animal's estrus cycle and/or pregnancy status. This is important to do in order to make sure the cows are bred back in a timely manner so that the cyclical clock of calving and milking does not skip a beat.

When I approached the tail end of the yak, Phurba got a bit nervous, politely reminding me to be careful back there. I informed him I would be very gentle. With that I placed my arm on the outside of the yak's rump, on the opposite side of the camera's position. This gave the illusion on the photo that I was actually palpating the beast.

The black yak danced around ever so slightly as it felt my hand glide across its hip. Phurba did a little dance too. I quickly vocalized that I was not just a climber but also the cattle veterinarian who came to help the yaks. A big grin appeared on his face as he eased back into a relaxed stance. The yak followed suit and went back into a relaxed position as well. I guess it too realized I only had external intentions. The resulting picture was priceless, definitely blog worthy.

As I stood in camp waiting for my first patients to arrive, I started to wonder how well they would stand for me while I placed a small blunt stainless steel tube inside their mouths. I didn't want this to become the highest rodeo ever recorded. There would be only one way to find out. The film crew was interested in documenting this event, especially if they needed extra footage for the show. I could see it now, "There goes Dr. Fox flying through the air, the result of a horn wedged up his backside!"

My ears then queued in to the characteristic guttural chimes approaching in the distance. One by one the yaks crested the rocky trail ridge just above camp. Phurba leaned over to inform me that these particular yaks belonged to his sister's herd. As a whole, Phurba Tashi's family owned around two hundred yaks. Ironically, this number worked out perfectly for the amount of dewormer available.

After finding out that information, I revamped my plans to solely teach Phurba how to deworm all of his family's remaining animals, because I knew he could get the job done and do it right. I also knew we had a busy month of climbing ahead of us and I wasn't sure how I was going to feel afterwards. The plan would be for him to use the product as soon as he returned to Khumjung after the climbing season was over. There he would administer the first dose to those we missed, as well as a follow-up dose approximately six weeks later to all the patients.

One sign of prosperity in the Sherpa culture is the number of yaks owned. And with almost twenty Everest summits under his belt (as of the 2011 climbing season), Phurba is a highly recognized and respected Sherpa in the Khumbu region. Taking this into account, along with all the yaks he owned, I figured that if the response to the dewormer was favorable the word would spread throughout the valley. Besides, being able to give back to Phurba and his family was the least I could do. He was the grease, which was making this expedition run smoothly. As lead *sirdar,* or head Sherpa, he had the daily task of organizing the Sherpas to carry loads of gear up the mountain to establish our camps and even the route high above.

Unlike Russell, who had grown up around livestock in the Western World, Phurba was uncertain of what I was about to do. You may be wondering the same. Let me explain. If you have a dog at home and are giving it a once a month product designed to prevent heartworm disease, in laymen's terms you are deworming your pooch. Mosquitoes carry the heartworm parasite. Since preventing a mosquito bite is not practical, the dewormer is an insurance plan to decrease the risk of infection from ever occurring inside your furry friend's body.

Grazing animals do not get heartworm disease but are prone to contracting other types of parasites (mainly intestinal worms yet also respiratory worms) from eating contaminated grass, the source often being each other or wild animals. In between climbing seasons (spring and fall) the yaks tend to be found living at lower elevations in the Khumbu Valley, grazing on the seasonal grasses growing in the warmer temperatures. Such temperatures often mean flies, which can transport parasites from one spot to another. Flies can also carry a parasite that can damage the hide of cattle and yaks, although I did not see much evidence of this in the Khumbu.

Unlike the non-mountainous areas of Nepal, I doubted the yaks high in the Khumbu had ever had much, if any, veterinary-related care. The product I was about to use is very safe. Given both points, I figured there was really no downside to working on the yaks. Of course the image of that horn up my backside lingered in the back of my mind as Phurba's sister's yaks walked calmly into base camp.

As if on autopilot, the yaks lined up and waited for our base camp staff to remove the supplies lashed onto their backs. The staff then put some food out for the yaks, not only as part of the routine but also a great distraction from what was about to happen. I approached the first one with caution, realizing it would sense me as a complete stranger. Besides, with my glacier glasses on, a do-rag protecting the precious marble on top of my head from the sun, and a strange contraption in my hand, I could only imagine what I looked like to the animal.

Along with Phurba, his sister, and the camera rolling, several Sherpas popped out of the nearby tent, curiosity getting the best of them. Phurba calmly wrapped a soft ribbon-like lashing around the animal's muzzle in an attempt to gently restrain its head. Before the yak could even think about it, I had inserted the applicator syringe in its mouth and squeezed the trigger. A swallow or two, followed by a few tongue licks and it was over. What a relief, the first one went better than I had anticipated.

Having witnessed how quick it went and how well the first patient reacted, Phurba and one of the Sherpas simply held on to the second yak by its bell collar. No muzzle restraint would be needed. This time I made sure Phurba got a good look at exactly how I was administering the product.

Phurba appeared to be right-handed just like me, so it made it easier for me to teach him. Standing on the yak's right side, I used the index finger of my left-hand, placing it gently but purposely in the corner of the animal's mouth to stimulate it to open. Once open the stainless steel tube slides easily just inside the mouth and the trigger is engaged. The white liquid squirts into the back of the mouth which then elicits a normal swallow response. A few good licks of the tongue are an indicator that the job is done correctly. One more and it would be Phurba's turn to try.

After getting comfortable with the applicator, Phurba and I picked out patient number four. Unlike my "finger in the corner of the mouth trick," he decided to lightly pinch the nostrils of the animal with his left index finger and thumb. This is an effective way of eliciting the same jaw opening response. Phurba's graceful action caught me off guard. He was a natural because before the yak even realized it, the dewormer was already on its way down the animal's stomach.

The remaining yaks were just as cooperative. I could tell Phurba was growing more confident after each successful application. At one point he even mock-treated one of the Sherpas who seemed to be really engaged in what we were doing. The Sherpas' sense of humor once again revealed itself.

I applauded Phurba's willingness to learn. I informed him that if the medicine worked, the yaks would start to feel better shortly after the final dose was given. By that I meant the female naks may in fact make more milk, the hair coat quality of both females and males may improve, and lastly we joked that the yaks might even be able to carry larger loads as they bounded up the trail.

After our first successful yak clinic was finished, Phurba and I laid out a plan for him to administer the rest of the product to the remaining yaks in his family's herd. My goal of giving back was now complete, at least for now. Later that day Russell asked, even though he already knew the answer, how it all went. I was happy to report that it went great, that I was thrilled to have worked with Phurba, and that I was even happier I could continue climbing without a horn hanging out of my backside.

With my mock palpation photo in hand I returned to my tent to post a blog about the yak clinic. My friend Eric Scott back in Wisconsin who works in the dairy industry for a large veterinary distribution company likes to use the self-proclaimed slogan "a happy cow is a healthy cow." I couldn't resist borrowing that phrase with a slight adjustment. The title of my blog ensued, "a happy yak is a healthy yak." I was elated to have worked on the yaks, and now I could fully concentrate on an even bigger goal ahead, I mean two miles straight up.

One of my first yak patients.
Photograph by Jon Hansen.

Chapter Nine

Time for Russian Roulette

April 25, 2009. During a team meeting, Russell laid out the roster for two teams, staggered by two days, for our first foray up to Camps I, II, and III. After reaching Camp III for a night, we would head back down to base camp. This was the next phase of our acclimatization, not to mention the ideal summit weather window was still weeks away.

As a result of my performance during the second Lobuche climb, Big Boss put me on the first team. The names of the teams were Yaks and Yetis, so having been placed on the Yaks felt like an omen. Remaining on the first team for the second and final trip up the mountain was not automatically guaranteed with this particular announcement. I wondered if it really mattered though.

Although I never felt like I was in some sort of race with anyone, I did challenge myself to move as efficiently as possible to show Russ and the guides I was a fit and competent climber. Remember my earlier comments about competition? It drives us to be successful. Yet whether our names appeared on the first or second team, success was about the effort. To quote Vince Lombardi, one of the greatest coaches in sports history: *Winning isn't everything but wanting to win is.*

Big Hot Gouda was part of the Yetis, so I had to find a new tent mate. Stuey was assigned to the Yetis as well. On Team Yaks, Grizz was paired up with Valerio Massimo of Italy, or "V" as I often called him. John Black and Moises became tent mates. Who would be my tent mate?

Eugène Constant from France was on the same team and fortunately we had gotten to know each other in between our

Lobuche climbs. We agreed to share a tent up high. Although English was not his native tongue and my French is virtually non-existent, I knew we would do well together.

I deeply admired Eugène's relationship with his mother. She actually had trekked to base camp with us and even climbed up Lobuche with Eugène. It was fun having her around and their relationship reminded me so much of the relationship with my own mother, less the climbing connection of course. It was obvious that Eugène was very committed to his family back home in France. His connection to them would prove very powerful after our stay at Camp III on the steep slopes of the Lhotse Face, halfway up to the summit of Everest.

As suggested earlier, perhaps the most dangerous part of the route on the south side of Everest is the notorious Khumbu Icefall. With its maze of enormous seracs and crevasses and the avalanche prone ice shelf above, it is like a game of Russian roulette entering the icefall. Although part of the same gameboard, the three dangers were like individual chess pieces, a matter of time before one of them would make its move, literally.

Similar to a frozen pond or lake in winter, the icefall is alive, hissing and popping, moving all the time. Depending on the ambient temperature, its movement may be minimal while other times flowing several feet per day. The eerie sound of the ice groaning under your feet is as good as any verbal dare. "Go ahead, take another step and see what happens."

The plan was straightforward. We would get up in the middle of the night in order to be into the icefall by around three in the morning. This would increase the margin of safety because the cold nighttime temperature meant less icefall movement. The colder air also reduced the risk of avalanches being spawned from the west shoulder. Sometimes as we slept in the safety of our base camp tents, we would wake to the distant rumble of one in the darkness.

April 29, 2009. Other than the occasional rumble of ice and snow, I usually slept quite well in my cozy base camp cocoon. Tonight was different as the anticipation of heading up into the dangers of the icefall meant a lot of tossing and turning. As a result, I didn't need an alarm clock or the base camp staff knocking on my tent door to tell me it was time to get up.

I knew I needed the calories. Choking down breakfast amidst the nerves already housed inside my stomach was difficult. I looked up from my dining tent seat to see Russell's characteristic early morning smirk. Big Boss made it a point to be up when both his climbers and Sherpas were up, to wish all a safe journey up the hill. Even Monica was awake to make sure we were all doing okay. The film crew was already busy too, filming our final preparations. The film crew planned on capturing us going up through the icefall and for some of us, including myself, they handed out an extra headlamp in hopes we would wear it on our sleeves so the camera people already positioned within the ice field could identify possible screen characters.

With handshakes and hugs we started filing out of camp towards crampon point amidst traditional Everest base camp. Crampon point is the area where we would stop to strap our spikes to the bottoms of our mountaineering boots. They would remain there until we reached Camp I, four to six hours away and another 2,000 feet above us, somewhere in the chilly and calm darkness. The twenty-minute walk to the crampon point was nerve racking.

No one spoke. All I could hear was the crunching of snow under our boots and my own heart, intensely beating within my chest. Halfway to crampon point, the light from my headlamp started to flicker. I tapped on it a few times only to see the beam become progressively weaker. As I approached the planned stop, the light was gone. I played with the buttons yet it didn't make a difference. Surely the batteries were okay, as I had just replaced them the other day. I decided to put new ones in versus getting my backup lamp out.

Fortunately the spare set of batteries I brought saved the day, or shall I say night, as I was once again graced with my own luminescence. The debacle used up precious time however, and our guides wanted to keep us moving as quickly as possible to keep ahead of the other teams, now starting to rouse within the numerous tents immediately around us.

Eugène was kind enough to wait for me. Nerves were taking over, as this minor setback seemed to snowball. It took me a bit longer than normal to get my crampons on. Add that my intestines felt a bit irritated and it was not the smoothest launch into the icefall I had hoped for. Finally, Eugène and I caught up to our team at the back of the pack, carefully picking its way up through the short pinnacles of ice in the lower portion of the ice maze.

About thirty minutes in, the first ladder crossing appeared. Luckily it was just one ten-foot ladder section and not as intimidating as I expected. Ironically, the darkness helped to ease my fears because I could not see the madness surrounding me or get a sense of the depth of the crevasse. From time to time the ice would groan. We would also hear an occasional distant rumble and be politely reminded of the dangers lurking ahead. If there was any time for tunes in my ear it was now! Instead I listened to myself saying, "Keep moving. Don't stop."

Surprisingly, the radio remained fairly quiet as we navigated the hellish maze of frozen water. Sometimes I would pause to listen to the clanging of crampons on ladder rungs up ahead, mentally preparing myself for another crevasse crossing. Other times it was the movement of Sherpas coming up from below, flying past me as if I were standing still. At times I was caught motionless.

The icefall was exhausting. Unlike a well-trodden path with a distinct direction, the route was constantly changing, up and down ice walls, around the steroid induced ice cubes. As dawn approached I found myself a few hours shy of reaching the safety of Camp I. The exhaustion continued to build. Eugène appeared to fade just a bit too, so we found ourselves being passed by a number of Sherpas and climbers from other teams. Then along came Phurba with several of our other Himex Sherpas. I couldn't believe their speed, let alone the fact that quite a few of them weren't even wearing crampons!

With his ever-present courtesy, Phurba said good morning to us and before I could even return the pleasantry, he was out of sight. The Sherpas would climb through the icefall in a matter of a couple of hours, less than half the time it took most of us Westerners.

It didn't help that my intestines wanted to join in on the fun. My bowels weren't going to hold out until I reached camp. I had to make a quick decision. I unclipped from the safety-line. In general, this is a cardinal sin when climbing fixed-line, but at least I wasn't on a steep pitch but a fairly flat spot amidst a maze of ice towers without crevasses nearby. I did not want to stray too far from the route, but I also didn't want to be seen by every passing Sherpa and climber on the mountain. I got my wag bag (as previously mentioned, we hauled everything off the mountain including "duty number two") in position, got my harness unbuckled, followed by a less than comfortable pose. Just in the nick of time!

I felt embarrassed but also a lot better. As I buckled back up I glanced up, only to notice I was perched directly under a forty-foot serac. What a terrific story for my children to tell their children: "Your grandfather went to climb Mount Everest and got crushed by a large ice cube while going to the bathroom."

I hastily clipped back into the safety-line and continued my way up through the maze. Around eight o'clock in the morning, I emerged from behind the last ice tower and could at last gaze upon the rolling landscape of the glacier above. Unfortunately for me, cameraman Mark Whetu had his camera fixed on me at the same time.

My tongue seemed to be swollen, if only imaginary, yet I had signed up for this and should have expected a camera here. Mark proceeded to ask me what I thought of the icefall. I replied that although I had to stop to relieve myself in such a dangerous place, I admired its beauty. I was also thrilled to have made it through the first time unscathed. With the interview over, I continued on towards our camp.

Camp I was set up between crevasses on the lower part of the Khumbu Glacier. The glacier actually starts over a mile farther up the snow and ice filled valley referred to as the Western Cwm (pronounced *coom*). Known as the Valley of Silence, the Cwm is bordered by the west shoulder of Everest on the left, 25,791-foot (7861m) Nuptse on the right, and 27,940 foot (8516m) Lhotse at the top by the start of the glacier.

With the peaks being so high overhead, the prevailing wind tends to go right over the top of the valley rather than within. Add to this fact the valley's ice covered bowl shape radiates like a desert during the day. For example, take a metal mixing bowl out of your kitchen cabinet and shine a flashlight inside it for an extended period of time. The bowl will be warm as it reflects and collects the heat of the light, just as the Cwm collects and radiates the heat of the intense sun at altitude.

It was remarkable to have climbed through the icefall in freezing temperatures, yet stand in Camp I by late morning with temperatures approaching seventy degrees Fahrenheit. It gets better, I mean hotter. By midafternoon the temperature would tease the triple digit mark!

Because of the rapidly rising temperatures, not to mention the fact that we were tired, Eugène and I, along with many others decided to hold up at Camp I for the night. Getting caught exposed in the sun higher up on the glacier was not a smart option. Camp II was only a three-hour climb away and about 1,000-feet higher, yet the growing altitude seems to slow time down.

Eugène Constant and I at Camp I in the Western Cwm.
Photograph by Shaun Hutson.

The next morning we departed from camp early while the sun was still behind Everest itself. The gradual climb up the glacier seemed to take forever. We had several crevasse crossings on the glacier too. With those added to the ones crossed yesterday, we successfully negotiated close to thirty ladder bridges on our way to Camp II. With two full round trips on the glacier and through the icefall that meant around 120 ladder crossings in all.

A full day of rest was planned at Camp II before tackling the next big obstacle, the imposing Lhotse Face. Rising for almost a mile in length with a pitch of forty to sixty degrees, Russell and the guides all said that the Lhotse Face would be our toughest day climbing Everest. Part of that day would be used just to reach our next rest stop at Camp III, perched around 23,500 feet above sea level, halfway up the wall.

Camp II was a miniature version of base camp and therefore appropriately named Advanced Base Camp or ABC. Spoiled once again, we would actually get our own sleeping tent. We also had a communal dining tent, cook tent, Sherpa tent, and even a toilet tent. Kyla, a member of the base camp staff, lived at ABC for weeks on end to cook for us and make our stay as comfortable as possible.

When we first arrived at ABC not all of the sleeping tents had been pitched so we decided to give the Sherpas a hand. We needed to first clear the platform sites so we began the process of moving rock and flattening out the ground as best we could. After tossing just a couple of rocks I was gasping for air. The Sherpas made everything at altitude look easy. After a lot of grunting and groaning I finally got my tent up. Eugène pitched his just above mine so that if we needed to double-up for any reason it would not be too far to carry our gear. I appreciated his efficient forward thinking.

After settling in, Moises and I decided to take a short hike over to the First Ascent camp sponsored by Eddie Bauer to try and meet Ed Viesturs. He is the first (and, at publication of this book, only) American climber to reach the world's fourteen highest peaks, all over 8000 meters or 26,247 feet. What's even more impressive is that he climbed them all without the aid of supplemental oxygen.

Currently living in Washington, he was born and raised in northern Illinois. Beyond originating from the Midwest we also had something else in common. Prior to becoming a climber and adventurer full-time, he used to be a practicing veterinarian. Needless to say, I was very interested in meeting him.

One of the First Ascent guides just happened to be coming back from an acclimatization climb to Camp III and informed us that Ed was still up there but would be coming back down tomorrow. I thought perhaps I would see him on the climb up but it wouldn't be a grand place to stop and chat so meeting this mountaineering icon would likely have to wait until I got back to base camp.

When we got back to our tents Jamie Berry, one of the cameramen stationed at ABC to film both Himex and IMG, decided it would be fun to have us test out a chest-mounted camera. With a cobra-like appendage mounted to a plastic chest shield and straps over my shoulders I looked like an alien from the *Star Wars* trilogy. After making sure the camera was secure and focused, Jamie asked me to walk around the frozen landscape, talk into the camera while acting a bit tired to help accentuate the effect of the surroundings. I politely informed Jamie that I really was tired so no acting would be required.

After a good chuckle and some bantering back and forth, I set off with the contraption dangling in front of me. While not Oscar material I managed to do as Jamie asked, struggle with my breathing, commentate about the effects of the thin air, and offer some panoramic shots of the outstanding scenery. Everest's summit, although just out of view, loomed high overhead with a characteristic plume of snow stretching out towards the east. I still had to pinch myself that I was truly here, knocking on the summit's door. Well, almost knocking that is.

Moises took a turn with the contraption as I snapped numerous photos to capture the moment. Just as he had done to me I yelled at him periodically to remind him how stupid he looked. After completing our movie role auditions it was decided that we better not give up our day jobs.

Kirsty Mitchell, another gifted camera-hand specifically assigned to Himex, had accompanied us on the climb up to ABC. Kirsty is also a fit climber, having been high on Everest's north side, along with climbing other peaks. She got her camera out to do some one-on-one interviews. As we sat on the icy moraine behind the dining tent, she began to ask me a series of questions. We talked mainly about my motivation for climbing the highest peak in the world.

I informed her that I wanted to show my kids that dreams could come true, if you work hard and believe in them. I then started to talk about my father and how I had brought some of his remains along with the hope of releasing them at the top. A trip like this magnifies one's emotions. I couldn't hold back the tears, my voice started to shake. After the interview she put the camera down and gave me a heartfelt hug, tears rolling down her cheeks too. Some of that interview would eventually become the backdrop of the show.

After a brief second night's rest, we started across the upper slopes of the glacier in the pre-dawn hours. A relatively low-grade pitch from camp, it still took us a couple of hours to ascend to the foot of the ice wall. Just before the bergschrund we clipped into the safety-line which would guide us up to Camp III, another 2,000 feet above, well out of sight because of the steep angle overhead.

A bergschrund is the large gap that forms at the start of a glacier as it pulls away from the mountain. Fortunately this bottomless pit had a significant snow bridge stretching across its span that allowed us to walk right up to the wall itself. From that point on, the most common view I had was the backsides of my teammates just above me.

The ice was extremely hard and, at times, the steps formed by previous climbers were mere dimples. The crampon skills I had learned from my prior climbs were now being put to the test. It was exhausting work putting one foot in front of the other. The rest step technique had renewed meaning on an ice wall of such magnitude.

There were only a couple of places to really catch my breath during the five to six hour climb. I started out fairly strong but after a couple of hours the fatigue was catching up with me. Dave McKinley, better known as Narly, one of Russell's other guides from New Zealand had been by my side since we left Camp I, two days earlier. I really appreciated his verbal support.

Once again my bad habit of taking off too quickly at the start of a climb was prematurely draining my gas tank. At one point I told Narly that he could pass me. I would eventually catch up at our tents. This was his first time on Everest too, and I didn't want to diminish his chance of success. He politely declined, telling me he was in no rush and wanted to hang with me. It was obvious he was committed to all of our success, something I really admired him for.

A bit of an adrenaline rush surged through me as I approached the first tent platform of another expedition. I soon realized, however, that our camp was another forty-five minutes or more higher. Darn it! To top off my frustration, an imposing forty-foot nearly vertical wall of ice had to be surmounted to even get to the first line of tents, a flat area that invited a much-needed rest.

With a titanic effort I labored up the obstacle. After some very deep breathing, along with constant urging and positive reinforcement from Narly, I finally reached the tents. Other climbers on the fixed-rope were going through the same agony, so everyone seemed to respect the rests. Still, not everyone was standing on a flat surface so Narly suggested we keep moving. I now fully appreciated why Russ and the guides said this would be the toughest day of climbing on the trip.

Finally, after five and a half hours I plodded into Camp III. Several days earlier our Sherpas chiseled the three tent platforms needed to accommodate our large group into the wall. Rolling out of bed at night, literally, was simply not an option, but oh, what a view!

We could see the tiny dots of our tents at ABC, as well as numerous crevasses of the Khumbu Glacier stretching through the Cwm below. The 23,494-foot Pumo Ri (7161m), the peak providing the vertical backdrop directly above base camp, now appeared as our equal. The view of the long snow plume above was spectacular. It was obvious the winds were still strong up at the summit. The triangular South Summit, just over three hundred feet lower yet still a mile higher than Camp III was effectively blocking our view of the top.

The views did not last long as a cold front descended upon the camp, along with it winds and blowing snow. Camp III was in essence shut down. The temperature plummeted to around minus thirty degrees Fahrenheit. Eugène had already made it to the safety of our tent and was getting the stove ready to melt ice for water.

Every movement here took longer than normal to perform. So far I had escaped a classic high altitude headache, yet here I could feel the blood vessels in my head throbbing with increasing intensity. Despite the frigid temperature outside the tent, the air within was stifling hot. Any remaining peaks of sun were cooking us inside our protective barriers. I felt like a veggie in a microwave steam bag. It was time to shed the down suit and force down some water to try and curb the pounding inside my skull.

I wanted to have Eugène take a picture of me holding my sponsor's banner here, similar to those I had taken at the lower camps, just in case I would not be able to return to this point due to illness or injury. In other words, I had intended to get that banner as high as possible, documenting its voyage for the company. After all, being here in Camp III meant we were now higher than any point in the world outside of the Himalaya Mountains.

Unfortunately, the wind continued to batter our tents and the clouds swallowed up what was left of a panoramic background for the picture. The picture could have been taken at base camp and you wouldn't have been able to tell the difference. The banner shot would have to wait.

Tomorrow morning we would head back down to ABC for one night's rest before returning to base camp. The thought of down climbing all the way back down, then humping it all the way back up to here and beyond was a bit overwhelming to think about. Except for our teammate David Tait, we knew this was still a vital part of our acclimatization schedule. David had already been to the summit of Everest twice before.

With Himex in 2007, he climbed to the top via the North Col route on the north or Tibetan side of the mountain. Instead of descending the same way, he came down via the South Col route on the Nepal side, essentially the same route we were now using. In other words, he did a complete traverse of the mountain. Phurba Tashi Sherpa had accompanied him on that incredible voyage. This time David was here to try and reach the summit without the use of supplemental oxygen, something only a handful of mountaineers have been able to successfully accomplish.

During the trek into base camp, I visited with David a handful of times. Usually he kept to himself, not because he was anti-social but because he had a lot of experience in such communal living arrangements here. Such close quarters in a third world country tend to increase the chance of contracting ailments such as respiratory viruses and gastrointestinal parasites. Without using supplemental oxygen, David needed to stay as disease-free as possible, all of his energy and strength put towards conditioning his body to prepare for the oxygen-deprived environment up high.

I appreciated the fact he was willing to visit with me. One day I noticed he was using the same type of PDA I used to post website updates and check emails. He made my blogging life a lot easier by giving me one of his extra PDA adapters. It allowed for quicker and more efficient transfer of my pictures from the camera directly into the PDA, removing the need to use the laptop and formatting software. I still use that adapter today and think of David every time I do.

Tait had actually been up to Camp III days ahead of us and as a result had also climbed above the yellow band, five hundred meters higher. The yellow band is an iconic rock band, easily seen from both Camp I and Camp II. It is made up primarily of marble. Marble is composed of several types of rock including metamorphosed limestone. Digging deeper into the geology lesson, limestone first forms under water. In this case the bottom of the ocean. Pretty amazing to look above and know that everything we could see was once deep under the sea. In fact, the Himalayas grow up to a quarter of an inch every year. The Indian tectonic plate continues to slide under the Asian plate, pushing the mountain range towards the sky above.

David was extremely fit and with his earlier acclimatization routine he sought Russell's permission to continue up the mountain instead of returning all the way down to base camp. After some debate, Russell agreed to let him travel with the Himex rope fixing team, led by Phurba Tashi. The weather forecast was showing a very short window coming up which would allow them to try and reach the summit, establishing the rest of the route as well. Russell's blessing meant David was given one of the earliest cracks at the summit for a Westerner.

Gaining altitude often means losing the desire to eat. I was definitely following that trend. Eugène and I picked out food from the Camp II cache that we hoped would help stimulate our palates. Yet even being raised in a state known for its cheese production could not help me engage in consuming the cheese we had just hauled up. I forced myself to swallow Ramen noodles and a few pieces of chocolate. I did manage to continue to drink plenty of water spiked with electrolytes.

This also meant that what went in had to come out, at least part of it anyhow. I dreaded putting my boots and warmer layers back on to go outside for nature's call. I struggled out of the tent and slowly made my way over to the designated urinal, placing each step with caution so as not to slip and end up almost half a mile below in the bergschrund.

I didn't realize until I reached it that the urinal area was just a couple meters away from a large gaping crevasse. On its far side laid the remnants of a camp from years past, some of it teetering on the edge. I began to have the sensation of vertigo, the first of its kind on the trip. I began to will my stream to start and end as quickly as possible. I wanted to get back to the relative safety of the tent. Looking into the abyss high on the face was as if the mountain was politely reminding me of the dangers that lurked everywhere.

That night, despite our best efforts to get some rest, Eugène and I continued to share stories and photos of our families. When the luxury of actually falling back to sleep occurred it didn't last long. This was not just because of the altitude. The concerns over the steep drop just outside the tent's backdoor coupled with the fact that our abode sat at a slight angle in its direction added to the insomnia. My side of the tent seemed to be a hair higher and as a result I found myself continually sliding towards my European companion, albeit slowly during each phase of rest.

I recalled that the French live in a reasonably open society yet the thought of actually ending up on top of Eugène was more than I could take. We joked about how glad we were that no one else could see the *Cirque du Soliel* acrobatics within our self-proclaimed "Dad's Tent." When morning arrived so did the extreme temperatures, the mercury plummeting to thirty degrees below zero with an overcast sky and snow flurries overhead.

It was once again time to struggle, sealing myself inside the red Santa Claus suit and overgrown banana-colored high altitude boots in order to protect myself from the weather outside. Despite the overnight Vegas-style tent show I felt surprisingly rested. I mustered up the mental courage in preparation for the descent back down the face to Camp II. Conversely, David Tait was getting ready to push up the mountain. We wished him Godspeed for a safe journey to the top.

One by one we clipped into the fixed-line. Going down is often harder than going up. Gravity challenges your balance, the leg muscles start to burn as if on fire, and the knee joints creak like old wooden floorboards. Proper crampon placement is a top priority to avoid taking a slide that could result in a less than happy ending.

Only fifteen minutes below, Himex guide Adrian Ballinger from the US, fellow teammate Valerio Massimo from Italy, and I got caught in a mini-traffic jam. Several members of the Russian 7 Summits expedition were coming up the rope just below us. We were on very hard blue ice angled on a nasty pitch. This made it difficult to get a good purchase with every metal point between my boots and the frozen water underneath. Unfortunately communicating with the Russian climbers proved challenging as well.

Adrian commanded the situation on heightened alert. With a firm yet polite voice he asked them to carefully go around us, pointing at the same time as if using sign language to illustrate his request. His gesture seemed to register. One by one they slowly continued their ascent. As each climber made the move to step around we would assist them with the procedure of clipping and unclipping their carabiners into the rope.

When ascending on steep pitches we use an ascender device known as a jumar clipped onto the fixed-rope and tied to our harnesses. The device slides one way in the direction of intended travel. If a slip occurs its metal teeth lock onto the rope, acting as a braking device. Climbing means backing up everything. In addition to going up with the jumar attached to the rope we also clip onto it with a carabiner (often shortened to biner) that slides along the rope as we move up.

When down climbing we don't use the jumar but rather wrap the rope around our forearms to create friction, which helps control the rate of descent. This technique is known appropriately as an arm wrap. Did I mention we face forward during fixed-rope descents? Going backwards, similar to Army Rangers coming down a tower wall, is called rappelling. Like them, we only rappel to get down vertical spots on the route. On Everest there are just a few locations where this is needed. The biner maintains its role as backup during a fall when arm wrapping.

Biners come in a variety of shapes and sizes yet perform the same. In general these solid metal rings are bent to form an oddly shaped "O." They are about as thick as your finger with a hinged gate on one side. The rope is passed through the gate to allow it to ride on the inside rim of the biner. If the jumar's locking mechanism should fail during a fall, the biner will slide along the rope until the next anchor is reached. As long as the anchor, usually an ice screw, doesn't pull out the fall is stopped. Assisting unknown climbers was considered professional courtesy on the mountain as safety for all leads to everyone's success.

I have to admit I felt a bit unnerved standing on the sixty-degree pitch, my legs straining to insure good contact between my crampons and the slick surface. Valerio was about five meters above me. Just as the last Russian climber was passing him, V's footing became jarred loose, which caused him to start sliding downward. Luckily I was close to one of the ice screw anchors, standing next to Adrian as V slid into home plate, in this case my upper leg.

After regaining my composure Adrian instructed me to continue down. V also appeared to need a minute to soak in what had just happened. I did not run into any other climbers coming up that section and within minutes reached the bottom row of tent platforms. The first rappel of the route was next in order to get down the vertical section just below the tents, the area that had taken such a huge effort for me to ascend yesterday.

Upon finishing the uneventful forty-foot rappel, a freak snow squall swept up the face creating extremely poor visibility in the process. In essence it had the making of a miniature blizzard. Mother Nature was definitely testing my nerves today. The fixed-rope was now not only a lifeline but also a guideline. Even though the route was located on a wide section of the face and away from visible crevasses, I cautiously felt my way down with a death grip on the rope.

I eventually caught up to Chris Jones. Back in base camp I had learned he was an avid dog lover, so we got along quite well. I was about get to know him even better. The reason I had caught up to him on the lower slopes of the face was not because I was descending quicker. Instead it was because an ascending climber further below, just above the bergschrund, had clipped into the wrong rope, the rope we were using to descend.

In general the red rope was used to ascend on while the white rope was placed for descending, mainly in spots too precarious for a one-way lane. As I worked my way down to Chris the mini-blizzard disappeared and the sun started to poke through the weakening clouds. The mystery climber below seemed to be standing still, just out of verbal range.

Chris and I debated what to do. We were now halfway between anchors and the angle was not friendly for passing. Chris grabbed an ice screw from his harness, rotating it into the hard ice which allowed us to clip to, in order to take the strain off of our legs, not to mention provide a bit more physical security. It looked like we were going to have to hang out here for a while because the guy appeared motionless.

Adrian and V were making their way towards us so we yelled up to let them know what was going on below. Luckily for them they were at a junction where both ropes were in close proximity. With no one coming up the red rope they clipped into it and unclipped from the white one Chris and I were now stuck on. As Adrian closed in on our altitude he yelled over that we were likely going to have to traverse over to him. He thought there would be just enough pendulum-like give to our rope from above to allow for it. Oh goody, I thought.

Chris went first and after some very cautious cramponing he reached the red rope. It was my turn. I reminded myself on each step to make full contact with my crampons. I had come this far and wasn't about to take a ride down the remaining three hundred meters. There was just enough slack in the rope to allow me to stretch out and grab the red one. Got it! No time to wipe my brow. I just wanted off the face.

After a couple more hours and no further incidents, Chris and I finally lumbered back into ABC. Waiting there were the smiles on the faces of my friends from the Yetis, Big Hot Gouda and Stuey. They had successfully made the trip up through the icefall the day before. It would soon be their turn to tackle the face. For now we relished the safety of ABC, once again enjoying the camaraderie of the group, all feeling the same effects of thin air.

A short rest helped me regain some of my strength so I decided to take a short walk, every once in a while looking back up the wall, thankful to be off it, at least for now. As I came around the dining tent I recognized a voice inside the neighboring expedition group tent. I peeked inside to see a familiar face.

It was Jon Shea! How great to see him. I am not a tenth of the climber Shea is. What he taught me in Mexico greatly contributed to where I was now standing. After a few laughs and a couple pictures together at 21,000 feet, it was time to depart once again. Even though Everest and the Himalayas are big, our chance meeting at ABC confirmed that the world truly is small. We knew we might see each other again on the route, yet it was not guaranteed. For now we shook hands and wished each other a safe and successful climb to come.

May 4, 2009. We awoke before sunrise to begin the descent down the glacier. Our hope was to be passing through the icefall well before the sun started to heat up the maze of seracs and crevasses. I found myself traveling alongside Gilad Stern of South Africa. A very polite middle-aged man, I always got a kick out of listening to him remind Robby to watch his tongue.

Gilad didn't always act his age though. Not in a bad way mind you. During our stay in Namche he prompted a few pictures of us guys with our shirts off. With a smile on her face, Megan quickly became our photographer. Gilad's wife Micky had been by his side for the trek into base camp. Her calm and pleasant demeanor was a welcome addition to our group, and I thoroughly enjoyed our conversations. Once we started climbing she made the long voyage back home to Cape Town.

We eventually caught up to the leaders of our pack near the remnants of Camp I. We took a quick break to change layers, drink some water, and eat a snack. One by one we entered the icefall but not before being instructed by our guides to travel in groups of at least two. I fell into the queue between Grizz and V. We agreed to stick together as a threesome.

These two had been extremely fast on Lobuche and continued such speed up the Lhotse Face a couple days earlier. Fortunately for me we were now going downhill and with the ever-shifting route I had a chance of keeping up with them. We worked very well together, holding up the ropes for each other as we approached anchors and crevasse crossings. Doing so made unclipping and clipping into the safety-lines go more smoothly, not to mention decrease the need to bend over as much, the entire process proving to be exhausting.

As we approached the halfway point one of V's crampons popped off. Not a big deal but as he was strapping it on a small cloud of ice and snow let loose from the ever-present ice shelf above. The look on Grizz's face said enough. With very few words we knew we needed to get moving. We picked up our pace, every once in a while turning to sneak a peek above. The sun was now starting to works its way over the top of Everest and Lhotse; as a result both the icefall and the west shoulder's ice shelf above would start to become less stable.

Gilad and Chris Jones were a few minutes behind us traveling with Narly. As Grizz, V, and I reached the lower portion of the icefall, well past the deep crevasses and threat of being crushed by a tumbling serac, we heard the characteristic crack. We spun around to see a modest avalanche envelope the route we had traveled through only moments earlier. We were very lucky to have kept moving as quickly as we did. Our minds then turned to Gilad, Chris, and Narly somewhere above on the route now obscured by a wave of snow and ice.

We waited to hear the radios come to life with a notification that everyone was okay. After what seemed like an eternity, Narly's voice broke the silence. They had been dusted but were intact. Later we learned that when the avalanche broke directly above them, Narly yelled out one simple yet definitive word, "Run!"

He knew all they could do was try and find some shelter behind the nearest serac and fast. They were fortunate enough to shield themselves behind several of the gigantic frozen stalagmites, just out of reach from the squall of snow swarming around them. Gilad even managed to capture a few pictures of the white fury as it passed. I could only imagine what it must have felt like to be surrounded by such chaos.

After reaching crampon point, I told Grizz and V that I would catch up with them at base camp. Before returning there myself, I wanted to see if I could locate and meet Ed Viesturs. I made my way towards the First Ascent base camp. As I gained the small boulder-ridden wall that seemed to guard their tents, I could see the iconic climber sitting in his tent. Although base camps here were less restrictive to visitors, I approached with caution and respect for Ed's privacy.

About to call out his name I debated if I should address him as Mr. Viesturs or Dr. Viesturs. Even though I wanted to be polite, I decided to take the casual approach, right or wrong. With a curious tone I said, "Hi Ed."

He looked up, crawled out of his tent, and with his own curious voice returned the greeting, "Hello." I'm sure he wondered who the guy with the blue buff and enormous smile was approaching in catlike mode. It was hard to contain my excitement. I was staring eye to eye with someone I had read about so many times and had watched on the big screen. In fact, he is a pivotal character in the book that sparked my dream twelve years earlier.

With outstretched arms we shook hands. For a moment I wanted to pinch myself. After formally introducing myself, I ad libbed a bit to let him know that I was a veterinarian from the Midwest here not just to climb but also do some work on the yaks. I could see from his body language that his comfort with me increased slightly. I didn't want to take up too much of his time but did manage to exchange some small talk. I couldn't resist sharing with him that prior to coming to Nepal I had given my mother his book *No Shortcuts to the Top* to read.

I informed him I had spoken to her recently and that she wanted me to know that she was "going to bed with Ed every night." That brought a smile to his face. Before leaving I asked if he would mind having a picture taken with me. He graciously handed my camera to one of his base camp staff as we posed for a couple of photos.

I left the First Ascent tents with a renewed vigor in my step. I had just met my climbing idol and was now even more anxious to be reunited with the rest of my friends back at Himex base camp. There, Monica and Russell sat waiting to welcome each one of us back after our first successful trip up to Camp III. Narly, Gilad, and Chris Jones arrived shortly after; meaning all members of Team Yaks were back in base camp. We would not fully rest; however, until all of Team Yetis returned in a couple of days.

Later that day I went on to post a picture of Ed Viesturs and me on my website blog. He was a genuinely nice man who took the time to visit with someone who had been following in some of his footsteps. I could never match the size of those footsteps but am humbled to have traveled in part of them. It was an up and down day. Meeting Ed was certainly the highlight. Of course getting through the icefall unscathed was another huge bonus.

Today was also the day Jon Hansen returned home to Wisconsin. Regardless of the day's events, I was glad to be back in base camp. Here I could at least sleep, eat, and recover.

One of the cravings I seemed to have after climbing was the need for a soda. Despite the fact that the local grocery store was not around the corner, Russell provided us as many luxuries of home that he could. This included bottled Coca-Cola and even the orange soda, Fanta. Whether it was the carbonation and/or sweetness, at almost 18,000 feet, both tasted incredible. I feasted on soda and crackers with a cream cheese spread called Puck. Puck ended up becoming a precious commodity. In fact, Billi would go on Puck scavenger hunts; often strategically hiding a jar or two amongst the three dining tents. By the end of the expedition, the Khumbu Valley, maybe even all of Nepal did not have a single jar of Puck left!

May 6, 2009. Today our teammates from Team Yetis, with the exception of Hiro, Takenori, Saito, Kyomi, and Megan would be back in base camp, provided all went okay on the route above. Megan and the Japanese remained at Camp II another day to help promote their lingering acclimatization process. Even though Megan had made tremendous progress while back in Lobuche, she still had not been able to climb it more than once. Russ felt an additional night at altitude would help her body catch up in order to participate in our final assault in a couple of weeks.

The morning was sunny with temperatures mild. Billi, Moises, and I sat on the edge of the Puja altar to act as a greeting party. One by one we watched our friends turn off from the main trail above into our camp, the icefall and west shoulder creating a magnificent backdrop. My eyes clued into Stuey's lime green La Sportiva boots making their way slowly towards us. I couldn't resist meeting him part way up the trail.

We embraced as I congratulated him on a job well done. He returned the pleasantry or shall I say increased it by reaching around to grab my rear end! It was nice to know that despite his obvious exhaustion he still had his sense of humor at the forefront. I couldn't help but laugh, especially after seeing the photo Moises took with my camera. He captured the flirting perfectly, something I will never let Stuey forget.

Big Jim was next to come striding down the trail. At first he missed the cutoff into camp so we yelled for him to make a hard right. The Big Hot Gouda deserved a big bear hug so that is exactly what I gave him. Today was special not just because of his safe return, but also because tomorrow we'd be celebrating his birthday. Birthdays were special to all of us because it meant cake for dessert after dinner.

Bruce Parker and Paul Robinson followed a few minutes apart so we met them partway up the cutoff trail as well. I was still getting to know my fellow American teammates. Bruce is from Utah while Paul lives in Indiana. This climb was momentous for Bruce as a successful summit of Everest meant he would complete his quest to become a member of the 7 Summits club.

Even though I did not get to climb with him much, Paul was interesting to talk to while in base camp. Turns out we had a common link. He is a researcher at the College of Veterinary Medicine at Purdue University. That meant he was a Boilermaker and part of the Big Ten athletic conference, the same conference my Wisconsin Badgers are a part of.

We repeatedly teased each other about how much better our respective teams were. He did slightly outdo me in displaying his university colors as he often wore a Purdue hat, not to mention constantly flying with pride a Purdue flag attached to his base camp tent. Sometimes I would throw on my Badgers party necklace yet it was my Packers pride that often led the way. My bright yellow Foamation Cheesehead hat made the trip and was a great way to protect my head from the intense sun. Okay, maybe not but as you can imagine it was an eye-catching piece.

The last two members of Team Yetis to welcome home were Alec Turner and Robby Kojetin. John Black joined the welcoming committee when he saw his friend coming. You have likely heard how opposites attract. Well standing next to each other these two were just that.

John is tall and lanky, a gifted runner, and also a very fast climber. Robby is much shorter than John, but what he lacks in height he makes up for with tenacity and incredible internal drive. During an indoor climbing accident several years prior to Everest, Robby shattered both of his ankles. Not just one or two fractures but nine in all. With metal holding them together, his doctors told him he would likely never be able to climb again. Yet here he was proving them wrong.

I found Alec to be intriguing as heck. He is a stonecutter from Fairbanks, yet in a prior life worked on a crab boat on the dangerous waters of the Bering Sea. Thus, he was no stranger to danger. He isn't an adrenaline junky, but rather someone who strives to live life as well as being an eternal optimist. Alec is a big boy, his outward appearance not necessarily pegging him as a climber.

Alec would go on to surprise all of us, supporting the concept one should not judge a book by its cover. On Lobuche and both climbs up Everest he was typically towards the back of the pack. Alec reinforced the concept that he was not competing with anyone but rather the mountain itself. During his final summit bid he blazed the trail for his team from Camp IV to the top in record time, outpacing everyone on the mountain.

We also welcomed back David Tait today. Two days earlier he made history by being the first Westerner to follow the rope fixing team to the top. It was also the first summit by a Westerner this season. A large congratulatory group formed around David and the Sherpas whom he followed. Not only did their return mean they were safe, but it also signified that the entire route was complete from bottom to top. The weather would now dictate when we could head back up. With a lot of high fives and hugs exchanged, David's success gave us all a deep sense of satisfaction that we were strong and ready to go for the summit as well.

The next day we anxiously awaited the return of Megan and our Japanese teammates. As mid-morning approached we heard on the radio the team was making good progress down through the icefall. Moments later a loud crack sounded, resonating through the lower icefall. The deafening rumble had a crescendo unlike anything I had heard before. I sprang out of my tent to see what my mind had already visualized. The explosion of snow and ice hurtled downward at an alarming rate, swallowing everything in its way. The white cloud began to mushroom as if an atomic bomb had just been dropped.

Some of us were able to snap a few photos of the gigantic freight train as it rolled down and across the vast expanse of seracs and crevasses. It was the largest avalanche yet, its fury sweeping all the way to the edge of base camp. As the roar subsided and the thick plume of ice crystals settled, an even greater commotion began. Sherpas began frantically grabbing shovels, ropes, and other rescue gear. The base camp radios crackled to life, alarmed voices dominating the conversations between expedition leaders, would-be rescuers, and base camp doctors.

A Sherpa and two Westerners were directly in its path when it swept over them, knocking the Westerners deep into crevasses. The Sherpa was nowhere to be seen. For hours a rescue party worked to finally extract the Westerners as well as search for the missing Sherpa. Russell dispatched many Himex Sherpas to assist in the search and recovery efforts to no avail. After several more hours the search was called off due to the ever-growing threat for another avalanche, and with it more injury and/or death. Sadly, only the Sherpa's backpack and one boot were located. His body would not be found, entombed inside the vast expanse of ice for years to come.

It was a haunting reminder of just how lucky we were to be standing in the safety of Himex base camp. We couldn't help but wonder where Megan and the Japanese were. Had they been on the route in the icefall too? Our radios came to life once again not long after the dust settled. Fortunately they had already made it to the safety of crampon point when Mother Nature's wrath unveiled itself from above. At last everyone was back in base camp. We were elated that no one from our team got hurt yet the death of the Sherpa created a somber mood around camp.

The avalanche claimed the first victim of the climbing season on Everest. In just over a week we would have to head back into the icefall on our final push for the summit. The same precarious ledge of ice and snow responsible for spawning such devastation would still be waiting for us. It was just a matter of time before the next wave of terror would come crashing down.

My biggest little hill in Wisconsin, Mosquito Hill.
Photograph by Lance Fox.

The first view of Everest from Tengboche.
With Christopher Macklin (on my right) and Stuart Carder.
Photograph by Moises Nava.

2009 Himex Sherpa and base camp staff.
Photograph by John Black.

Front row (L to R): Dr. Monica Piris, Hayden Fisher, Hiro Kuraoka,
Shaun Hutson, and Dave "Narly" McKinley. Back row: Russell Brice,
Shinji Tamura, Adrian Ballinger, Dean Staples, Mark "Woody" Woodward,
Kirsty Mitchell, Mark Whetu.
Photograph by John Black.

The spine-tingling airport runway at Lukla.
Photograph by Lance Fox

The Sherpa village Namche Bazaar in early April 2009.
Photograph by Lance Fox.

Wisconsin on display in Himex base camp.
Photograph by John Black.

With climbing legend Ed Viesturs at traditional base camp.
Photograph by First Ascent base camp staff member.

Deep within the Khumbu Icefall.
Photograph by Lance Fox.

A short ladder crossing.
Photograph by John Black.

The imposing Lhotse Face and Yellow Band above.
Photograph by John Black.

Looking up at the South Summit and Southeast Ridge above Camp 4.
Photograph by Hiro Kuraoka

Dawn high on Everest.
Photograph by Hiro Karaoka

View from the South Summit of the Cornice Traverse.
Photograph by John Black.

The Hillary Step.
Photograph by John Black.

The view of Lhotse and the final summit ridge from the top of Everest.
Photograph by Lance Fox.

Megan Delehanty's victorious return to Himex base camp.
Photograph by Lance Fox.

Post-climb celebration for Team Didi
(Billi Bierling on my right with Ellen Miller).
Photograph by Moises Nava.

Alec Turner and I after the climb.
Photograph by Moises Nava.

Moises Nava and I showing off Wisconsin colors inside the Tiger Dome.
Photograph by Christopher Macklin.

Reunited with Big Boss and Phurba, Himex Everest base camp 2011.
Photograph by Claire Windeyer.

A happy and healthy yak during the 2011 Healthy Yak project.
Photograph by Lance Fox.

Chapter Ten

Preparing for War

May 8, 2009. With everyone from Himex off the mountain and back in base camp, Russell could relax a little, at least until it was time to send us back up. Despite the fact that David and the rope fixing team reached the top a few days earlier the jet stream winds returned to shut down the upper reaches of the mountain. The weather was now in charge.

Russell utilized a meteorological service out of Europe, thousands of miles away to monitor the jet stream patterns. The reports had been pretty darn accurate to date, even those predicting the weather a week or more in advance. Other expeditions picked up on this so Russell asked those of us who were blogging to refrain from talking about potential weather windows, even though we weren't quite sure at this point exact dates. All Russ could tell us was to be patient and that our time was coming.

With the acclimatization process over, we needed to learn how to use the supplemental oxygen system. The plan was for us to use it once we reached Camp III again. Russell called for a meeting in the Tiger Dome for an oxygen debriefing. He methodically went through the various parts of the system: the mask, regulator, and oxygen bottles. He then showed us how to attach the regulator to the tank and complete the system with the mask and hose

Big Boss warned us to wear gloves when changing oxygen cylinders up high. Doing so would prevent us from getting intense frostbite on our fingers from the extremely cold oxygen releasing from the bottles while screwing on the regulator. While in the warmth of base camp over the next few days, it would be important for us to practice this procedure a few times. Even though guides and Sherpas would be with us high on the mountain, we needed to be as self-sufficient as possible.

From base camp we would carry our own regulator and mask up to Camp III. The Sherpas had already cached dozens of oxygen cylinders up high. Some were at Camp III while most found a home at Camp IV, ready to be used during the final twenty-four hours of the summit assault. Each tank would provide close to nine hours of gas at a two-liter per hour flow rate.

Even with a slightly higher flow rate, Russell figured each of us would use up to two cylinders from Camp IV to the summit and back, typically a twelve to sixteen-hour climbing day. He allocated a total of four to five cylinders per person for the climb above Camp III. With a price tag of approximately five hundred US dollars per bottle the oxygen was not only valuable physiologically but also monetarily.

Back home mothers across America were celebrating Mother's Day, so I made certain to call my own to wish her a happy one. Even though I got an answering machine, I left my second mom, Lucy Ruffalo a message as well. I dialed Kathy next. After well wishes and making sure all was okay at home she handed the phone to my mother-in-law, then each of my three sister-in-laws. The ladies surprised Kathy by driving up from their respective homes in southern Wisconsin to spend the day with her. Although hearing their voices was wonderful, it made me miss being there with them to celebrate this special day.

I spoke to the kids, reminding Jordan to give his mom an extra hug from me. It was my conversation with Bailee, however, that tugged on my heart even more. With her sweet voice she reminded me they were counting the days until I got home. Although I had a lot of work and some uncertainty ahead of me, I reassured her that the days would go by quickly. The cardiac pull followed, "Do good, Daddy." Normally it's the parents' job to provide encouragement for their children, yet here was my eight-year-old daughter turning the table on me. As I hung up I knew I couldn't let her down.

Despite the emotions it was such conversations that made me thankful to have brought the communications kit. During his three weeks in base camp Jon used it to stay in touch with his own family as well. Occasionally Grizz and Stuey, along with Big Hot Gouda used the satellite phone to call and the PDA hookup to email their loved ones. I had purchased a block of minutes in advance, yet whenever more was needed it was a simple charge to my credit card.

I didn't mind making the technology available to my friends, as I knew how important it was to stay in touch. All they had to do was ask and no one abused the privilege. Russell also had a computer for emailing and a satellite phone for calling, both for a nominal fee.

After reading my blogs, I started receiving numerous emails from my teammate's family members and friends. Macklin's older brother Andrew wrote to thank me for mentioning Grizz in the blogs so that they could keep track of him. A climbing buddy of Stuey's from Michigan wrote, as did several of Big Hot Gouda's friends back in "Da Burgh," local slang for Pittsburgh. It was fun getting to know all of them even if just through cyberspace. I had no idea at the time that I would actually get to meet several of them face to face in the future.

I had more emails sent than I anticipated. Most were well wishes in support of the climb ahead. Even a complete stranger from Germany who had obviously stumbled across my blogs took the time to send me words of encouragement. There were three emails that stood out. It was their humor that set them apart.

My friend Mike Turba of Platteville, Wisconsin had been emailing me throughout the course of the expedition. One of his emails was the classic fun-loving Turba I had come to know. In one of the pictures from my blog about the Puja ceremony he recognized an object that caught his attention, something only a true Wisconsinite would inquire about. He titled the email "Beer," the question that followed read, "What kind of beer you drinking on the mountain?"

Yes, I had given up beer for the year leading up to Everest, yet here at the foot of the mountain I indulged in a few. After the Puja, tradition mandated we all have a drink as part of the overall celebration. Taboo to break tradition, it was a great excuse to taste the barley water on my lips once again! I decided to keep my reply to Mike short and sweet because I knew I had been busted: "Carlsberg and San Miguel, both are pretty good."

The second unique email followed my blog about the food cravings I was having, specifically my desire to have a bacon cheeseburger pizza from the local pizza parlor, Jolly Rogers in New London. Mike O'Connell, a guy from the area fired a reply: "The bacon cheeseburger pizza at Jolly Rogers is good, but have you tried their chicken alfredo version?" Although it made my cravings intensify, it was refreshing being able to sit halfway across the world and compare pizza notes. The winter after returning home from Nepal I would actually meet the Jolly Rogers' chicken alfredo pizza lover. I was standing in our local middle school gymnasium watching Bailee during basketball training camp. A gentleman I did not recognize walked up to me.

"Are you Lance Fox?"

"Yes, I am."

"I'm Mike O'Connell." The blank look on my face tipped him off that I didn't remember who he was. "I'm the guy who sent you the email about the Jolly Rogers' chicken alfredo pizza."

Fate was once again at work! As it turns out, Mike and his family live on the other side of town from mine. Our daughters actually ended up playing on the same youth softball league team during the summer of 2010. Needless to say, our conversations went beyond talking about pizza.

Doug Stayrook, a friend and former co-worker of mine, had also been periodically emailing me, telling me to stay focused and strong. Several of my friends within the company did the same, but it was Doug's last transmission right before heading back up the mountain for the last time that put the pressure on me, albeit with a fun twist.

Doug had traveled to Missouri to work with David Officer, another friend and former co-worker. Driving down the road one day they noticed some heifers grazing out on a pasture. Keep in mind cattle grazing in Missouri is not a unique observation but to see a donkey in the same pasture is not the norm. It gets better. With a bit of gusto in his step the little fellow vigorously chased one unsuspecting heifer from behind, the unfortunate victim of her own estrus cycle.

Doug's email quickly turned from sharing their detailed observations to one of inspirational analogy. "If you have even half the determination that donkey had, you will have no problem reaching the top of Mount Everest!" I pondered for a minute that maybe instead of referencing the little engine story I should be thinking *The Little Donkey That Could*!

On a clear day I could download a dozen or so emails in about one to two minutes–pretty amazing considering it was all done via satellite as I lay in a tent deep in the heart of the Himalayas. One morning's email session started working on thirty minutes duration as a single large email was taking its sweet time filtering into the PDA. I knew I had no choice but to let the clock keep ticking, along with the $1.20/minute charge.

The inspiring donkey story was certainly fun to read, but what finally downloaded put the "M" in motivation for me. My stepfather Ira had taken the liberty of sending a picture of Ryan's family, my stepbrother Chris' family, Kathy and the kids, as well as mom and him, all together during Easter at their home. What set this photo apart from any other family snapshot was that they were all wearing the "Quest for Success" shirts. My friend Debbie Thompson from the corporate office had graciously shipped them to Wisconsin while I was on my way to Nepal. Even Mom and Ira's dog, Feather, was wearing one.

Upon opening the picture, my concern for racking up a big download bill was instantly replaced with pure joy and tears of happiness. Seeing my family's support of the climb was worth every penny. Of course the photo also made me drool as I knew I had missed a terrific meal of ham and all the fixings.

The waiting game at base camp meant my mind was spinning in several different directions. I realized I had no picture taken of Russell and me together. There weren't too many times where we would see Russell just sitting around waiting for a photo op, so I hated to bother him. Nevertheless, the downtime seemed like it was now or never to ask.

As predicted, I found him busy as ever, this time with an ice pick leveling the ice formations outside of the dining tent area. I quietly approached, "Big Boss, would it be okay to get a picture with you?" Laying down the pick he turned around with a crooked smile and replied, "Would be happy to. I might put you to work in exchange though."

Turns out he wasn't joking. After a couple poses he handed me the extra ice pick that just happened to be lying nearby. After quite a few swings, the number of which was surpassed only by the number of breaths needed, the area was flattened. My body actually welcomed the miniature workout, endorphins now pumping wildly through my bloodstream. The greater bonus was breaking the sweat next to Russell Brice.

The waiting game typically found Russell downloading the daily weather report every afternoon. Those reports started to read as if May 18-22 would be the first window of opportunity for summit attempts. That meant we had at least another week before climbing. Adding to the mystery was the announcement of who was on which summit team. The rumors started flying once again that three teams instead of two might soon be announced.

I may have been on the faster team the first time up, but I was typically close to, if not the last to arrive into the various camps. I told myself that no matter what team I was placed on I would simply be happy to get my shot at the top. My biggest fear, however, was the longer we waited in base camp the greater the chance that the weather window could prematurely fall apart. The remaining days of the trip were now in Mother Nature's hands.

While contemplating that possibility, I discovered that my newfound tent mate would not be heading back up the mountain. Eugène made the decision to leave the expedition to return home to his family. Apparently he had been having a recurring dream, a dream that would make anyone think twice about heading back up. The image in his head started a couple weeks ago, yet he kept it to himself until our return to base camp from Camp III.

As he watched from above, the haunting scene mirrored itself from the time before. His lifeless body was lying face up in the snow, the oxygen mask still in place. His wife and children were standing over him mourning their loss. Since we had not yet worn the oxygen system while on the mountain, it was clear to Eugène that this was a warning to not visit the upper slopes of the mountain. While I was sad to see my *Cirque du Soliel* tumbling partner leave, I respected him for listening to what his inner voice was telling him.

Depending on how the teams panned out I wondered who would be my new tent mate. It couldn't be Gilad either because he too decided to leave without climbing back up. Gilad's close call with the avalanche in the icefall, not to mention the avalanche on the seventh that took the life of the Sherpa haunted him. He felt it was better to return home safely to his wife Micky back home in Cape Town with the hope of returning to climb another day.

Although Christophe had made it up to Camp II during the Yeti's first climb his body once again was not happy with the altitude. He was unable to make it to Camp III, so Russell devised a plan to send him back up with a guide and one or two Sherpas to Camp II with the hopes of a successful second attempt to Camp III. This would give his body a chance to acclimatize like the rest of us for the summit bid yet to come. Despite his physical ailments at altitude Christophe relished the chance to try again. He was committed to seeing his challenges through to the end, no matter what the outcome.

Guided by Narly and with the help of our Sherpas they led him back up through the icefall. Even though he couldn't hear us, we were cheering him on. On the radio things sounded like they were going fine, but once again as they reached the upper slopes of the glacier the altitude induced Christophe's repeated illness. The team had no choice but to turn around. Christophe's dream of climbing to the top of Mount Everest was over.

Back in the safety of base camp, Christophe asked Russell to arrange a helicopter flight for him from nearby Gorak Shep to Kathmandu. During Christophe's last night in camp he politely challenged me to a game of checkers in the Tiger

Dome. Christophe is a methodical thinker. Even as he finished one turn I could see him processing the future moves it would take to win. The game persisted just long enough for me to be humbled. After admitting defeat I shook his hand one last time. The next morning he was gone before dawn. To the end Christophe epitomized what it means to be a true competitor and a good sport.

Christophe had given us something to cheer about, and we applauded his efforts. We hated to see him leave, yet as it turned out, the helicopter ride he requested not only delivered him directly to KTM but Russell also arranged for it to transport to us fresh salmon! The base camp staff and Haydn prepared an absolutely wonderful lunch for us that day. After a month of chicken, canned fish, and pasta, the meal was to die for!

Downtime at base camp continued to linger. We started to watch climbers heading up through the icefall, wondering when it would be us. The weather reports were still a bit sporadic in terms of ideal days to reach the top safely. Life in the Tiger Dome though now included an electronic racecar driving set.

After our second ascent of Lobuche, Chris Dovell, a native of England as well Russell's part-time neighbor in Chamonix, France, arranged to have the set brought up to base camp. It was a welcomed addition to the already lavish luxuries of the now famous Himex base camp centerpiece establishment. At least it made the days a bit less routine for some.

Something else we did to pass the time was to adjust our tent platforms. Being perched on the edge of a moving glacier meant, over time, tents tended to shift. The rising spring temperatures also contributed to lumpy sleeping surfaces and even threatened some tents to act like Noah's ark in the rising waters.

Along with Megan and Haydn, Mark Whetu and Kirsty Mitchell were positioned on the lower tier of tent rows just below John Black, Robby, and I. This meant the majority of the thaw tended to pool in between their tents. We ended up moving quite a few large boulders to accommodate a new raised platform, particularly for Mark's saturated area. It was good to have these mini-construction projects to keep our minds from fixating on when we would get the green light to climb.

Mark has been to the top of Everest multiple times and used to be a guide for Russell. While not guiding this time he still had a heavy responsibility, literally. As a high-altitude cameraman he was one of three guys assigned to carry a shoulder camera to the top. Built like an ox yet as kind as a kitten he comes across with an exuberance towards life. He is no stranger to danger and what it means to persevere.

During one of his previous Everest summit bids he, along with another climber were caught high on the mountain in a raging storm. After surviving a bivouac (a night on the mountain without proper shelter), just meters below the summit, his climbing partner never made it off the mountain. Mark managed to make it down, losing toes to frostbite from the ordeal. Except for one, our team had been fortunate to avoid frostbite to this point.

Grizz, unbeknownst to him, had a torn liner inside one of his gloves during the first trip up to Camp III. After returning to base camp the tip of his index finger became quite swollen. Dr. Piris treated it aggressively, eventually having to lance it open in order to drain the enormous blister that eventually formed. Doing so helped him avoid losing the end of that finger yet his football and snowball throwing days in base camp were done. I couldn't resist chucking a snowball in his direction from time to time. Of course in return he would offer a few unconditional words of wisdom.

May 14, 2009. Russell called for a meeting outside the white pod to announce the summit teams as well as lay out the plan for the five-day climb to the summit just ahead. The weather in base camp was spectacular and the meteorological reports allowed Russell and the guides to predict a suitable summit window. Big Boss immediately put to rest the rumors of three teams.

One by one Russell announced the members for the first summit team, which meant those not called, would make up the second and final summit team. Dean Staples from New Zealand would be the lead guide for the first team, assisted by Adrian and Shaun. As expected Phurba Tashi would be the lead Sherpa. The names Dovell, Valerio, ZQ (short for Zi Qiang Qiu), Billi, Moises, Chris Jones, Tommy, Thomas, and John Black all rang out. Then I heard my name, the "a" pronounced with a long "o" or British sounding tongue. Another pleasant surprise followed. Stuart made team one too. Ellen Miller would also join team one and once above Camp III she would branch off with her Sherpa to climb Lhotse.

Stuart had been getting stronger with each step of the expedition and had proved to Russell that he was definitely ready for the summit. I waited to hear Chris Macklin's name to no avail. I looked over to see the disappointment on his face. Grizz had remained at the top of the pack throughout all of our acclimatization climbs, yet Russell was concerned about the frostbite on his finger. It appeared to be mending but still needed a few more days to completely heal. Suffering another bout of frostbite would result in amputation.

I reminded Grizz that Russell's decision was about looking out for his well-being, not about performance. I could only imagine how he was feeling inside. Despite that, he smiled and congratulated those of us chosen for the first team. Grizz knew he was still headed to the same place, just a couple days later than he originally planned.

The rest of team two included Jim, Alec, Robby, Paul, Bruce, Megan, Kyomi, Saito, Takenori, and Antoine Boulanger from France. Similar to Megan this was Antoine's second attempt on Everest. Although I did not know him as well, he had been climbing in a style I describe as stealth mode. Tall and thin with a strong native tongue, he quietly climbed and never complained. Woody would be their lead guide assisted by Shinji, Hiro, and Gnarly.

Russell then revealed the really big news. The first team would leave base camp early on May 17. We would bypass Camp I for two nights at ABC, then Camp III for one night, followed by a half-day push up to Camp IV on May 20. Provided the weather held we would leave high camp late that night for one last push with the hopes of standing on the summit early on May 21. Team two would follow just two days later with the same itinerary, their projected summit window the morning of May 23.

The excitement was hard to contain, yet out of respect for Russell's earlier request we avoided blogging about the teams' plans. There were too many other people on the mountain with the same goal in mind. Given how well Russell had nailed the weather so far, if others caught wind of when we were headed to the summit we might face serious traffic jams up high.

When Big Boss was done, Stuey and I looked at each other and knew we would make good tent mates up high. Stuey's levelheaded thinking and our banter made us a complimentary pair of Everest first timers. Knowing Stuey was going to be by my side on the final climb helped calm the nerves I felt inside. I was disappointed, however, that I was not going to get to climb one last time with Grizz and Big Hot Gouda, along with guides Narly and Shinji.

May 15, 2009. It was time for Russell to introduce us to our Sherpa partners. The plan was to have them climb with us from Camp IV up the final slopes of the mountain. We gathered outside the Tiger Dome forming a large circle, Westerners on one side and Sherpas on the other. My excitement grew as I waited to hear my name called out, followed by the name of my Sherpa.

"Lance will be accompanied by Tashi Tshering Sherpa." As we entered the inner circle to formally meet Tashi reached out to shake my hand. I couldn't help myself but to pick him up off the ground in a bear hug sort of way. The group broke out in laughter. I was thrilled to meet the young man who would be by my side during the last vertical day of climbing. Even though the Sherpa culture readily accepts social contact the bear hug caught Tashi by complete surprise.

Along with the introduction, Russell then informed us that Tashi would have some additional weight to carry. The film crew decided I would be one of four climbers on team one to be filmed going up the mountain's final slopes. That meant Tashi would need to wear a climbing helmet rigged with a small camera, appropriately named a Sherpa-cam, that would be connected to an antenna in his backpack, the entire system designed to beam live images down to the tent Russell and another member of the film crew would be sitting in, just above base camp at the foot of Pumori.

Also inside that tent were small television monitors to allow Russell to watch our progress while those same images would be fed directly into a nearby computer. V, Chris Dovell, and Billi would also be filmed on the upper slopes of Everest for team one. Robby, Alec, and Grizz would be filmed on team two. There is nothing like having a little more pressure on us up high, yet we signed up for the possibility. I only hoped I wouldn't have too much frozen snot adhered to my face on summit day.

Before heading back to my tent I handed Tashi my spare digital camera in hopes he would want to capture some of his own photos up the mountain. It was also my backup plan in case my main camera malfunctioned or worse, I lost it again.

Later that day I decided to send one final blog before departing base camp for the summit, now less than forty-eight hours away. While not mentioning dates, I introduced Tashi as well as the great news that we were getting ready for the summit push. Knowing I needed to remain focused and positive about the outcome, regardless of whether I made it to the top or not, I faced the reality that bad things can happen up high.

With that on my mind plus the fact that I decided I wasn't going to blog during the final climb I wanted to close the dispatch strong so that anyone reading would not be afraid but rather be inspired to live their lives. In particular I knew my kids were reading the blogs back home. I dedicated the following final words to them: *Dream big, pursue your passion, smile often, and laugh a lot. Life is short so live it to the fullest.*

With less than twenty-four hours before heading back into the icefall everyone was busy organizing and reorganizing gear and clothing. We needed to keep our packs light. For the next seven days (five up and two down) we would be adding and subtracting layers of insulation as needed. We would add our down suits and high altitude climbing mitts to the layers once we reached ABC, now acting as a temporary stashing depot.

In preparing for the trip I overlooked bringing a thermos for summit day. I had planned to carry a small bottle of water inside my down suit with the remainder stored inside my backpack. The problem is that extreme outside cold temperatures up high will accelerate the possibility of having frozen water inside the pack even if a bottle insulation sleeve is utilized, which is exactly what I brought along.

Once again Moises came to the rescue. No, unlike the miracle at Tengboche he wasn't able to change the fact that it was going to be very cold two miles higher. Instead he let me borrow one of his extra thermoses. I comfortably continued organizing my gear knowing I would now have almost two liters of thawed water on me for summit day.

Whetu decided to film us preparing our packs for the two-mile vertical endeavor just hours away. He asked me to overview each item as I placed them inside my pack. Other than the standard backup gear, snacks, and extra layers I made certain to show the camera the most important item I had been carrying all along, the container holding my father's remains. Similar to Kirsty at ABC, Mark inquired about why I had them along. This time I maintained my composure as I once again revealed that this climb was in part, a tribute to my dad.

I then pulled out to show him a compression sack that contained another precious item, maybe not as sentimental as the ashes yet one of Wisconsin pride, my cheese wedge hat! Call it a spur of the moment decision yet that little voice inside me told me to take it up the mountain. Before finding its place inside the compression sack I had everyone from the Himex team put his or her signature on it.

Russell called for one last meeting, this time within the comfort of the Tiger Dome. The mood inside had shifted from casual and jovial to one of both sincerity and seriousness. We were about to embark up the slopes of the tallest mountain in the world. Although we were as fit and competent in our climbing abilities as we were ever going to be, the mountain could change at a moment's notice, fooling even the most experienced mountaineer.

Russell was acutely concerned for our safety. He reminded us the summit was only the halfway point, that getting home was success and not just the summit. He reiterated that we would need at least 30 percent of the energy used to go up in order to come down safely. His voice started to quiver slightly, the soft side of him revealed, "I cannot get inside your body, your head..."

It was now up to us to muster up the strength and courage, both physically and mentally, to get to the top and make it back down alive. He was sending his soldiers off to war, not knowing for certain who was going to return. I have to admit my eyes started to well with tears watching Russell's do the same. Fortunately my ball cap strategically covered mine; Big Boss' would be visible to the world on film months later. As he fought back the tears, he finished the emotional pep talk with a smile, "Come on. Let's go."

The Khumbu Icefall and Everest, as seen from above
Himex base camp (lower left).
Photograph by John Black.

Chapter Eleven

Chomolungma's Invitation

May 17, 2009. Timing is everything, right? The past few days saw a nasty diarrhea run through our camp. While not everyone was affected I could not escape its grip. I broke with just under forty-eight hours on the countdown timer. While I was not completely over it the early morning hours of the seventeenth, I counted my blessings to be past the worst of it. The next week contained some of the most grueling climbing of the entire expedition, so having a full head of steam was important. All I could do was hope it would not flare back up as we gained altitude.

Most of us had retired to bed right after dinner the night before, knowing that in a few short hours we would commence the climb of our lives. Between the runs to the toilet tent, I managed to get very little sleep. Before I knew it the clock struck one in the morning. With an excitement driven by nerves I emerged from my tent to cool crisp air and thousands of brilliant stars lighting up the night sky, the flow of the Milky Way galaxy directly overhead.

Although normally a breakfast person, choking down food so early in the morning proved difficult, just as it had the first time we headed up the mountain. Stuey calmly walked into the dining tent with his usual morning grin and jovial "morning, my love" gesture. Moises popped in jolly as ever. John Black cracked a smile indicating he too was ready to step into the unknown.

V was still up at his tent for good reason. He was busy saying goodbye to Alexandra Bliss-Owens (better known as Alix, at the time his girlfriend and now his wife) who had graced us with her presence in base camp since May 4, the day V and the rest of us on Team Yaks returned from our first foray up the mountain. She had been a breath of fresh air. A joy for V too, of course, yet I'm sure he was already thinking about reuniting with her in just over a week.

Billi strolled into the dining tent along with Jones and Dovell. Tommy and Thomas were back to making some jokes which helped break the nerves circling within the chilly night air. ZQ, a Chinese-American Ph.D. physicist from the University of Berkeley seemed poised to take on the mountain as well. Although soft spoken, ZQ had proven himself a strong climber to this point. Team one was assembled with Deano, Adrian, and Shaun ready to lead the way. Kirsty was busy filming our final preparations and subtle jokes.

Like our first early morning departure a couple weeks ago, Russell and Monica were awake to see us off. Russell knew he was not going to get much sleep over the next nine days. He was sending us into harm's way, an incredible level of responsibility and stress no doubt. Not until everyone from the second summit team walked back into base camp would his mind rest.

With his direct way of communication he looked each one of us in the eyes, wished us luck, and shook our hands. Monica gave us a hug as one by one we filed out of base camp, following our guides like ants on their way to a picnic, only there was no feast where we were headed. No one spoke during the twenty-minute hike up to crampon point. Reality was sinking in deeply; we were about to take on the highest mountain in the world in its entirety.

Once again I extended my welcome at crampon point a little longer than the others. Both Stuey and I seemed more challenged than usual to get our crampons on, no doubt nerves the biggest culprit. With Adrian now leading our pack into the icefall, Deano remained at the point in order to make sure no one was left behind. Shaun floated in amongst the team. As Stuey and I entered the maze of upside down icicles characteristic of the icefall's lower area all we could see in front of us was a world that reminded me of some deep cave never explored before. We couldn't see our teammates' headlamps or hear them clamoring through the icefall anywhere. There were no human tracks to be found.

Where are the wands marking the route? How far from the trail are we? Although we were not panicking, Stuey and I tried to rationalize our whereabouts. We gazed back towards the tent lights of traditional base camp near crampon point. Suddenly several headlamps appeared, heading our way. We could hear our guides on the radio conversing about the team's progress, Deano not realizing he was missing two of his climbers. Too embarrassed, Stuey and I held off from entering the conversation to ask for turn-by-turn directions.

The mysterious headlamps turned out to be from another team that had just left crampon point. They thought we were on the trail and simply followed our lights. They weren't impressed when they finally reached us only to find out we were out for a casual stroll in the middle of the night.

We scanned in the direction of the west shoulder, its silhouette highlighted in the clear air. A repetitive flicker of light several hundred feet away appeared. Just for a moment I couldn't help but wonder if the men in the crow's nest on the *Titanic* felt like this when they suddenly caught a glimpse of something in the water. In our case, we actually wanted to steer towards the ice which held our comrades deep within.

Stuey and I humped it as fast as we could in the general direction of the light that now acted like a beacon. Finally, after a few concerned minutes we stumbled back onto the path. I didn't stop to look at Deano's facial expression when we came up from behind him. Moments earlier we heard him ask Shaun on the radio if everyone was together. What a surprise it must have been for him to discover the two climbers passing him were actually two of his own. Yeah, another smooth start on icefall day.

We had gained some significant ground to catch up to our teammates. The early morning sprint was not something I had planned for. It was hard to keep up with the faster members of our group. Fortunately, small ladder crossings early on created queues of climbers which allowed us to catch our breath. Sherpas from our team and of other expeditions passed us. It was déjà vu.

As we continued winding up through the now gigantic ice towers we came to a ladder section sitting at a forty-five degree angle across a very deep crevasse. One of the cameramen had perched himself nearby to get additional footage of us dealing with such awkward crossings. I tried to gracefully balance on the cold metal. Halfway up, the words rolling out of my mouth to be forever etched later on the show, "Ladders aren't just for painting anymore!" Although I was deep within one of the most dangerous places in the world, deep inside myself I was elated to know I was actually here.

Eventually Stuey, Jones, and I fell into a somewhat comfortable pace together through the maze of seracs. Thomas was poised just ahead of our threesome. Despite the trots back in base camp I did not have to stop and find a secret hiding spot to relieve myself like the first time. Other than the early morning navigation problem, traveling through the icefall for the third time went pretty smoothly.

Emerging from the icefall, we worked our way up onto the lower part of the glacier where Camp I used to be. Only a couple tents from other expeditions littered the area. With the morning shadow of Everest overhead the air remained quite cold. Deano had exited just ahead of us with an incredible burst of speed towards the top of the icefall. With Jones being a steadfast climber perhaps Deano figured Chris would keep the wanderers on the right path! We joined him, along with Tommy, for a quick breather.

Deano had brought along his small handheld video camera and had done some filming of us back in the icefall. As we approached, he hit the record button. Jones was in the lead with Stuey forming the Lance sandwich. Deano interviewed me for a couple of minutes as our threesome came to a stop.

My shifty enunciation was being exacerbated by the glacier's cold breeze. Yet I figured why not, this would be a great way to document the final climb. Deano thought additional footage might be needed for the show. I was thinking that maybe if I talked to Deano nicely after we were done I too could acquire a copy of the footage.

After a few wisecracks on film it was time for us to get moving to ABC, another 1,000 feet higher. Like the first trip through the Cwm we needed to be across the majority of the glacier before the intense heat of the rising sun slowed us down. Not even thirty minutes had passed and I felt the energy draining from my body, as if I had sprung a leak in my gas tank. Jones and Stuey were on a comfortable pace ahead so I told them to keep going.

With the route clearly marked, the glacier was relatively safe with a handful of ladder crossings. Despite their quicker pace, they would use the crossings to catch their breath and wait for me to catch up. We would then hold the safety ropes taut for each other as we moved across the ladder bridges, just as we had done in the icefall. It was an efficient system but the sun was really starting to heat the Cwm up. The climb up the Lhotse Face paled in comparison to how I was now feeling.

Once across the last crevasse I felt like my tank was on empty. ABC looked like it was twenty miles away when in reality it was less than a mile to reach. Going from freezing temperatures to sultry heat in a matter of hours really zapped my reserves. Knowing there were no more ladders to deal with I told my comrades to continue on at their stronger pace. Thomas had gotten his second wind, shooting up the remaining wasteland of snow and ice.

Every once in a while I would catch up to Stuey and Jones, not because I picked up the pace but rather because they were kind enough to wait for me. Their concern for me was like the three musketeers' motto, "All for one and one for all!" I could not have been more grateful. The process repeated itself over and over.

As I finally reached the rock formations, signifying the start of ABC for all expeditions, I was over the worst of it, or so I believed. This time Stuey and Jones had been waiting for me for quite a while. I yelled up to them to go on ahead to camp. I felt bad to hold them up. This time I convinced them that I would soon be in camp with them.

It took a herculean effort to remove my crampons, but it was good to feel the rock and melting snow directly under my boots. I drank some water and ate my three hundredth candy bar of the trip. Once I got going again Stuey and Jones had covered a lot of ground. Every once in a while they would pause to make sure I was still upright and on the move in the right direction. A simple nod or wave told them I was okay. Inside, however, I felt wasted. The triple-digit temperatures of the Cwm had baked me like a fish both inside and out.

Every step forward was agonizing; each one slipped backward just a little, the wet ground underneath creating loose traction. Conversely, my frustration leapt ahead exponentially. Wanting desperately to simply sit down, I forced myself to keep moving. All of summit team one was in camp except me. Russell and the guides were chatting on the radio about everyone's arrival when my name popped into the conversation.

Fighting the sandbag feeling in my arms I reached for the call button on my handheld. I let the guides know I was in the vicinity of ABC but that it was taking me a while to close the gap. I didn't want a search and rescue team being deployed. Deano came on the radio, "No worries, mate. Take your time and conserve your energy. It's not a race." I appreciated his ease, yet I was longing for the confines of our dining tent and a comfortable seat under my exhausted bottom.

What the heck was wrong with me? I looked at my watch. I had been on the go now for almost ten hours. Over half of that was just between camp locations, the most gentle and least vertical part of the climb up from base camp. Surrounded by hundreds of feet of thick ice and dense snow, heat exhaustion was taking its toll.

After another grueling two hours I could finally see the Himex tents. Phurba was standing amongst a group of Sherpas, and his eye contact with me and kind wave resulted in my own weak arm flailing, my appendage now feeling like a fifty-pound log. It took tremendous effort to raise the hunk of wood connected to my body in order to reciprocate Phurba's gesture. I should have been here hours ago. Instead, the average three-hour trip from camp one to ABC took over seven.

Fighting to keep my balance, not to mention my poise, Moises appeared from the maze of tents. His warm smile was a welcome sight for me. He was upholding his self-induced role of being the welcome committee. As Moises closed the gap between us I struggled to speak. I lacked the energy to form the words, and he knew it. He gave me a big hug as I broke down.

The only good thing about my dehydrated state was that I couldn't produce a steady flow of moisture from my eyes. Thank goodness, as I felt so embarrassed. I had no idea that Russell's analogy of preparing for war meant that defeat could come on the upper slopes of the Khumbu Glacier itself.

My parched mouth managed to expel, "How the hell am I going to climb this mountain, Moises?" He reassured me that once I rehydrated, ate, and rested that I would feel better about things. I could only hope that he was right. Taking my pack, Moises escorted me on the final steps into camp. Unlike asking Stuey to hand my pack back to me during the final steps on the trek into base camp weeks earlier I didn't turn down Moises' assistance. The mountain had won the first day of the five-day bid to reach its summit.

It was such a relief to be in the shade, safety, and comfort of our dining tent. Most of the team was inside enjoying tea and a snack. One by one they welcomed me. After an hour of sitting down, a couple liters of water, and a few snacks I began to regain some of the energy I had lost during the day's event. Although my pride had been hurt, the silver lining was that I never had to walk up from Camp I to ABC ever again.

The lining quickly changed to reality and a much bigger slap in my face. In less than thirty-six hours round two on the Lhotse Face would start. I knew I had to get my act together and fast. A full day of rest was just what the doctor ordered and what this doctor needed! No doubt a direct result of my body's extreme fatigue, I slept surprisingly well, waking quite refreshed. Moises' predictions were spot on.

Instead of walking around today with a chest-mounted camera like last time at ABC, Jamie Berry handed us his shoulder camera, asking if we could do a self-recorded video diary to home. While the intentions were pure the concept was that if something bad should happen to us our families would get a copy of the footage.

Sitting down at the door opening of my tent I grabbed the camera from Jamie and pushed the record button. Depressing the button seemed to start the flow of tears from my eyes as well. It was incredibly hard talking to my family, sobbing like a baby wondering if this would be the last image they would see of me. Afterwards, Moises admitted he too had cried while talking to his daughter on film. Somehow I knew the tears shed at ABC wouldn't be my last of the trip.

With the diary out of the way it was time for some fun. Cricket at 21,000 feet! I had never played the game before, but ironically the boredom of lying around ABC got the team's imagination going. In between our acclimatization climbs on Lobuche, Russell had put together an impromptu cricket team for Himex. This was in response to hearing that cricket teams from the United Kingdom had converged upon Gorak Shep, the tiny establishment an hour's walk down the valley from base camp.

Their plan was to play the world's highest match of cricket with the *Guinness Book of World Records* there to document it. During the final trek back up the valley from climbing Lobuche, I stopped to take in a few minutes of the competition. I was trying to concentrate on walking and breathing in the thin air and here were a bunch of guys hitting a ball and running around like madmen. I had never witnessed this particular bat-and-ball sport being played live before.

Now it was our turn to beat that record. Well, in our minds anyway since Guinness was nowhere to be seen at ABC. We took turns pitching the ball, known as bowling. Several tried their hands at batting the ball. Even Phurba got into the makeshift match with us.

Our ice pad prohibited the intricacies of a professional game, but it did make for some hilarious fielding. Instead of two batsmen and an official wicket keeper we set up with the bowler and one striker generously apart, the three wooden stumps, and several fielders. After Phurba's surprisingly well-executed abilities as a bowler it was my turn to give it a try. All the snowball throws in the world could not prepare me for the unique and somewhat awkward bowling.

Deano stepped up to face the American bowler. While I did not give him a plethora of good balls to bat he managed to keep the guys behind me busy slipping on the ice. With one final delivery I managed to knock over one of the wickets. Deano stood for a second in disbelief. He then handed the bat off jokingly yelling, "Can you believe it? I've just been bowled out by the American!" Let's just call it beginner's luck.

May 19, 2009. For a second time we headed up the glacier towards the bergschrund and the bottom of the enormous wall of ice looming above. Similar to the icefall Adrian led the way, Shaun floated in the middle, and Deano swept the bottom of our column. Halfway up the glacier Thomas started falling behind. Still feeling strong, Tommy decided to stay with his Norwegian partner as they stepped to the side while we methodically marched upward.

Reaching the start of the safety rope at the base of the face, I looked back to see Thomas heading back down to ABC. I wasn't sure if Thomas was feeling the effects of the diarrhea bug or if altitude sickness had struck. After some debate on the radio it had been decided it would be best for Thomas to descend to try and recover. With a bit of hesitation, Tommy turned to continue the climb up. As it turns out, Thomas would give it another formidable try later in the day yet his sickness prevented a second trip up the Lhotse Face. His summit bid was over.

For some reason Billi was not on her usual brisk pace as we traded places a couple of times on our way up to Camp III. This worked out well for Deano as he floated between the two of us, filming both at various points on the face respectively. During our last rest break together, just below the first tent platform, he snuck in the last interview of the day.

We talked about the climb and what it felt like to be here high on the wall. He also picked my medical brain about the diarrhea that seemed to be spreading rapidly about the team. With the camera off Deano then scampered up the small vertical shelf of ice to get footage of Billi and me trying to follow in his footsteps. After my less than stellar performance Billi seemed to regain her steadfast pace, Deano right behind her.

The last couple hundred meters to our tents proved to be just as exhausting as the first time, but my mind became distracted from the agony. As I rounded the area just above the first platform of tents, I could see that Deano and Billi had stopped momentarily to visit with a Sherpa and Westerner from another team. The unknown pair then continued descending towards me as my teammates progressed upwards towards our tents.

When the unidentified pair reached me I could tell that something was wrong with the Westerner. His breathing was extremely labored and his legs periodically buckled at the knees. With what sounded like a European accent, he informed me he had succumbed to HAPE or High Altitude Pulmonary Edema while at Camp IV 2,500 feet above.

The unpredictability of HAPE means it can affect anyone at any time. Left untreated, the leaking blood vessels in the lungs cause a person to essentially drown in their own bodily fluids. Rapid descent to lower altitudes is the treatment of choice.

The Westerner had no choice but to descend. Giving up his summit bid would be a small price to pay in exchange for saving his life. All I could do was wish him a safe descent and returned health as I continued up to our tents. As the distance between us grew I heard a loud thud.

Just before the bulge of ice that hid the first row of tents the man collapsed. His Sherpa began tapping and yelling at him to get up. During our brief conversation I found it odd that the man was not wearing supplemental oxygen given his condition. I called up to Deano on my radio to see if I should head back down to try and help them, not exactly sure what I would do when I got there but nevertheless I felt bad for the guy.

Deano informed me that the two did in fact have an oxygen setup on them and that I really wouldn't be able to do anything for them. I turned around to see the man finally stumble to his feet. Moments later they disappeared around the corner. I, in turn, stumbled up and into our camp. As if on autopilot, Moises had come out of his tent to greet Billi and remained there to cheer me on into our tiny platform ledge.

As Moises' habit of playing greeter I continued to play my role of arriving last into camp. I called down to Russell to report in as required. Normally his response was short and sweet, along the lines of "Roger, Roger." Apparently I caught him in a good mood.

"Big Boss, Big Boss, this is Lance, once again I'm bringing up the tail end of team one into camp three."

"There's something about you veterinarians. You sure like the rear end!"

Even though tired, I appreciated the humor coming from Russ. I couldn't help but laugh. Heck, I figured it was better to be late than never, right?

The night here would be different and not just because I would miss doing the encore tent performance with Eugène. Instead, we donned our masks and started breathing supplemental oxygen. The plan was to suck on the precious molecule for the remainder of the climb until we got back to this point in two days, if not all the way back down to ABC.

Even though it was still difficult to sleep soundly at close to 24,000 feet, I have to admit the precious O's allowed me to rest more deeply. Already running on very little, sleep would be an increasingly rare commodity over the next forty-eight hours. I was about to head higher than I had ever gone before, not to mention venture into some of the most inhospitable terrain on the face of the planet.

May 20, 2009. We stirred to a beautiful crisp day, our camp still engulfed in the early morning shadows of Lhotse's ridge high above. The peaks to our west were already enjoying the warmth of day's first light. One at a time we clipped into the rope, funneling into a line of dozens of other expedition climbers, all with the same goal in mind. Passing here would be next to impossible, so the slowest climber above would dictate our initial pace. Shaun accompanied Stuey and me, our steps now in sync with the enormous span of climbers heading up.

After a couple of hours of quadriceps-burning terrain we reached the yellow band. As I waited my turn to climb up this historic rock formation I couldn't help but think about its origin, my gloved hands touching earth millions of years old. With some careful crampon placement coordinated with the jumar in one hand and rock in the other, the band was now below me. The band itself caused a natural separation between climbers so we were able to catch our breath at the top before starting the traverse across the face.

As I stood there I looked up to see a couple familiar climbers descending towards me. Despite their identical First Ascent climbing suits it was easy to pick out Ed Viesturs. He was not wearing an oxygen mask, his face exposed below his eyewear.

As he approached I took my oxygen mask off in hopes he would recognize me. I reached out to shake his hand, "Congratulations on making the summit." He thanked me in one fluid motion, as the line of climbers wasn't going to allow for detailed conversation.

I then reached out for Peter Whittaker's hand, owner of Rainier Mountaineering Inc. Even though he didn't know me, I credit RMI for helping me get to where I was now standing. After an identical salutation Stuey, Shaun, and I started the traverse. Making certain we had good crampon contact with the ice and snow beneath our feet we picked our way along the narrow and crusty path. One slip would mean a nearly mile-long uncontrollable slide to the bergschrund below.

Moments into our traverse Stuey's pace rapidly dropped off. It was as if someone turned his energy switch off. Shaun and Stuey pulled off to the side of the trail as best they could so Shaun could have a look at Stuey's oxygen system. Rather than create a traffic jam I moved ahead slightly to a less crowded spot. It was hard to not focus on the glimmering ice slide below shining in the morning light.

It was not a great place to hang out for too long, especially since the luxury of two ropes was not available for the two-way traffic. A number of climbers were on their way down. As each approached I couldn't help but wonder if they had made the top. I made certain to hold on to either their free hand if they offered it or part of their harness as the process of clipping and unclipping methodically occurred with each pass. Doing so also insured that neither of us would hopefully lose our balance. I was essentially acting as a temporary anchor.

Shaun called to Adrian on the radio to inquire if he could send a Sherpa from Camp IV to bring a replacement regulator and a fresh bottle of oxygen for Stuey. It sounded like his regulator was contributing to irregular oxygen delivery. That explained why he started to slow down so quickly. After a short wait they were able to get his system back in working order.

We continued towards the Geneva Spur. Named by the 1952 Swiss expedition, this enormous rock outcropping at the end of the traverse is the last imposing obstacle before a somewhat gradual trail concludes into Camp IV on the South Col. With the glimmering ice now behind us Shaun continued towards the top of the spur while Stuey and I paused to reflect on the day so far. After trying to choke down a bite of food and some water, we set off for the final push of the day.

The trail grew in width yet that did not increase our comfort level. The drop to our immediate left was even steeper and full of rocks jutting out everywhere. At each anchor point we held the ropes up for one another to make clipping and unclipping less strenuous. As we approached the actual spur we joined a mini-traffic jam.

Several climbers deep, each lined up waiting for their turn to surmount the twenty-foot jagged rock wall. As one or two climbers came down, another one or two would go up. Finally, like standing to place an order at the meat counter our numbers were called up. Knowing the relative safety of our tent was only thirty minutes away we heaved our weary bodies up and over yet another historic landmark.

That last half hour seemed like half a day, the thin air contributing to time standing still. Yet seeing the tents come into view as we rounded the last corner of the massive rock face caused a surge of adrenaline to rush through my body. It had taken us almost eight hours to reach our high camp. One of the cameramen approached. I removed my mask and proclaimed, "A tough day but a good day." After all, I was now standing at 26,000 feet, 3,000 feet closer to seeing the pinnacle of my dream become reality.

Far below I could see the tiny colorful dots of ABC. The South Col is the dipping saddle of the ridge that intimately connects Everest with Lhotse. Between the ridges of each mountain it is no longer than a couple of football fields and about half that in width. At opposing edges lie drop-offs of over a mile, so straying too far from the tents is not an option.

It is a desolate place with nearly constant winds. Standing amongst the wasteland of rocks reminded me of pictures of our moon's surface. The view above towards the Southeast Ridge of Everest is unbelievable as well as daunting. From the tents you cannot see the true summit but rather the 28,700-foot South Summit, our planet's second highest point. Tired and now over twenty pounds lighter than when I first arrived in Nepal, my energy reserves were being taxed heavily. Pausing to stare at the steep route above, I wondered how the heck I was going to complete the journey.

Moises suddenly replaced my weary thoughts. He could have simply stayed in his tent to recuperate yet walking over we embraced. Moises kindly agreed to take a picture of me holding my sponsor's banner. I knew that if I escaped to join Stuey inside our tent the chances of getting back out of my tent to get that photo were slim. I failed to get a picture of the banner at camp three twice, so I didn't want to strike out a third time. The banner and I were now officially higher than ever before.

Within an hour of arrival, our guides checked in to make sure we were feeling okay. Phurba even stopped by our tent to say hi. Our personal Sherpas paid us a visit as well with the gift of ice they had chopped. Like other camps we needed to melt the ice for our water. Not only was the physical exertion parching, but the extremely dry air also robbed moisture from our bodies with every breath we took.

Later that afternoon Moises surprised us with a visit to see how we were doing. Poking his head into our tent, Moises' uplifting spirit was a welcomed addition to our slow motion life at the highest campsite in the world. After a few oxygen consuming laughs and a couple pictures of Stuey and me in lethargy mode, Moises headed back to join John Black in their tent. We waited patiently to get the word whether tonight was definitely going to be game night. Around five o'clock Deano ventured back over to our tent. Russell had given the green light so Deano informed us that we needed to be ready to hit the trail around 11:30 pm.

Deano then surprised us that we had a bit of a time test ahead of us. Russell and the guides felt that if we could not reach the Balcony in less than six hours we would likely not be in position to make it to the summit and back safely. Fifteen hundred feet above us, the Balcony was the planned location for our first oxygen cylinder exchange. To think we had come so far only to take a climbing pop-quiz. It added to my existing stress load, yet I respected the concept.

With a sidekick cameraman, Deano then handed me a small wireless microphone to carry. The film crew wanted to get additional audio of me in conjunction with Tashi's Sherpa cam. I told Deano I would try to avoid swearing, something that was entirely possible under the circumstances. He said they could "beep out" that stuff if the footage made the show. Just a little more pressure countering the decreasing atmospheric pressure!

I placed the microphone in the inside pocket of my down suit, now a permanent fixture attached to my body, in order to keep the batteries warm. In fact, all battery-operated devices needed to either be in a pocket or at least within our sleeping bags, close to our body heat. Add to the stuffing list our water bottles and cozy is not a word one would use to describe the setting. With oxygen bottles next to us while continuing to breathe the bottled air our tent took on the image of a triage center.

Even though we rarely talked about it, all of us knew we might see the bodies of deceased climbers lying on the route. The area in our atmosphere above 8000 meters is known as the death zone. The human body is not meant to survive for very long above this invisible line in the sky. Supplemental oxygen merely prolongs the inevitable.

Over two hundred people have died trying to climb Mount Everest. The majority of them have perished within the death zone. In fact, I had read about several climbers who supposedly sat down and died on or near the route itself. Some were mountaineers with more experience than me so I could not help but wonder what went so terribly wrong for them. Could the same thing happen to me?

I started to think heavily about my family and friends back home. I decided to call my wife and kids. I desperately tried to sound upbeat and confident during the satellite link. Bailee, Jordan, and Kathy all sounded well. Perhaps they too were masking their own fears. I told them I would talk to them again soon, telling each one of them I loved them. It was hard to hit the "end call" button.

I also needed to hear my mother's voice. Forever that pillar of strength in the family, she encouraged me to stay strong and be focused. The emotions began to stir violently inside me. Moments after hanging up the lump in my throat swelled to the size of a grapefruit. I glanced over at Stuey. No words were needed as the floodgates opened once again.

My emotions had just reached their own summit. Stuey put his arm around me and pulled me into his shoulder. Unlike the video diary back at ABC these tears were different. As they ran down my cold cheeks they took along with them the fear of the unknown that had been building within. Stuey had warned me not to call home. Yet he also sensed my fragile need to stay in touch with loved ones. I will never be able to thank Stuey enough for his gentleness, understanding, and compassion the night of May 20, 2009.

That moment on the Col was the best thing that could have happened. It was a wakeup call of sorts. I would not let myself forget about my own mantra, *No Place but UP!* After regaining my composure Stuey and I decided we needed to rise and shine at nine o'clock. We knew we would need at least two hours to get our gear on, melt ice, and boil the resulting water. Of course sleep would evade us over the next few hours. Every twist and turn left us craving for oxygen. Several times we couldn't help but laugh at how silly we looked.

Just the simple act of trying to light a match was exhausting! Of course the lack of atmospheric pressure wasn't helping the process of lighting our stove, not to mention the fact that the Nepali matches we had were less than stellar. Stuey and I would pass them back and forth after just a couple failed strikes. After twenty minutes of match play, a successful spark ensued and the flame from our stove lit up the vestibule of the tent. The process of preparing water bottles and thermos containers was finally underway.

Like the stove flame, my gastrointestinal system decided it also wanted to suddenly light up. For the past thirty-six hours I had not had a bowel movement, an event that readily dismisses itself at altitude. Simply put, normal bodily functions slow down the higher you go. Of course, taking a few Imodium tablets from time to time had the same effect. With diarrhea running through our team, taking a preventive dose was warranted and I made no exception to that rule.

I looked at Stuey and said "Crap, I have to make an unexpected trip out onto the Col, to do just that!" While the winds were not excessive, the ambient temperature was still well below zero. I lumbered out of our tent, headlamp guiding my way across the Col. I charged out as fast as I could about fifty yards from camp, still well away from the mile long drop off yet also far enough from our miniature tent city.

Like most everyone else's down suits, there is a two-way zipper arched directly over the hind end area. It is appropriately named a moon door. With blinders on I reached around to let the cows out, so to say. My moon door did not want to open. The zipper was stuck. I had no choice but to strip down.

The moment was eerily reminiscent of my veterinary practice days back in Wisconsin. When I needed to do surgery on a cow to fix a twisted stomach, I often did so without my shirt on in order to sterilize my skin before it came in contact with the cow's flesh, even on the coldest winter day. Surely I could handle relieving myself half exposed engulfed by extreme cold and darkness at 26,000 feet. Of course it wasn't my upper half that was going to be exposed to the freezing temperatures!

Boy I was glad the camera guys weren't out filming. After the difficult balancing and aiming act I successfully sealed up my wag bag and redressed. Modesty is definitely out the door during expedition life, especially high on the mountain. Unbeknownst to me, Phurba had been watching the flicker of my headlamp the whole time, no doubt wondering what I was up to.

Upon my return to our tent Stuey's bowels were in action. In a flash he too headed across the Col. I guess the nerves and anticipation of what we were about to attempt finally caught up with both of us. I could only hope Stuey's moon door wasn't frozen shut. Upon his return the look on Stuey's face spoke volumes. We were both relieved, literally!

With our dueling bathroom visits over, we waited for the water to start boiling. It had taken almost an hour to melt enough ice. Eating something was not on our minds, the effect of high altitude shining. I reached inside my suit to test the microphone Deano had handed me hours earlier. I wanted to make sure the batteries weren't dead. Where did it go? I searched inside my sleeping bag thinking it must have fallen out of the pocket during my tossing and turning.

Then it dawned on me. It must have slipped out of my suit when I stripped down to relieve myself out on the Col! There was very little snow on the wind-swept plateau so retracing my steps would not be possible. It wasn't like I had any distinct landmarks to identify with either, just rock after rock. I felt so guilty for losing it, so I headed back out onto the Col to try and look for it.

After ten or fifteen minutes of searching I had to call the search and rescue operation off. I couldn't believe it; I lost the film crew's microphone on the Col. Back at the tent Stuey told me not to worry about it. Ninety-minutes had now passed and our pot of water just started to boil. We called it good enough and filled our bottles. With supplemental oxygen flowing we slipped back out of our tent one last time to get our crampons on, the last procedure before heading up into the night sky.

It was a struggle putting mine on. Eventually I got the first one strapped on tightly yet had to sit down to catch my breath in order to even think about repeating the procedure. Phurba sensed my growing frustration and kindly came over to assist me. He made everything look so easy. I mentioned that I lost the film crew's microphone. My guilt was getting the best of me.

Ed Wardle, one of the cameramen came over to film our departure from Camp IV. He had actually accompanied IMG's climbers to the summit the prior day, so he was simply adding complimentary footage as we began our final push for the summit. I let him know I lost the microphone and apologized repeatedly. He could tell I was a bit frazzled so instead of filming he lowered the camera. He placed his hand on my shoulder while looking up in the direction of the summit enveloped in the night sky high above and exclaimed, "Don't worry about the microphone, Lance. You've got bigger things to worry about."

His kind gesture had a calming effect on me, which made the rough start begin to smooth out a bit. I promised him I would look for the microphone when I got back to the Col, hopefully in about fifteen hours or so. With that I was ready for the most physically challenging day of my life.

Our guides fell into what seemed to be their customary positions. Adrian led our stretched queue of Himex climbers and Sherpas through the dark abyss. Shaun once again floated in the middle of the pack and Deano graciously acted as the caboose of our train, making sure everyone left Camp IV on time.

All of team one was now on the way to join the growing queue of climbers from other expeditions heading across the expanse of the Col. It was fitting that I seemed to fall into last place for our team as we approached the fixed-rope. Just ahead of me, Stuey and his Sherpa trailed Billi and her Sherpa. A couple unknown climbers were having an even rougher start so we politely passed them while we could.

Before reaching the steep section of mixed rock and snow leading up to the Balcony, Billi's pace started to falter just a bit. In order to maintain our slightly faster pace Stuey and I clipped ahead on the rope. Deano maintained his caboose spot just behind Billi and her Sherpa. We would later find out that her oxygen system had been acting up. Despite an inconsistent supply of oxygen she performed amazingly well, her inner spirit a primary catalyst.

We continued steadily up the mixed terrain, resting for a second or two every twenty to thirty minutes, mainly because the queue dictated it. We were now in a place less friendly for passing so we were once again at the mercy of the climbers' speed above us. During one of the short breaks I happened to look over my right shoulder into the darkness, a flash of light catching my eye. On the southeast horizon a spectacular lightning show was on display. Seeing the clouds from above as they repetitiously ignited into bright plumes of white was incredible to gaze upon.

Looking up, the stars themselves put out their own brilliant show of sparkling light. At sea level I might revel in the twinkling show, yet the fact that I was now well into the death zone cut the tranquility short. I could see the headlamps of my teammates, some now five hundred feet or more above me. They were nearing the Balcony. Well above them, perhaps another 1,000 vertical feet or more I could see a pearl-string line of lights. Climbers from other expeditions were already closing in on the silhouette of the South Summit.

Just below the Balcony, Stuey started to slow down. It appeared that something was once again not quite right with his oxygen system. He and his Sherpa pulled off to the side to let the rest of us by. It wasn't long before they sorted things out and were coming up just below us. We arrived at the Balcony well under the six-hour cutoff mark, one less thing to worry about. I was elated that I wasn't going to be told to turn around.

Tommy and his Sherpa arrived just moments later, as he too had pulled off the side to catch his breath a couple hundred feet below the Balcony. Although I wasn't quite sure which headlamp was hers, it looked like Billi was not too far below us. Everyone from our team would make the six-hour deadline and therefore be able to continue the climb towards the summit.

Catching a breather at the Balcony also allowed Tashi to attach a fresh bottle of oxygen to my regulator. The partially used cylinder would remain here for our team's use as needed during the descent back to the Col later in the day. Although it was very dark, I could sense the ever-growing void on the other side of the Balcony.

We were now perched at 27,500 feet. Tashi placed an extra full bottle of oxygen in his pack to carry to the South Summit. That was our next official stop. There we would, once again, exchange partially used cylinders for fresh ones. The last full cylinder would be enough to reach the summit and back to that point, if not all the way back to the Balcony. The cold was starting to settle in so it was time to get moving again.

Shaun led out from the Balcony up the southeast ridge with ZQ moments behind. I followed with Stuey trailing me. Tommy joined in just below. There were numerous headlamps still climbing to the Balcony so we knew Billi and Deano were in the pack somewhere. It was hard not to think about how she was doing. Our group had become close and everyone's success was important to us all.

The southeast ridge connects the Balcony to the South Summit. It is here where I encountered the second defining moment for me on the expedition. About halfway up the ridge the sun pierced the eastern horizon. I stood there in awe as light started to filter the planet around me. I was standing above the clouds, now a sea of puffy white waves over a mile below. Standing there reinforced the translation of Sagarmatha, "standing with my head above the clouds." The moment also reminded me of how small we are in this world.

It was also the first time I could actually see the incredible drop immediately to my right, over a mile and a half in depth. It was the East or Kangshung Face leading back down into Nepal far below. To my left another large drop, the South Face falling back down into the Western Cwm, well over a mile below. Until now I thought the ridge was wider than it actually was, the pitch black of night concealing its true identity. Man we were exposed and yet there was still more to come!

Up until that point ZQ had always been in the lead pack on our acclimatization climbs. Today was different. He had been stopping more than I expected. The altitude was affecting all of us. I could only hope he wasn't coming down with the intestinal bug as well. Passing was definitely not an option here. Despite his frequent breaks, ZQ's determination never faltered and we were able to keep a fairly decent pace.

Daybreak high on the ridge reminded me a lot of dawn on a cold Wisconsin winter day, less the 28,000-foot difference of course. This is the time of day that sometimes offers an exaggerated yet temporary cold snap even on the coldest of days. This ended up being the only time of the day where I felt the need to put my big insulated mitts on. My thin liner gloves had worked well enough to this point and would again take over as the primary barrier for my hands as the day progressed. Keeping my toes warm turned out to be another story.

Boots tend to be temperature-rated based not only on the level of insulation or the material they are made of but also on the amount of body heat generated inside them. In other words, continuous movement promotes body heat with the construction of the boot responsible for retaining the heat as well as shielding out the elements.

With the added unplanned stops I noticed my big toes were starting to feel a little numb. I began to consciously wiggle my toes and stomp my feet whenever possible, trying to facilitate blood flow and warmth to curb the onset of frostbite. As it turned out, despite losing the feeling in those toes for three months following the trip I did not donate any toes to the mountain. The $100 per toe price tag was money well spent.

Daybreak also produced a little more wind, mainly in the form of sudden gusts. These bursts would cause the large collar of my down suit's hood to blow into the inlet valve on the side of my oxygen mask. When this happened I would get the sensation of suffocating, as if trying to breathe through a plastic bag. It was a bit unnerving the first few times it occurred, until I finally figured out what the heck was going on.

During one of these encounters I discovered that my hood was nowhere near the mask. I yelled back to Tashi to ask him to turn the flow rate up on my regulator. I continued to struggle to breath. It then dawned on me that the condensation from my breath might be icing up the inlet valve, something Russ had talked about back in the white pod days ago. Sure enough, a few firm taps with my hand and my breathing became less labored. In an oxygen rich environment these would be little annoyances but up here they provided plenty of concern.

As Tashi and I made our way closer and closer to the South Summit we locked into a rhythmical beeping sound. Similar to the warning sound a delivery truck makes while backing up, we realized the noise was coming from Tashi's Sherpa cam. The signal with Big Boss was nonexistent high on the southeast ridge due to a lack of direct line of sight. For now there would be no images anyway nor could we call on our radios. All we could do was hope the gusts of wind would carry the annoying sound down into the void below and away from our ears.

Nearing the slope leading to the South Summit, ZQ got his second wind. The area looked like a narrow staircase. Previous climbers had created fairly decent steps in the snow leading straight up to the crest. About a third of the way up I met the first climber of the day coming down from what I presumed had been a successful summit a few hours earlier. My excitement grew upon seeing several more making their way down.

My exhaustion was no match for my desire to keep going, to see what was over the next ridge. Some of the most notorious climbing in the world was still to come. It didn't matter because all I could think about was catching a glimpse of the true summit.

Just before seven in the morning, Stuey and I reached the South Summit. The view looking down to my right over the now 10,000-foot Kangshung Face was breathtaking. To the left was an 8,000-foot plunge back down into the Western Cwm. Seeing such drops made me love the fixed-rope that much more. Peering up I could see the tiny figures of climbers slowly making their way up and down the summit ridge but the top itself was still out of view. Straight across lays the famous Hillary Step with an exposed rocky skin poking out from behind a large mushroom of ice and snow on its right side.

The knife-edge ridge connecting the South Summit to this historic step is called the Cornice Traverse. With mile-long drops on either side, narrow and tortuous describe its appearance. To its left lies mostly vertical rock. To the right, the notorious drifts of snow called cornices. Snow cornices take on the look of a dolphin's dorsal fin. Essentially they are snowdrifts on steroids, formed by the jet stream winds blowing the snow in one direction over the ridge.

They appeared even bigger on the final summit ridge above the step but the area up there looked appreciably wider. Historically, without the use of fixed-rope guiding the way, straying out too far onto one of these fins was possible.

Without adequate earth underneath punching through meant free falling back down into Nepal. Even though I already had a lot of admiration for our Sherpas, knowing they were the first people of the climbing season to make tracks up here to fix the ropes and route made me appreciate their courage all that more.

At around seven in the morning we dropped over the South Summit's crest. Just underneath, at the start of the traverse we stopped for the second mandatory cylinder exchange. Chris Dovell and Phurba Tashi had just finished the traverse for the second time after having reached the summit earlier in the morning. Back in base camp we had celebrated Dovell's fortieth birthday. His wife's gift to him was her blessing to climb Everest with Russell. By being the first Himex climber of the day to reach the top he also successfully opened that birthday gift. With a high five, I yelled my congratulations to him through my mask.

Phurba had just topped out for the second time this season. It was incredible to think that a couple more and he would have twenty under his belt. I congratulated him with a handshake and pat on the back. With his game face still on Phurba turned to instruct Tashi to replace my used oxygen cylinder with a fresh one. Phurba continued preparing Dovell's cylinder so they could continue their descent back down to the Col.

Shaun had arrived at the oxygen cache moments earlier and had already sent ZQ out across the traverse. ZQ was obviously back to his normal self, as normal as one might expect anyway deep into the death zone. My mind then turned to Rob Hall. It was somewhere around this area where the famous New Zealand guide perished during the *Into Thin Air* disaster of 1996. I had mentally prepared myself to see him sitting near the route, yet unbeknownst to me his body had been removed from the route years earlier. For now I had escaped seeing any dead climbers, the darkness of night likely hiding several from view earlier in the climb.

What was present here was the ability to hear Russell on the radio again. He was already asking Phurba to take a look at Tashi's helmet camera. The request confirmed what Tashi and I had been suspicious of. After wiggling wires and making sure all the components were tight on the camera, Shaun recommended we get going. Barring human traffic jams or other problems, there was about two hours of climbing left.

A traffic jam did in fact occur earlier. While climbing up the staircase to the South Summit a large one had formed at the base of the Hillary Step. The blockade of climbers, including teammates John Black, Moises, and Valerio stretched out across the Cornice Traverse. Not the most comfortable place to hang out on, both physically and mentally. Standing still up here greatly increases the risk of frostbite as well as using up precious oxygen. Remember, we use it not just to reach the summit but also to get back down safely.

Dovell and Phurba had made it down the Hillary Step just in the knick of time, avoiding being stuck on the summit ridge above. Adrian had been with them throughout the course of the morning but on the way down chose to remain at the top of the step, morphing into the role of traffic cop. With my teammates waiting their turn to ascend the Hillary Step it was obvious to Adrian that someone needed to hold up the descending traffic from above in order to get the queue moving again fairly in both directions.

On the radio we could hear Adrian referencing the jam up. I pictured him holding up a badge. His words clearly rang out on the radio "Move fast. Take no prisoners!" That line become part of the drama depicted in the show, detailing what can happen when too many people pack the slopes of Everest, not to mention the loss of climbing etiquette.

As we prepared to follow Shaun across the traverse, Stuart glanced over at me and said, "I am turning around buddy, this is my Everest." I wasn't sure I heard him correctly so I asked him to repeat himself. At first I thought maybe the lack of oxygen up here was getting to him or that his oxygen system may not be working quite right again. Hypoxia or low oxygen on the brain can have a funny way of showing up. I admit that I felt like I was in another world altogether. Every movement was taking twice as long to clearly think through.

Unbeknownst to us, Stuey's Sherpa never removed the partially used bottle of oxygen from his pack back at the Balcony. At just under 10 pounds fully loaded, one tank was plenty of weight yet Stuey never wavered on his pace. He was quite surprised to discover the additional tank when we arrived at the South Summit and rightly so. Maybe the added weight had finally caught up with him, his body now craving oxygen more than ever. I tried to process what he said, concerned there was an underlying medical issue brewing.

He then eased my concerns by confirming that he was content standing here at the second highest point on our planet. He had promised his wife before the expedition that if he saw anything on the mountain that told him to not continue or if he ever felt threatened, he would simply turn around. The route above did in fact look intimidating, so even though I needed to ask him if he was certain of his decision, I understood the promise he made to his wife.

Hours earlier I cried on Stuey's shoulder. He had been my rock when I needed something firm to lean against. Selfishly I wanted him to continue to the summit with me, yet who was I to argue with such wise decision-making?

With a firm handshake and a heartfelt hug I asked him to be safe on the descent back to Camp IV. With his soft British voice he replied, "Good luck, buddy." Before turning I assured him, "See you in a little while, mate." He then joined Phurba and Dovell for the descent.

Kami, Stuart's Sherpa had never been to the summit, so Phurba agreed to allow him to continue with Tashi and me on the final steps to the top. I have since joked with Stuey that his turn around meant I had "two Sherpas for the price of one." As I sadly watched Stuey head up over the crest of the South Summit and out of view, I knew it was time to get moving, the summit was beckoning me to visit.

Shaun kept a steady pace across the traverse, glancing back occasionally to make sure I was still right behind him. About halfway across we came upon a bare rock ledge dangling to the left at an unnerving angle. Without sufficient ice and snow on top of it, crampons would have nothing to bite into. To put this in perspective, it's like fingernails on a chalkboard, yet this chalkboard wasn't located inside the safety of some classroom at sea level.

The slab was several feet wide and a little bit more in length. A large cornice shielded it to the right with nothing but open air to the left. Add to the excitement a bunch of older tangled ropes cluttering its surface. It was hard not to gaze upon the mile and a half drop on the left, Camp II straight down below.

I regained my focus to watch Shaun commence his crossing, clipping into the newest looking red rope that also appeared to be the most taught. He leaned back slightly to add some tension to it in order to increase the stability of his crampons on the rock to prevent them from sliding too much. Without incident he glided across to the other side.

It was now or never, so I made sure I was properly clipped into the rope. Rattled with the procedure would be an understatement as to how I felt, yet after what felt like an eternity I was across without even so much as a slip. Rattled was quickly replaced with thrilled as I felt my crampons contact snow underneath.

We now had a fairly clear run to the base of the Hillary Step. I would have to wait my turn to surmount it, just not quite as long as my teammates had earlier. Although I couldn't let my guard down, the wait allowed me to soak in the views. Jagged Himalayan peaks poking through the clouds stretched as far as my eyes could see. I leaned over the waist-high snow wall guarding us from the Kangshung Face. Man, it looked steep and long!

While I felt fairly certain I could successfully navigate my way up the various hand and footholds, I have to admit I was overwhelmed thinking about the level of courage Sir Edmund Hillary must have had back in 1953. After all, I had a rope guiding my way up which I could attach my jumar device to for added security. If I should slip, the combination would catch my fall, at least theoretically.

Hillary did not have the luxury of a fixed-rope. What he did have was an ice axe and a rope attached to his partner, Tenzing Norgay. Most importantly, he had determination. He scanned the buildup of ice and snow loosely adhered to the rock, wondering if it would hold. There was only one way to find out.

Just before tackling the Step, one of my teammates appeared at its top. It was Moses coming down from on high! Even though he was not holding stone tablets, Moises had successfully reached the summit. When he got to the bottom of the Step it was my turn to greet him with a hug, "Congratulations, amigo!"

"It's your turn, bro," the excitement on his face adding to the comment. Moises started across the traverse while Shaun began his climb up. A few minutes later he pulled himself over the top and was out of view. I waited patiently for a couple of unknown climbers to make their way down the one-way street. This was it, now or never.

Although the jumar is not supposed to be used to pull oneself up a rope, no matter what the pitch, it was hard to not pull on the device as it locked into the rope. A few handholds, some careful cramponing, and a couple deep breaths later I was at the top. I just successfully climbed the most famous step in the world! I couldn't help but wonder how Sir Edmund Hillary must have felt to be standing here, knowing he was the first to overcome it, all the while being on ground never touched by a human before.

I had hoped to have a clear run to the top from here. Unfortunately I couldn't completely avoid being caught in a traffic jam. Numerous climbers lined the curving rock ledge just above, each waiting patiently for their turn to drop over the Step. I thought the traverse was a bad place to stand but it was much worse here. I wondered how I was going to get around the climbers or how they were going to get around me.

With faces covered, I couldn't recognize any of the climbers in queue at first. The identical Michelin Man suits didn't help. I could feel the mass of climbers edging forward. I started to get pushed outward over the drop to the left, my nerves now on red alert. I then spotted Chris Jones.

I lowered my mask to shout through the wind to get his attention. I quickly congratulated him on reaching the summit then asked if he wouldn't mind helping me get around the queue. Similar to the security he provided us back on the first descent of the Lhotse Face he was again lending a welcomed hand. As I stepped forward I unclipped one carabiner and reached around Chris's back, blindly feeling for the safety-line. I knew my crampons were teetering on the ledge's edge so I wasn't about to look down at the 8,000-foot drop below.

The climber behind saw what I was trying to do, reaching out to guide my hand and help clip the carabiner back onto the rope behind Chris. As I began my tiptoe move around, Chris held on to my harness while I grabbed onto his. He then unclipped my second carabiner in front of him. As he handed it to me I could feel both of my crampons coming into full contact with the rock ledge. I yelled thank you to Chris but knew we both had to keep moving in our respective directions.

After sneaking around a few more climbers I finally had a clear path leading up to the final summit ridge. John Black appeared over the sloping crest ahead. I could see a smile on his face. As he approached he informed me that the summit was approximately forty-five minutes away. After a quick hug and congratulation he continued down.

There was just enough sloping angle up ahead that I could not see the summit. Every few steps, like a young child peering over the top of a candy counter, I would pop up onto the tips of my boots in hopes of catching a glimpse of it. Tashi and Kami were not far behind with Shaun just minutes ahead. As I had read, the final ridge was not that steep yet the altitude required a lot of work for every step. Sometimes it took a half-dozen breaths per step. But now my adrenaline started to kick in full force.

Gaining the last of the rocky outcroppings I caught a glimpse of something in the distance. At first I wasn't sure if my eyes were playing tricks on me. Then I realized it was not a mirage but prayer flags flickering in the wind. I was staring at the summit! Twelve years of dreaming was within my grasp. The reality set in that I was actually going to make it. You would think I had no more tears to shed after all the crying down below. I told myself to knock it off because the tears were freezing to my face almost as fast as they were being produced.

May 21, 2009. Whether it was a lack of oxygen or the overriding effect of the adrenaline surging through my veins the last one hundred meters are kind of a blur. Maybe it was tunnel vision because I became fixated on the bundle of prayer flags, now getting bigger with each step. At 8:50 in the morning local time, I couldn't climb any higher. A flurry of emotions swirled around inside my head. Was I really standing on top of the world?

I radioed down to Russell informing him I had made it, thanking him in the process. "Well done, now would you please talk into the camera?" Even at 29,035 feet I appreciated his directness. Apparently Tashi's Sherpa cam was still not working properly. The cameraman for the show who had topped out with V and the others had to descend with them, capturing Tashi and me as we waited to climb the Hillary Step. From there it was up to Tashi's camera to snag footage to the top or at least that was the plan.

From here it was a straight line of communication over to Russell's tent at the base of Pumo Ri. The film crew was hoping to capture some live images of my stay on the summit. I sat down on top and began to talk into the camera while staring at the horizon, now slightly curved. After a few taps with his hand, Tashi and I realized the camera was not working so he took the helmet off in order to be a bit more comfortable as we shared the views three-hundred and sixty degrees around us.

ZQ took a break from taking pictures to shake my hand. We congratulated each other after which I turned to Shaun. I could not thank him enough for being here with me. With his characteristic green hat shrouding his ball cap and oxygen mask on he told me how proud he was of me.

Although my body was craving oxygen, I somehow knew it would be okay to take off my oxygen mask. The air was crisp and cold yet inviting. Blue skies predominated. The wind was mild with occasional gusts. Without the wind chill factored in, the ambient temperature was around ten to twenty degrees below zero, just another mild Wisconsin winter day!

I felt surprisingly warm, my thin liner gloves protecting my hands. Other than their use at daybreak on the Southeast Ridge, my large over mitts dangled gently below my wrists, attached firmly to me by way of their built-in security straps. Interestingly enough, an alternative name for such a strap is "idiot cord." When removing your mitts you don't want to have to hold them because you may drop them and gravity does the rest or worse, strong winds blow them off the face of the mountain. Cinching the cord around the wrist is an idiot's insurance plan to avoid losing fingers as well.

I sat down right on the top of the ever-growing blossom of prayer flags. Perched like a bird on a pedestal I gazed back at the spectacular view of Lhotse. The nearly vertical gulley of snow and ice that Ellen Miller was to follow up to its summit the next morning looked intimidating. I paused for a moment not only to admire the difficulty of the route but to also pray for her safety while climbing. We would have to wait until we got back down to Camp II to see her and find out in-person whether she reached the top.

I scanned the horizon over to the left. At 27,765 (8462m), Makalu rose well above the clouds, an impressive looking mountain which reminded me of a shark's dorsal fin. Back to my right I traced the path of the Khumbu Glacier and the Icefall, Base Camp somewhere at its foot under the clouds, two miles below. Just behind me was Tibet, the Rongbuk Glacier flowing from the foot of Everest's north side. I could see footprints from climbers who had traveled up the North Col route earlier, yet for now, it was just my teammates and me sharing the highest place on our planet.

Although my mind was dulled, I knew I needed to thank Chomolungma for allowing me to visit her summit. I reached into my backpack to retrieve the roll of prayer flags for her. Kami was there too so he used my camera to take a few pictures of Tashi and I together on top. I then handed the Lung Ta to Tashi, asking him if he wouldn't mind attaching it to the bundle of flags we were now comfortably surrounded by. It was Tashi's first time to the summit as well so he kindly agreed to my request.

Tashi and I thanking Chomolungma moments after reaching the summit.
Photograph by Kami Tshering Sherpa.

I continued on with the business at hand or at least what I could remember to do that is. I made certain to pull out my sponsor's banner from inside my pack. Weeks earlier I noticed that David Tait had a small banner that he had carried to the summit. Having been to the summit before, he had tied it to his pack using a short length of accessory rope. Similar to the concept of the idiot cord, it was a way of making sure that a sudden gust of wind didn't spoil the photo op. I liked the idea so I did the same with my banner. After all, I didn't want to have to explain to upper management how I reached the top but failed to get a picture with it. A return trip was not an option!

I realized Tashi had my backup camera as he had been snapping a few photos, but to be safe I handed him the camera I was carrying. I proudly held the banner up while he clicked away. The Quest for Success was now fulfilled. I could not have been more thankful for Alpharma's support. My sponsorship contract with the company stated that while I was not required to make the summit, something that can never be guaranteed, I would try my best to get the banner as close to it as possible. Having fulfilled a contract never felt so good!

The business side was over. The moment had come to make good on my own personal goal of honoring my late father. I pulled on the ends of the tape I had used to secure the lid of the container holding my father's remains. The cold temperatures caused the tape to become more like a thin layer of rotten cement rather than an easily removable adhesive, splintering in small pieces as I tugged away. For a split second I felt my frustration build only to subside when I remembered I brought along a pocketknife. I carefully cut the tape away from the lid. Before opening the container I asked Tashi if he could take a picture of me spreading my father's ashes.

He looked at me with bewilderment, not sure what I meant. I pointed at the container and with a motion raised my hand to show him that my intentions were to release its contents. The light bulb went on inside his head, "Okay, I count to three, you release." I popped the lid off and as if on autopilot, the moment I heard him say the number three I gave the ashes a light toss up into the gentle breeze swirling around me. It happened so fast that all I could do was hope that the act was caught on film.

As he handed the camera back I thanked him for being part of the moment. I couldn't wait to check the photo so I fumbled with the menu buttons. Tashi had pushed the button at exactly the right time. The photo revealed my father's remains hovering over my head and is what you see on the cover of this book.

My brother was right: my father had been riding on my right shoulder throughout the expedition. I also knew that for over the past two decades he had been watching us from above and would continue to do so. I'd like to think that in that split second I guaranteed his lofty presence until we meet again someday. Despite every day wishing he were still alive, I somehow knew he was watching me, smiling like never before. Had it not been for his contributions early in my life, I would not have been sitting on top of the world, close to him as humanly possible. It was the highest tribute to him I could make, both figuratively and literally.

Twenty minutes had already gone by. Russell knew I had enough steam left in me and the weather showed no signs of deteriorating. My mind was obviously stormy, however, because it never dawned on me that I had Barry's photos inside my pack, including the one of our late friend Richard which I had hoped to get a picture holding. I also managed to forget that I was wearing my altimeter watch. Up until Everest I made certain to take a picture of its digital height display on every summit.

I did remember to do one last thing before leaving. I reached back down into the bottom of my pack. Shifting the oxygen cylinder to one side I pulled out a grapefruit-sized compression sack. Tashi turned around to see what I was up to. With both his goggles and oxygen mask off I could clearly see his expression.

The look on his face when I opened up the sack will be etched in my mind forever. I only wish I would have taken a picture of him as my Wisconsin cheese wedge hat sprang out of its compressed state like a jack-in-the-box! I believe his priceless gaze and slight shake of his head confirmed for me that in his mind I truly was a crazy Westerner.

Removing my goggles now too, I proceeded to put the now autographed wedge on. With all of the Himex team member's signatures, everyone was with me on the summit. I had sacrificed some food and water to haul that baby up to the top, my Wisconsin pride having gotten the better of me. As Tashi snapped a few more photos I couldn't help but chuckle wondering if this would constitute a record in the Guinness Book of World Records: the highest cheese wedge in the world!

After the fun was over, we welcomed Tommy to the summit. I could see Deano making his way up the summit ridge as well. Upon arriving there were more high fives. It didn't take Deano long to pull out his video camera and start recording. I stood up and with arms stretched high overhead I yelled, "Top of the world, baby!"

Chapter Twelve

Only Halfway There

For years I dreamt of reaching the summit of Mount Everest. Now, after enjoying this magical place for an incredible forty-five minutes, a stronger sense of reality slapped me in the face, "I have to get down." I thought a lot about Russell's final speech to us back in the Tiger Dome. Success was not the summit but rather reaching the summit and getting down safely. With nearly 80 percent of mountaineering accidents on Everest occurring during descents, I knew I had to muster my remaining energy.

Climbing up is demanding on the lungs; going down adds further demands on your legs, particularly the quadriceps muscles. The adrenaline that helps push you to the top is now all but gone. The mind is already dulled and the euphoria of reaching the summit numb. I started to think a lot about my family waiting for me back home. Part of me wanted to call them from the summit, yet I did not want to jinx the day. Not to say those who have done so were wrong in doing so, but there have been some who did only to later become tragic statistics.

In reverse order we departed from the top of the world. ZQ shot down the summit ridge with Shaun a few steps ahead of me. I turned to thank Chomolungma one last time for allowing me to visit this special place. As we neared the bottom of the ridge Billi appeared, steadily pushing upward. There was no doubt in my mind she was going to reach the top. As we met to make the carabiner switch around one another I yelled through my oxygen mask, "Nearly there, baby, nearly there." Moments later the final member of team one stood atop the world.

Fortunately the narrow ledge above the Hillary Step was empty by the time we reached it, only a couple more ascending climbers had been trailing Billi. Tashi and I had a clear run to down climb the step, both doing so uneventfully. Before continuing across the traverse towards the South Summit I glanced up at the Step, still in a bit of shock over where we had just been. Celebrating would have to wait.

I carefully approached the rock shelf with the precarious angle and incredible view of the Western Cwm far below. Its surface continued to beckon me to give it the old fingernails on a chalkboard try. Crossing it on the way up went off without a hitch. Navigating it this time would not be as friendly.

I double-checked to make sure both of my carabiners were secured to the red safety rope and that the pencil diameter ropes connected to them and my harness were intact. My nerves seemed to be in overdrive. I placed my right crampon onto the smooth surface. With my left crampon on the rock it was up to my balance and careful foot placement to get me across.

About halfway across I could feel both crampons start to slide out from underneath me. Slipping, I collapsed to my hands and knees with a loud thwack. The void started pulling me down from behind. For a split second I thought my life was over, that I was going to become part of the 80 percent statistic. I have heard that seeing your life flash before your eyes as death draws near can happen. For me, I yelled at myself for being such an idiot.

I came to an abrupt halt, my harness tugging firmly on the small of my back. I thought my heart was going to leap out of my chest. My incoherent mind forgot about the safety-line, my own gear doing exactly what it was designed to do. There was no time to be joyous, only the need to get up and get across the rock slab and onto the snow-covered route ahead. Without further incident and a more manageable heart rate I stopped to contemplate what had just happened. I was able to relax a little more when I reached our oxygen cache nestled underneath the South Summit. The traverse was now behind me.

ZQ was already up and over the crest above. Shaun, Tashi, and I assessed the oxygen cylinders in our packs. We had plenty to get down to the Balcony. After calling down to Russell to check in we headed over the South Summit. Before dropping below I took one last look back at the summit ridge and the Hillary Step. I was sad knowing I would never see them up close again, yet I was also elated to know home was that much closer.

We arm-wrapped down the staircase ridge at a fairly brisk pace. Our progress was unexpectedly halted as we neared the exposed steeper section a couple hundred meters below. An unknown climber was sitting right on the route, alert yet apparently unable or unwilling to move. As we approached we could see by the color of his suit and patches that he was a member of the Russian-led 7 Summits Club expedition. With some rudimentary international lingo Shaun tried to communicate with the stranded man. He was not wearing any eye protection, and it soon became clear that he was suffering from snow-blindness.

From what we could gather he had either forgotten or misplaced his goggles earlier in the day. At this altitude the ultraviolet light is so intense that it takes very little time for the retina to be damaged without the use of protective lenses. Fortunately snow-blindness is a temporary condition, albeit a painful one. Medication, eye patches, and time provide the cure.

In 2001, American climber Eric Weihenmayer became the first blind person to successfully climb Everest. It was an incredible feat, which I admire to an even greater extent having stood where he stood. His accomplishment is a terrific reminder that vision isn't always about what we see with our eyes but rather what we see with our mind. Still, I was concerned for the Russian climber, at the same time feeling very fortunate to be able to see where I was placing my feet.

Although fully prepared to assist, Shaun called down to Russ and Monica to draw awareness to our discovery and seek any additional treatment suggestions. Russ followed through with a radio call to the 7 Summits base camp to let them know one of their own was in trouble. After Monica weighed in, Shaun got out a syringe of dexamethasone as well as some eye medication from his medical kit. Administering the eye medication was going to be the easy part. Given the language barrier, injecting the man in the thigh with the syringe was going to be interesting. With as clear of words as possible Shaun yelled, "I am going to poke you in the thigh now with this needle?"

Without further delay he then drove the needle through the man's down suit and layers underneath, penetrating the muscle below. Without flinching or even a Russian word in vain (not that we would know if one was being said or not) the shot was over.

Tommy arrived moments after the excitement. Shaun instructed us to continue descending. He was going to wait for Deano to help him with getting the Russian climber down. Conversely, the 7 Summits team was already in the process of sending a couple of their Sherpas up from Camp IV to assist the rescue.

After about thirty minutes of descending it was apparently time for more excitement. With Tommy fifty meters or so above me, I maintained a controlled descent with a firm arm wrap on the fixed-rope. Scanning ahead for the next anchor I caught a glimpse of something abnormal in the line a couple meters ahead. It was split wide open with only its stretchy chopstick-size core intact. The core holds little to no strength but is rather what the strong nylon strands are wound around.

I quickly scanned the older ropes close by to see if any could be used to continue the descent. One single white rope appeared to be in good enough condition although there was no way of knowing if it would hold until after I clipped in and continued the arm wrap. I yelled back up to Tommy to warn him of the danger yet I wasn't sure if he could hear my words given the distance between us. I then radioed to those above me in hopes they would understand where the problem was. Had I been rappelling and hit that section I believe I would have taken a very long tumble down the Kangshung Face.

With Tommy and me past the danger we started to make better time towards the Balcony, the Southeast Ridge now at a more manageable angle. We planned a short rest at the Balcony to reassess our oxygen cylinders before continuing down to the

Col. The sun was heating things up, giving me a flashback to my now infamous second climb up through the Western Cwm.

As the Balcony neared, I welcomed the opportunity to shed a layer, getting rid of my thicker hat in exchange for my characteristic blue do-rag. I also needed to get my big goggles off in exchange for my lighter glacier glasses. I could feel a layer of sweat building up so the timing could not have been better.

This was also the first time I felt like drinking water since we left our tents almost twelve hours ago. Tashi and Kami arrived minutes ahead of us, arranging the partially used cylinders all of us had cached during the early morning hours. Despite a lack of appetite, Tashi offered me a piece of gum, which I gladly welcomed. My mouth felt terribly dry. Tashi then told me he would carry an extra empty cylinder of oxygen so that I would not have to. I admired his strength and willingness to help.

Tommy decided to rest a bit longer so Tashi and I decided to head down. Other than a couple of other unknown climbers at the Balcony, the route below appeared vacant. Tashi and I were in our own little world of sorts, albeit once again a steep one. The snow here had loosened up a bit from the rising sun in contrast to our nighttime ascent. Numerous rock outcroppings meant carefully cramponing and balance work as we twisted down through the maze.

The view of Camp IV on the South Col far below the Balcony.
Photograph by John Black.

The tents were slowly getting bigger yet still seemed so far away. I felt the need to rest every so often, mainly to ease the fire burning inside my thigh muscles. We were about 1,000 feet or so above the Col during one of our breaks when I happened to catch a glimpse of something about fifty feet lower and just off the route to the left. As we approached my mind started to register.

At first I thought it was fabric from a collapsed tent strewn about the snow. Oh how I wish it had been that inert. Instead, my brain screamed reality. It was a human body. Until that point I had been lucky to not see any deceased climbers. The early morning hours had hid dead climbers from view. Seeing it now was no blessing, yet witnessing it during the ascent would have made the push to the summit that much more daunting.

It was hard not to stare, my mind's numbness spiking. The body was large in stature, too big to be female. Wearing a light blue down suit, he was lying on his back, with legs bent at the knees and arms slightly elevated as if he had been reaching out. His face was covered with snow. Some of the carpal bones in his fingers were exposed; the gloves shredded by the wind. I was surprised to see such decomposition at this altitude, yet fluctuating temperatures had obviously dictated this. With Camp IV in sight, the body was a humble reminder how lucky I was to be alive but also reinforced that I wasn't completely safe until I was off the mountain. Who was it? When and how did he die? The questions kept popping into my head. I would later describe the body to a couple different individuals. While I debated about it at the time, describing the body to others revealed it was quite possibly Scott Fischer, the elite mountaineering guide from Mountain Madness who died in the 1996 tragedy.

Tashi wondered why I paused for so long, so I pointed over to the body. No words were needed to know he wanted to get moving as quickly as possible. I didn't argue, and we picked up our pace. Just before reaching the Col we intersected two 7 Summits Sherpas coming up the rope on their way to assist with the rescue of their blinded climber. Finally, we exited the rocky slopes and onto flatter ground, the safety of our tents less than thirty minutes away. I was elated to unclip from the safety-line. It was the first time over the past fifteen hours I could actually let my guard down just a bit.

The first person to greet me at camp was one of the cameramen, "How do you feel to be an Everest summiteer?" Despite my exhaustion, I removed my oxygen mask and with a big smile I yelled out, "I'm going to Disney World!"

Stuey emerged from the tent with a bottle of water in his hand. I was so happy to see my British friend, embracing him as tight as I could. With some hydration within and my crampons finally off Stuey and I slipped into our tent. Even at 26,000 feet the sleeping pad felt plush as I stretched out like a beached whale. Some of our fastest climbers of the day like

Dovell, Moises, Jones, and John Black had continued their descent to ABC.

I admired their strength yet knew I would be better off resting at the Col for the night, even if still on the edge of the death zone. Besides, even if I had the strength I would have been pushing the amount of daylight left to tackle the steep Lhotse Face. Russell's words kept running through my mind. "Success is not the summit. Success is getting home safely."

Our tent's vestibule door was open to allow ventilation. As I lay there gazing out across the Col, I noticed a familiar figure walk by. Low and behold a smiling face suddenly peered into the tent. It was that of my friend and former guide, Jon Shea. He was stretching his legs a bit as he prepared for his own summit bid in just a few hours.

His infectious smile brought one to my face as he congratulated me on reaching the summit. A tremendously strong climber, Shea did not need luck, yet I still offered him some and told him to be safe. I then informed him that I expected to see him one more time back in base camp. We slapped hands before he strolled back to his tent.

As the chill of the night air approached, I couldn't help but think about calling home to let my family know I reached the top. I struggled with the idea for a moment. I still wasn't in the safety of base camp, yet I felt confident that in two days I would be. The temptation was too great.

I powered up the satellite phone and hit the speed dial button. My wife answered. After informing her I had made it to the top and was now back at high camp, she asked if it was everything I had expected. I mustered up, "Although exhausting, it was." Both Bailee and Jordan were excited, and I wish I could have talked to them longer. Before hanging up I told each one of them that I loved them and that I would call in a couple of days from base camp.

Mom was next on my list. Before I could get it out she asked, "Did you make it?" I told her that Dad made it with me and was now high above. She then asked if she could tell the rest of the family and friends who were waiting to hear the news. While I was not opposed I wanted her to realize I still had a long way to get off the mountain. Before hanging up she told me how proud she was of me. It was the icing on the cake.

I wanted my brother Ryan to hear the news from me directly. He had been diligently following my blogs, along with Megan and Valerio's, not to mention those from other expeditions. He knew we were somewhere high on the mountain and that our final push had to be close at hand. It was good to hear his voice. I thanked him for allowing me to carry the coin and finished the conversation by telling him that I would be in touch soon. Unfortunately I got Barry's voicemail next but was still happy to relay the news.

Before powering down the phone as well as myself, I wanted to let my sponsor know that the corporate banner reached the top of the world too. Who better to call than Carol Wrenn? Upon answering the phone I told her where I was and where I had just come from. She congratulated me. I thanked her again for her support. I knew I would likely make one or two more calls yet couldn't call everyone on the company list, so I asked her if she wouldn't mind sharing the news with the corporate office.

Alongside Carol, Jeff Mellinger and Mark LaVorgna too had pushed internally to get the financial support needed to make the trip become reality. I would have kicked myself had I not at least tried to reach both of them as well. Unfortunately I got Jeff's voicemail but was a bit luckier to have Mark answer his phone. He was happy to hear I made the summit yet even happier that I was getting out of the death zone and on my way down.

Despite the altitude, the reduced stress of having summit day over meant I was able to rest a bit more comfortably that evening. As I shifted positions a couple down feathers appeared, suspended in the air. One more shift and a few more graced the confines of our tent. I realized they were coming from my suit but where? Turns out it had two punctures, one in the leg and one on the buttock area! Who knows how long I had been shedding my plumage.

I did have an unknown climber slide into me on the Cornice Traverse, yet it wasn't a big deal at the time. Apparently his crampon though caught my leg and over the course of the day, the suit's thin skin finally tore open. However, that gap paled in comparison to the one on my rear end. As I rolled over for the exam, Stuey politely chanted that I had a hole in my arse. Tell me about it.

Good ole duct tape came to the rescue. I like to carry it taped around my ice axe just in case quick fixes are needed. I also had some taped to my water bottle as backup should I lose the axe, so there was plenty to do the trick. I handed Stuey my ice axe and he began to unroll. After a few forceful taps on my rear he exclaimed, "You need some meat on your bones, mate!" He jokingly finished up by massaging the tape into place in order to get it to stick and seal out the feathers. No wonder my bottom cheek had felt cold.

Before lying back down, I commented to Stuey that my eyes felt like they were on fire. I had taken my goggles off on the summit for about ten minutes, completing forgetting about the rule of doing so. In essence, that short amount of time allowed the UV light to reach my retinas–a minor discomfort that would only last a few hours, but a hard lesson learned.

We woke to increased winds and some snow starting to blow across the South Col. The plan was to be on the trail by nine in order to be off the Face and back to ABC by midafternoon, before any potential storms could brew. With less frustration Stuey and I managed to get our stove going to melt more ice to fill our water bottles. Yet our appetites were still somewhere down below waiting for us. As we made final preparations to leave, our handheld radios came to life.

It was Shaun talking to Russell and Monica. What we could make out was that Deano had awakened to severe swelling in his throat such that it was impeding his ability to breathe properly. The first medical attempts relayed by Monica had failed. I could sense a bit of panic in their voices as decisions on what to do next were being contemplated. A tracheotomy was even thrown into the discussion. I started to think that I should head over to Deano's tent to assist with the procedure should it indeed be needed.

Monica offered up one last medical trick before resorting to the surgical option. As it turns out gargling water with aspirin tablets dissolved in it opened Deano's airways enough to cancel the need for his windpipe to be opened up. Although I had never done a tracheotomy on a human, I had on animals. I was relieved to hear that I didn't need to experiment on Deano at 26,000 feet.

With the news that Deano was feeling better, Stuey and I rolled out of our tent and into the start of a miniature blizzard. The winds were incredible and visibility quickly diminished. Phurba came over to our tent and suggested we get a move on to join the last group of Sherpas. Billi, ZQ, and Tommy were already on the trail. Shaun and Deano planned to rest a bit longer to make sure the swelling in Deano's throat continued to subside before tackling the steep ice of the Lhotse Face.

I followed Stuey along the route towards the Geneva Spur. The storm seemed to be building with each step. We weren't very far out of camp when we recognized Hiro and our Japanese friends fighting their way through the winds to reach the safety of the tents. They had left Camp III hours earlier only to get caught in the storm as they traversed the ice wall.

As we approached the Spur the moisture in the air had increased as well. The cold temperature caused it to instantly freeze onto our goggles. Stuey and I stopped several times to try and scrape it off our lenses but as quickly as we did, a new layer of ice formed. We were down climbing blind.

I thought for a moment it was the mountain's way of getting back at me for making the satellite calls last night. The experience made me appreciate that much more the accomplishment of Eric Weihenmayer. Originally I had thought that not seeing the incredible drops on the route might prove less nerve racking, yet now being blinded myself, my fear of not seeing things two feet in front of me had grown exponentially.

With extreme care we negotiated the Spur one by one, luckily not having to wait as long to go down as we did to go up a couple days earlier. I couldn't have relied more on the rope that day for it truly was my lifeline to get down, not only preventing me from falling to my death but also providing me a "yellow brick road" by which to follow.

As we continued down across the rocky outcropping just below the Spur, we crossed paths with several more of our teammates from team two coming up. Even though covered from head to toe I was able to pick out my friends. The fact that the moisture had finally stopped instantly freezing to my goggles helped too.

I wished each one of them a safe climb as we passed. Grizz seemed to be doing well, yet an alarming sound prevailed around him. A loud hiss was coming from his oxygen system. He said he wanted to reach Camp IV before stopping to see what the problem was. It was apparent he still had enough of the precious gas to help get him there. Besides, it wasn't like there was a rest area on the route here, only a huge drop down the Face. I knew he was in good hands with guides Hiro, Shinji, and Narly, so I told him to be safe, and that I would see him in a few days.

The number of climbers coming up was dramatically less than when we had departed Camp III for the Col two days earlier. A lot less passing in either direction made the descent a bit less stressful. The weather continued to ease up as well, although the winds stayed fairly steady until we reached Camp III. It was now down to just a few tents for temporary shelter as the Sherpas ahead of us had already dismantled part of the tent site.

We needed to stop to put our helmets on before continuing the descent. Several items dropped by climbers had narrowly missed several of my teammates during the previous two climbs up the ice wall. This included an oxygen tank, a sleeping pad, and even someone's helmet to name just a few. Add to the list the chunks of ice that naturally break off and the wall's level of danger heightened beyond that of just falling.

Seconds before leaving Camp III, a wave of lethargy splashed over me. I told Stuey and the others to go on ahead and that I would catch up down below. I reassured them that I would be right behind them. On the ledge just below the last tent platform sat the small vertical wall of ice that required a rappel to get down. After sending the rope through my figure eight descender I became locked up, unable to move in either direction. Stuey was nearby so he came over to see what the problem was.

I had done this the last time we were here without so much as a hiccup getting in the way. Stuey and I stood there in bewilderment trying to figure out why I was locked in place. With a growing sense of frustration I disengaged from the rope and headed over to the other anchored rope. It was a sign that the mountain wasn't quite done with me yet.

Below the wall our small group got stretched out. Once again I brought up the rear and this time quite a ways back. After what only seemed like a few minutes everyone had vanished from my sight. It was as if I was the only person on the route. Despite the tranquility, the winds now absent, my mind began to wonder if I was going to be able to complete the descent. After just a few minutes of down climbing I would have to stop and rest twice as long. The process repeated itself over and over. Where the hell was the bottom?

Finally I could see the bergschrund. It was still a couple hundred meters below. I had to stop yet again. Sitting there looking out over the haze encrusted Western Cwm I wondered if I was actually dying. I couldn't move. I had a hard time focusing on the task at hand.

Then images of my family popped into my foggy mind. How could I let them down after having gotten so far? Perhaps it was the Hoffman black belt in my pack calling to me. Somehow I managed to get my weary legs out from underneath me. I needed to finish this thing.

As I approached the snow-filled bergschrund I glanced out onto the glacier to see someone in a yellow down suit coming up the route. Well below the start of the fixed-line the person stopped and stood there motionless. Was it my greeting party or a rescue party? It had taken me a long time to get off the Face so maybe there were concerns in camp?

The first time I reached the one-story vertical rise immediately above the bergschrund I rappelled down it. This time I was simply too knackered to even think about stopping to rig up the rope for a rappel. So I made sure I had a secure arm wrap on the rope and went face forward. Two steps down and I lost control of the wrap, my body swinging wildly around in a circle. Plop, down I went the rest of the way. Luckily the soft snow cushioned my stop, not to mention the fall was out of view from the mystery yellow suit out on the glacier.

Whew, nothing like finishing the Face with the white stuff on my own face. At least I wasn't hurt, except for my pride of course. I continued out onto the glacier, unclipping from the final section of fixed-rope. The yellow suit was in fact one of our Sherpas, sent to make sure I was okay.

I felt bad he had made the climb back up the glacier to check on me, yet I was also glad to see him. His presence reassured me that I would soon be back in the safety of camp. Knowing the Face was forever behind me retrieved some energy within. I picked up my pace a bit to try and stay within shouting range of the Sherpa, still a tough task even if 8,000-feet lower than the previous day.

As I approached the area of rock and ice at the bottom of the glacier, near the outskirts of ABC, another Himex Sherpa appeared. This was definitely intended as a welcoming committee rather than a rescue operation. He handed me a cup and filled it with warm lemon tea. It tasted so good. I thanked him repeatedly between gulps.

I could see a cameraman working the tri-pod mounted camera near the edge of ABC. I raised my arms up in triumph. Not only had I made it to the top, but I successfully down climbed the Lhotse Face one last time. Okay, maybe the descent wasn't graceful but at least it wasn't caught on film.

The greeting party had done their job and, knowing I was safe, returned to the Himex camp. I was in no rush, not to mention I no longer had the necessary energy to keep up with them. I weaved my way through the rock and ice, finding a suitable spot to remove my crampons. I was thankful to be alive despite being in such a desolate place, the warm air shrouding camp in a mystical haze. ABC was exceptionally quiet this time around, a number of teams having already left the mountain for good. The strange tranquility added to the peacefulness I was starting to feel inside.

Dovell, Moises, Black, and Jones along with Adrian had already left Camp II for base camp, over 3,000 feet below. I dropped my backpack off at my tent and stumbled over to the dining tent. Handshakes and hugs spread amongst my remaining teammates including Tommy, ZQ, and Stuey. Ellen was there too after successfully climbing Lhotse. Not only was she in an elite category as the first American woman to climb Everest from both sides, she could add to her climbing vitae being one of just a handful of women in the world to summit the fourth-highest peak in the world. I was happy for her as we exchanged hugs and congratulations.

V was also present which at first surprised me, so I immediately wondered if he was hurt or not feeling well. Even though he had descended from Camp IV yesterday he decided to hang around to rest another day before tackling the icefall. I was relieved to hear he was okay. We then joked that there was no Puck in ABC so we needed to get back down to locate the last of the hidden jars. Yeah, we had a number of reasons to want to get off this mountain.

Yesterday I thought I heard a sketchy report on the radio that my buddy Jim Holliday, the Big Hot Gouda, had to abandon his summit bid before reaching the Lhotse Face during his team's climb to Camp III. The reasons were unclear so I asked the group. It turns out Jim had collapsed before the fixed-rope, apparently stricken with the bug that had been spreading through our camp causing severe diarrhea. After regaining his strength here at ABC he returned to Base Camp. I was just glad he was okay and out of harm's way.

Deano and Shaun suddenly appeared at the door of the dining tent. They must have been hauling butt to be here so quick considering their late departure from the Col. Aside from Phurba, who elected to remain at the Col to help the second summit team, our group was all either here or farther down the mountain.

Kyla, our cook at ABC, brewed up a mean batch of instant potatoes. I had never been a big fan of these back home, but today they tasted almost better than the real thing. In fact, Kyla had to make a second batch, our appetites coming back with full vengeance. Of course anything tasted better than plain noodles or the hundreds of candy bars I had eaten over the past several weeks.

Despite the revelry inside the dining tent, we were exhausted. Tomorrow was the last official day on the route. Yet it involved one last trip through the dreaded Khumbu Icefall. Before retiring to my tent for a few hours of rest I gladly pulled out my toothbrush to polish my not so pearly whites. I left it here to conserve weight higher on the mountain. I had the cheese wedge to carry up after all.

Despite not having eaten very much up high my mouth still felt like it had moss growing in every nook and cranny. Just like the simplicity of those yummy instant potatoes, cleansing my teeth was a natural high. Who needs altitude to get high? With pearly whites shining through once again it was time to try and catch some long overdue zzz's.

I knew deep sleep would be impossible. I wrestled inside my sleeping bag, thinking about the icefall, wondering if it would allow me to pass unscathed. As a group we decided to get up very early in order to increase our odds of an uneventful trip through the maze of towering ice blocks and widening crevasses. Personally, I was very willing to give up several hours of rest to reduce the risk of being blasted by an avalanche or crushed by a serac.

May 23, 2010. Five o'clock came early, or so it seemed, yet one last surge of adrenaline kicked in to get my body moving. I had taken a few minutes last night to organize my gear, so all I had to do was roll up my sleeping pad, stuff it into the bowels of my pack, and get my boots on. It was also time to free myself from my aromatic down suit for the last time. I had lived in that thing for over two weeks and even though it performed beautifully, it was definitely time to say good-bye.

A cup of tea and a few mouthfuls of food and I was ready for the descent. The faint glow of daylight started to work its way into the Cwm. I started to think of team two. They should be above the Balcony by now, somewhere on the Southeast Ridge. I wondered if the winds had calmed down from what we had experienced during our exit from the Col. I turned my radio on in hopes of hearing my friend's names called out one by one as they reached the summit.

I had no idea that Grizz was not only fighting for the summit but also against the same dysentery that turned Big Jim around. I knew I needed to concentrate on the descent, yet my mind drifted to our teammates who were now battling gravity and whatever Mother Nature was dishing out high above. I politely asked Chomolungma to keep my friends safe and to grant them access to her summit.

We thanked Kyla one last time for all his wonderful efforts to keep us fed while at ABC. With that we donned our packs and headed down the trail towards the glacier. It didn't take us long to reach the spot where crampons would be needed for the remainder of the trip down. Despite duct tape and a couple extra screws, mine had held together well, so I could only hope they would last until we reached crampon point at base camp.

Before our final voyage up the mountain I discovered my crampons took a terrible beating on the rock on Lobuche, exacerbated by the first trip up to Camp III. The plastic plates on the bottom that prevent snow from building up were loose and a couple screws had fallen out. I also noticed that the strap on one was sliced in half.

Attached to the crampon, its purpose is to act as a leash. When the crampon is attached to the boot with its metal clip in the back, the strap is wrapped over the top of the boot and cinched back down through the frame of the crampon. Should the crampon accidentally pop off the bottom of the boot the strap pulls tight, preventing the crampon from disappearing down the mountain or into a crevasse. The tear was something I could fix using the duct tape.

For the other problem I tracked Phurba down to inquire whether the Sherpa tent might have some extra screws for reattaching the plates. Scanning the crampon over he kindly gestured, "Let me see what I have." About an hour later he appeared at my door, "Here you go." He had drilled some extra-long screws through the plates and into the metal frame of the crampon. Problem solved.

Saying thank you seemed like such a meager response so I dug through my gear to see if there was something I could give to Phurba in exchange for his help. I had already planned on giving the Sherpas some of my gear when the expedition was over, so for now I pulled out several brand new pairs of high-altitude climbing socks which I was not going to use. I know, socks might seem like a weak gesture yet Phurba was pleasantly surprised by my show of appreciation.

We continued our brisk pace down the heart of the Khumbu Glacier for one last time. By now we had become experts at the ladder crossings, hardly noticing the obstacles in the way. As we approached the area where remnants of Camp I still stood, we came upon a group of climbers from the 7 Summits expedition taking a short break. We paused to do the same, shedding a layer of clothes in the process. Even though we were still in the shadows of Everest, the sun would rise over the top in a couple hours and with it the temperature too.

Small talk was exchanged between our guides and the Russian guides. Ironically, one of the older gentlemen sitting in the group turned out to be the blinded climber we came across below the South Summit. Realizing Shaun was one of his rescuers his guide translated how grateful he was for Shaun and Himex's help in getting down the mountain. Although still painful, his vision had returned. With the good news we exchanged good-byes and entered the icefall.

This time there was no drama of avalanches coming down or seracs collapsing, just one ladder bridge after another. Like clockwork the daily fatigue I seemed to be plagued with started to rear its ugly head again. About two-thirds of the way through, my energy rapidly evaporated into the atmosphere. Fortunately the bottom third of the icefall had few ladders to cross so falling behind didn't concern me.

I tried to keep within earshot of the team, every once in a while catching a glimpse of my teammates skirting in and out of the ice maze. Descending farther and farther into the thicker air brought along with it a moisture-consumed fog. The damp air was warmer. It was as if we were walking in the Moors of Scotland.

The wands in the very last section that marked the route seemed out of place, the route now closer to the west shoulder than a week earlier. With the ladders now behind me I simply wanted to get out of the everlasting maze. I started to see some of the tents of traditional base camp periodically poking through the ice towers. They looked so far away. The new route made me feel like I was never going to reach crampon point.

By now I could no longer hear my teammates other than listening to them call into base camp on their radios as they reached crampon point. I continued along the marked route. The process repeated. Up a small ice formation, down a small ice formation, each time trying to get my bearings at the top. I could finally see the Himex storage tent at crampon point.

As I rounded the last outcropping of ice I could see Billi and Valerio taking their crampons off. Billi, V, and I exchanged hugs. I was finally out of harm's way. Alix was standing there too. I hugged her as she handed me a plastic glass, a bottle of orange soda in her other hand. It was incredibly kind of her to bring the pseudo champagne! It tasted incredibly good, the carbonation feeling like it was saturating my pores. It was just the revival I needed.

I decided I would sit for a few minutes and catch up with everyone back down at base camp. I needed a few minutes to soak it all in. On the way down I had heard the names of my friends being called out one by one as they too reached the top of the world. I thanked Chomolungma one more time.

Alec Turner had played my counterpart on his team by also historically bringing up the rear into the various camps. Yet this morning he led the charge to the summit from Camp IV in record time. With battered ankles, but not a battered spirit, Robby reached the summit through sheer determination and tenacity. Having pushed through her own pain and discomfort, Megan made good on her second summit attempt.

Our Japanese friends, including the petite yet formidable Kyomi made it. Sitting there on the rock at crampon point, I couldn't help but wonder if Saito may have swam the last few meters to the top like he had done back on Lobuche. My dear friend Grizz, although sick with diarrhea most of the climb from Camp IV, relied heavily on his inner strength to put one foot in front of the other all the way to the top.

Bruce and Paul were no different. Paul had done something genuinely sincere when he reached the summit. Big Jim had come to place his mother's picture there so before Paul continued the climb up from Camp II, he took that picture up on Jim's behalf. Even though not the original plan the gesture was extremely kind. I know it meant a lot to Jim. Rounding out team two were guides Hiro, Narly, and Shinji. Snow and clouds may have marred the view from the summit on May 23, 2009, but the spirits of my friends had been high, both literally and figuratively.

We would not rest comfortably, of course, until all of them were back in the safety of Himex base camp two days from now. I got up from the rock and headed towards our camp. Traditional base camp had grown quiet, multiple expeditions having already pulled out. The route back was now slushy, the rising spring temperatures giving the area a substantial face-lift. Slumbering along in my own little world, I thought about my friends back in base camp, no doubt already celebrating.

As I approached the cutoff trail leading to our tents I could see a lot of people standing outside the Tiger Dome. Rounding the final ridge near our ceremony altar the group erupted in noise. Pots were clanging matched only by a number of cheers and whistles. It was the official base camp greeting given to all climbers returning from the top of the world. I had a hard time holding back the tears, my emotions again getting the best of me. I stopped briefly at the Puja altar to toss a handful of barley over my left shoulder, extremely thankful to be back with my friends in Base Camp.

The pandemonium grew louder as I turned to walk the final steps into camp. Kirsty was manning a tripod-mounted camera near the dome capturing every moment. So who was the first to officially greet me? I had missed him up at the camps on the way down but not this time. Moises emerged from the group, embracing me in a heartfelt hug. We had not only come together as teammates, developing a friendship in the process, but we were now forever bonded as Everest summiteers.

Big Jim was next in line. During our embrace he congratulated me to which my response was, "I am just glad you are okay, brother." Even though Jim was stripped of being able to reach the top, he was alive and for that I was grateful. He was alive to fight another day on Everest.

The hugs and handshakes continued. It was a surreal moment to say the least. Last but not least I needed to shake hands with the man that made it all possible. Although he too would not be able to completely relax until everyone was off the mountain, Russell cracked a smile as I grabbed his hand.

I wanted to give him a big bear hug, yet I settled for a firm handshake with the simple words "I cannot thank you enough, Big Boss" rolling from my mouth. "Well done," he said and with that, he checked my name off his ledger pad.

It was time to rehydrate and clean up. Yes, a well-deserved beer was part of that process, and I admit it tasted oh so good! Even better than the one I had after the Puja over a month ago. Sitting in the dining tent, we enjoyed each other's company while we shared stories from above. Yet after a week of climbing it was time for another well-deserved treat. A shower! I couldn't imagine what it must have been like not to take one for eighty or more days during the early expedition years on Everest. The word *whew* may not do the thought justice.

May 25, 2010. After two nights of catch-up rest, we woke to damp overcast conditions. Light snow was already falling, blocking our view of the icefall. Our friends from the second summit team were somewhere in its bowels. We anxiously listened to the radio waiting to hear their names as they checked into crampon point. Being able to participate in the pot banging ceremony overjoyed me.

One by one they emerged from behind the stone alter, exhausted and worn, yet every one of them wearing a smile on their face. It was amazing to see how Everest changed us physically. Personally I had lost over eight pounds of weight just on the final seven-day voyage up and down the mountain. Alec must have lost more. He looked like half an Alec as compared to his arrival in base camp back in early April. As Robby rounded the final corner he was greeted not only to our cheers but also to a giant hug from John Black. They were now part of a short list of South Africans to have climbed to the top of Everest.

Bruce Parker's return meant he had just become one of less than a hundred Americans to join the 7 Summits Club, having successfully stood on each of the continents' highest points. It is truly an amazing accomplishment and one that is well deserved. As Paul Robinson entered camp, the first thing I noticed was how white his beard had become. Granted, it had numerous white strands in it prior to leaving for the summit a week earlier, yet I remembered more gray ones too. His appearance reminded me of the story of Moses (no, not Moises) coming down from Mount Sinai. Nevertheless, despite being a Boilermaker I was happy for him and what he had just accomplished.

When Megan came into view the smile on her face said it all. She was elated to have finally made it to the top. The walk back into camp was definitely the icing on the cake for her. With her return Megan joined just over two hundred women to have reached Everest's summit, only a fraction of who are American.

Antoine, our quiet French teammate held up his hands as we continued the racket. Similar to Megan this was his second attempt. A third would not be needed. In a few days he would be reunited with his daughter who would arrive in Nepal to share in her father's celebration of having reached the top of the world. How great is that?

I anxiously waited for Grizz. His body had taken a serious beating up high. As he emerged from the snow and fog he too momentarily stopped at the stone altar. I could see his eyes fill with tears. He looked frail with his cheeks sucked in. I wanted to tease him that his scruffy beard did in fact have a purpose. As I snapped away on my camera Stuey approached, wrapping him in a gentle hug. I put the camera down, tears of my own now building. I put my arms around him choking out the words, "Welcome back, Grizz. Congratulations, mate."

We stood and cheered until every member of Himex walked into camp. Our mighty Sherpas brought up the rear, each receiving their own respective heroes' welcome. Without their support, not a single one of us would have reached the summit. Phurba Tashi Sherpa walked in with the final group of Sherpas, all carrying large loads of gear from the higher camps.

Our welcoming committee erupted with even greater noise. Phurba had orchestrated the Sherpas with perfection and we knew it. With all of the Himex members off the highest mountain in the world, we could finally relax.

With a final check on his ledger, Russell closed the book on his most successful season guiding climbers to the top of the world. Between Sherpas, guides, camera crew, and paid climbers, almost sixty people stood on top of the world for Himalayan Experience in 2009. No fatalities and no major injuries had occurred on our expedition either.

Out of the twenty-eight paid clientele with Himex, twenty of us made it to the top. Historically, one of every three climbers reaches the top and typically about twenty percent of first timers are successful. Of the twenty-three of us who were there for the first time, fifteen made it up. Himex 2009 far exceeded both historical statistics. Teamwork, leadership, weather, luck, and the willingness of Chomolungma to allow us to reach her summit all played a part in making our success possible. As Everest summiteers we joined the ranks of less than 4,000 people in the world to stand on top of the world. It was hard to believe that after forty-five days on the mountain it was time to finally go home.

The plan was for us [clientele] to depart base camp in two days for the three-day trek down to Lukla in order to catch flights back to Kathmandu. As the day progressed it was evident that Mother Nature wanted to test our patience one last time. The snow became progressively heavier as evening approached. By the next morning we woke to almost two feet of new snow and it didn't appear to be letting up anytime soon. Some of our tents were starting to collapse so several of us kept busy clearing the snow from our shelters as well as digging out the footpaths in between.

I was anxious to get home. Russell could see that several of us were concerned about being stuck in base camp for a few more days. He calmly and politely reminded us that expedition life is about being flexible. After all, we couldn't control the weather so why not enjoy the last hours of life together at the foot of Mount Everest? He was right and with that the bottles of jubilee were placed one by one in the growing snowdrifts outside the Tiger Dome to begin the chilling process.

May 26, 2009. Russell hosted a grand celebration in the Tiger Dome. With snow in the air outside, champagne corks filled the air on the inside. Russell commenced with a touching speech. It was his first time leading an Everest expedition from the south side. He thanked all of us for the team spirit. Russell finished with a respectful reminder, "Not one of you would have made it to the top had it not been for our Sherpas." With that the Tiger Dome erupted in cheers and applause. Nothing more needed to be said. Only hugs, handshakes, and revelry followed deep into the night.

As quick as she dumped on us, Mother Nature gifted us the next morning with deep blue skies and the warmth of the sun. Over a meter of snow had blanketed base camp over the past two days. Unfortunately the deep snow prohibited the planned arrival of the yaks to carry our gear to Lukla so Russell came up with an alternative plan. A messenger was sent to the tiny village of Gorak Shep where porters waited to be hired for such tasks. One by one they arrived at base camp, loading their backs with as much gear as they could possibly carry.

It was time to say good-bye to our Sherpas, the Base Camp staff, Dr. Piris, our guides, and of course Big Boss. One by one I exchanged hugs and handshakes with those whom helped me reach the top of the world. Everyone had become like family, and it was hard to say good-bye, not knowing when or if I would ever see them again. The knee-deep snow made the initial thirty minutes out of base camp anything but fun yet Bruce and I fell into place joking how we better not complain given where we had just come from.

Stuart and Big Jim were close by with the rest of the team spaced out either in front or behind us. Before losing sight of it, I turned to get one last look at base camp. It had been home for the past month and a half. In a crazy way, I was going to miss its simplicities, yet I also longed to get back to my permanent home halfway across the world.

After a brief lunch at our Lobuche camp, several of us stopped by the cairns that line the ridge before dropping into the valley below. In between Lobuche climbs I had found Rob Hall's cairn back near Gorak Shep. I paid my respects to him as well as several of the other climbers who died on that fateful day high on Everest back in May of 1996. I had yet to find Scott Fischer's memorial but knew it was somewhere here on this particular ridge.

Big Jim pointed it out. I paused for a moment to pay homage to Scott while reflecting back on the image of what I believe was his body high above Camp IV. Standing there looking at his cairn was a somber reminder of how fortunate I was. With mixed emotions we forged through the snow to navigate the wet and muddy trail leading down into the valley.

As we descended, the snow rapidly disappeared. I paused after seeing the first blades of grass and then a flower. It was almost overwhelming. Out in the fields the newborn yaks were still trying to figure out how to coordinate their gangly legs. I relished in the joy of witnessing life and not death.

The group I was traveling with made good time to the lodge in Pheriche where we would rest for the evening. As I sat in the dining room admiring the historic climbing memorabilia on the walls and in the glass cases, John Black arrived. Robby was not with him. Apparently his battered ankles had been slowing him down during the trek out. As dusk turned to night there was still no sign of Robby, and the concern on John's face was evident.

He did not have to contemplate much. John put his headlamp on one more time and headed back up the valley to find his friend. You might think it would be easy to stay on the path leading down the valley yet numerous times we came to a fork in the road. What if Robby turned the wrong way and was now lost? Several hours passed before John found Robby, still plodding along but at least on the right path. Even though they did not summit on the same day they did start the journey together and John made certain they would finish side by side.

Our final night in the Khumbu Valley found us back in Namche Bazaar. The hand planted potato paddocks that had appeared so desolate and lonely almost two months ago were now full of green foliage. As we made our way back into the village, Alec, Moises, Bruce, Paul, Big Jim, Grizz, Stuey, and I gathered at the local bakery shop for a celebratory feast of excessive carbohydrates.

Dovell even made it for he was one of the lads who had a late evening in the Tiger Dome celebrating and as a result got a wee bit late start trekking out. The thicker air had obviously helped him recover from the festivities allowing him to regain his standard fast pace. We repeatedly teased him about his weathered look, and the need to keep his shades on. A hangover at sea level is bad enough yet thousands of feet up it's a whole other story.

After pigging out, I fulfilled my vow to revisit the shop next door. Fortunately the man who had been so kind to help me on the trek in with the necklace my daughter made me was there tending his goods. At first he did not recognize me yet I did not expect him to. After all, I was almost thirty pounds lighter and I'm sure not the most pleasant vision.

I showed him the bead necklace around my neck. The smile grew on his face as he recalled my previous visit. I then handed him the silk *khata* that he had presented to me for good luck on the journey towards Everest. I wanted to return the goodwill. He then draped around my neck a new silk *khata* for the journey home. I finished my visit by purchasing a couple yak bells to take home, just as I had promised weeks earlier.

By the following afternoon we strolled into Lukla. As long as the weather stayed good, we would fly to Kathmandu early the next morning. With several unique eating establishments in Lukla we broke up into small groups to once again feast on the cuisine which was now starting to appear and taste more and more like Western food. There was even a Starbucks-style coffee shop. What a treat to not be drinking instant.

The last few hours of the trek were uneventful, yet our last night in the valley turned out to be anything less than calm. Around four o'clock in the afternoon my intestines started turning inside out, quite literally. This would be Big Jim's and my last night together in the same room and what a memorable one it would be.

Not long after I started making trips to the bathroom his GI system started performing the same song and dance. Like clockwork we alternated the bathroom chorus line of heaving and squirting. This went on every thirty minutes until the sun came up. We were lucky we had an actual working toilet in our room.

It turns out that three others had come down with the same overnight problem as well, Kirsty, Bruce, and Megan. Food poisoning was high on the list of culprits. It really didn't matter; our flights were leaving with or without us so we forced multiple Imodium tablets down our throats in hopes of providing at least an hour's worth of relief. Jim and I were nervous about having an accident on the plane. After all, there were no bathrooms on board so we stuffed several small trash bags into our pockets as backup. Like the mountain, modesty would have to take a backseat for now.

Fortunately the plane ride was the only thing that went smoothly as the Imodium kept everything where it was supposed to stay. I wanted to kiss the runway at the airport back in Kathmandu. Instead, I needed to reach the hotel as soon as possible. I could feel my insides weren't quite done with me yet. Big Jim and I have since labeled our final concert in the Himalayas as the "Lukla Pukla Event."

Because of flare-ups, Big Jim and I missed the evening festivities later that night, Billi and Valerio having arranged a farewell dinner at a nearby restaurant. Since our return to Kathmandu was a week earlier than expected I was able to catch a flight home scheduled for the following afternoon. Trots or not, I wasn't going to miss that flight. Missing the dinner though meant not getting to say good-bye to a number of newfound friends.

The next morning Stuey needed to do some last minute things in town, so we planned on saying good-bye to each other just before noon. That was when my taxi was scheduled to pick me up to take me out to the airport. Fortunately my guts had slowed down, so I ventured down to the Thamel district to visit Mansukh at YAQOOT.

I walked into his store, not sure he'd recognize me. I pulled out the note he had given me, reminding him of the necklace and what I had come to Nepal to do. Before he could say much I interjected, "I made it to the top, brother." The hairs on his arms stood up as he repeatedly shook my hand in congratulations. It was a special moment.

With all my bags packed, I made my way to the hotel lobby just before noon. Despite my guts returning close to normal my mind was churning over the notion of saying good-bye to Stuey. We had been through so much, my thoughts drifting back to our time at Camp IV, particularly when I cried on his shoulder.

Normally I am a punctual person yet when the taxi arrived early I hesitated to get in. The driver became adamant about taking me to the airport versus waiting any longer. I tried to put him off for a few more minutes, my bags now in the trunk of the car and his annoyance building. I wanted so badly to give Stuey one last hug, yet I admit I feared the good-bye.

Just minutes shy of noon I wondered if Stuey might have gotten caught in traffic somewhere. I wasn't able to hold my taxi driver off any longer. With regret I headed to the airport but vowed to myself that I would see Stuey again someday soon. I discovered later on that Stuey dreaded the good-bye as well. Perhaps it was fortuitous that we didn't have one last hug while on Nepalese soil.

June 1, 2009. As I landed in Detroit, Michigan my excitement grew. I was now only a couple hours away from seeing my family. My brother Ryan and his sons, Benjamin and Nicholas, my mother and stepfather, as well as Katherine, Jordan, and Bailee were all planning to welcome me back at the airport in Appleton, Wisconsin. Alas, the trip had one more surprise up its sleeve.

As we sat on the plane now parked comfortably at the gate, the pilot came on the PA to announce that the ground crew was having difficulties getting the cargo door open. Behind that door was our luggage. The only way to successfully proceed through the final stages of customs is with your luggage in hand. We disembarked to at least start the customs process. As I stood at the baggage carousel waiting for my gear, I began to stare at the clock. As the minutes ticked away I realized I was going to miss my last flight of the adventure.

Luckily there was still another flight a few hours later that day so I was immediately rebooked. The missed connection was out of my control, just like the weather had been on Everest. Still, there was only one thing to do to forget about my disappointment, head to McDonald's in the terminal and satisfy at least one of my food cravings.

Even though my gastrointestinal tract had just gotten over a high-wire circus act just twenty-four hours earlier I couldn't resist devouring a double quarter pounder with cheese, fries, and a large Coca-Cola. It would be just a matter of time, only a few days in fact, before I would eat that Jolly Roger's bacon cheeseburger pizza and indulge in my third and final craving, a Dairy Queen peanut-buster parfait.

The unplanned delay meant the greeting party in Appleton would be three people shy. My brother had to be on police duty that night, so I would have to wait for the reunion with his family and him. My mother and stepfather decided to make the hour-long drive from their home for a second time. Kathy, Bailee, and Jordan would be waiting in the airport too. It was hard to contain my excitement as I walked off the plane and back onto Wisconsin soil.

As I approached the secured exit of the terminal, I could see my kids holding up a large white congratulatory banner they had made. The kids and my mother were wearing t-shirts with one of my climbing pictures plastered on the front. One more time the floodgates opened as I embraced Bailee and Jordan together.

I didn't want to let them go, yet I wanted to hug Kathy. I had placed a lot of responsibility on her shoulders over the past two and a half months, not to mention induced an emotional rollercoaster as well. How could I ever thank her? Back on March 25, close to the same spot we were now standing, I told her I would return. I felt like the luckiest guy alive to be able to fulfill that promise as I wrapped my arms around her.

I continued the circle by hugging my mother, the tears welling up in her eyes. Her fears too could now finally be released as she told me how proud she was of me. I completed the circle with a firm handshake from Ira. He had been kind enough to capture my return on his camera, pictures worth more than a thousand words indeed.

The reunion with my family will be etched in my memory forever. Standing on top of the world may have been the highest point of my dream, but returning safely to my family was the true summit. The journey was now officially stamped a success.

Not long after my return home, after speaking about the adventure at a large veterinary convention, I was asked, "How could you leave your kids for sixty-nine days?" Without hesitation my response was simple and direct. "I left for my kids." I want my kids, as well as yours to know, that dreams do come true.

Chapter Thirteen

More than a Mountain

It would take the remainder of 2009 for me to regain the strength I lost on Everest, not to mention the thirty pounds of muscle mass the mountain had devoured. Burning ten to fifteen thousand calories per day had been the norm and on a good day of eating, only a fraction of that was replaced. Despite the temporary loss of weight as well as the feeling in my big toes I believe I was able to retain most of my brain's gray matter. Of course some of my closest friends try to argue that I had already lost some of my sanity well before heading off to climb Everest.

Just days after getting home I made the short drive over to the elementary school in Wild Rose. One of the third-grade classes had tracked my climb, using it as a classroom project to learn more about Everest and the surrounding region. Back in base camp I enjoyed answering the numerous questions they posed including one that I got a chuckle out of, "Have you seen the Yeti?" Knowing how much they enjoyed corresponding and the fact that they would soon be on summer break, I wanted to visit the children in person.

Pulling my roller bag of gear through the school's front doors, I was greeted by dozens of children, all simultaneously yelling, "Welcome, Dr. Fox!" Several tiny escorts led me down a long hallway. At the end of it was a contingency of third graders standing in front of an enormous mountain poster they had constructed just outside their classroom.

I was in complete awe as one by one the students formally greeted me with a monologue of sorts about their project, images from the climb strategically placed all over the poster.

There was even a red string attached to it, which represented where I had been on the mountain during the various climbs. One by one they read their lines perfectly. A sense of pride escalated inside me. To this day I give credit to those students for teaching me that Everest is actually twenty-five Empire State Buildings high above sea level.

We filed into the classroom where I proceeded to do a show and tell presentation and answer their questions. There's nothing quite like the innocence of a child. I have since fielded on numerous occasions the same question, which was asked in Wild Rose, "How did you go to the bathroom up there?"

The short answer is, "Very carefully." The long answer is the same but as you can imagine a bit more complex. It is an important one to ask though because it allows me to tell my audiences the importance of taking care of Mother Nature.

After numerous autographs, pictures, and hugs from the children it was time for me to head back home to try and gain some sense of normalcy about life. It was their last day of school, a day which I could only hope ended on as big a high note for them as it did for me. What exactly would a normal day be like after having stood on top of the world? Getting home a week earlier than expected allowed me to use the time to mentally prepare myself to get back to routine life.

Every night of that first week home I fell asleep early in the evening. My body wanted to hibernate, to conserve what energy it had left inside. I was physically exhausted beyond belief. Mentally I was a bit taxed. Still, there was more mental anguish to come.

I had repeatedly called and emailed Jon Hansen in the days following my return home. All of my messages went unanswered. At first I didn't think too much about it. I figured he was probably busy with work. As the days progressed, however, my concern grew. The last time we spoke was back in base camp when I called him on the satellite phone after my final trip up and down the mountain. The conversation was brief but it was a good one. I had no premonition that our relationship was in trouble, but now my gut was telling me something entirely different.

During that conversation I informed Jon I wanted to give him the Cheezehead flag I carried to the summit. It wasn't a consolation prize but rather a gesture of appreciation, a thank you for having been part of the journey that made the summit possible. Despite admitting he was a little envious, he was appreciative of the offering. Since I wasn't sure exactly when I'd see him, I mailed him the flag, along with a digital copy of all the pictures taken with my camera during the entire trip. As quickly as the items were received they arrived back on my doorstep. No note accompanied the return package.

I immediately picked up the phone only to be greeted by his voicemail once again. Days turned into weeks without a response. Why was he ignoring me? I had never had anyone in my life act this way towards me. Sure, there was the occasional short-lived disagreement with a friend or two growing up, all part of the process of fitting in amongst peers.

Ironically, my best friend Barry Ruffalo and I had the longest period of non-communication. Our little spat lasted for all of two weeks during our freshmen year of high school. Why? It turns out we had eyes for the same senior girl. Our blinding hormones were in overdrive. Even though I lost the girl, I didn't lose my best friend and for that I will always be grateful. We joke to this day about how silly we had been to fight over her.

It wasn't until early March 2010 before I heard from Jon, nine months after I returned home from Nepal and almost one year to the date of our departure together for Everest. His delayed correspondence came in the form of an email, one that prompted me to pick up the phone. Sadly, Jon felt like I hadn't done enough for him during the expedition. Countering with specific examples refuting such an idea didn't matter. I was stunned to say the least.

No one could have prevented or cured Jon's physical ailments or the mental anguish that followed. The Discovery show aired in December of 2009, two months prior to that unfortunate telephone conversation with Jon. Jon and I ended up being two of several featured climbers on the fourth episode titled *Death Zone Gridlock*.

Our friendship, performance differences, and subsequent results on the mountain became individual storylines, respectively. With no acting and no scripts, the show revealed the effect the mountain can have on climbers, good and bad. Maybe the revelation of his performance on television added to his frustrations, which eventually boiled over in early 2010. I certainly couldn't blame him for being upset but to think any one individual contributed to his demise completely caught me off guard.

While the conversation ended amicably, I was saddened to know I had indeed lost a friend. Yet I could not let what happened between Jon and I tarnish what had been accomplished. In fact, I am not mad about the situation but rather am grateful. There is a silver lining in everything, and in this case, I learned a valuable lesson about communication and true friendship: never take either for granted.

I not only reached the summit but also, and more importantly, acquired a number of new friends to add to a long list of special people in my life. I have been fortunate enough to stay in touch with many of them on a regular basis. Since Everest I have been able to rekindle old friendships, some dating back to my days in high school. It is the integrity of such people, which has renewed my confidence in the definition of true friendship. Author Samuel Johnson's words speak volumes regarding the formula needed for such a relationship: *There can be no friendship without confidence, and no confidence without integrity.*

So what would life be like without a few challenges along the way? It turns out that losing a friendship paled in comparison to a more significant hurdle following Everest. After the traditional holiday season break, my kids headed back to school like hundreds of other students. The start of what should have been a normal spring 2010 semester turned out to be the start of a very tough year for my family.

Since it's not uncommon for kids to pick up viruses in commingled settings, Kathy and I weren't alarmed when Jordan contracted what appeared to be a run of the mill gastrointestinal bug. Yet unlike other kids who had experienced similar symptoms, Jordan's vomiting persisted well beyond just a couple of days. As the end of week one passed his vomiting showed no signs of slowing down. Kathy and I suspected that something more than the ordinary influenza was at play.

After several visits to the physicians and even a couple trips to the emergency room, our physicians remained puzzled. So Jordan was referred to Children's Hospital of Wisconsin where we met with a pediatric gastroenterologist, a doctor who specializes in intestinal disorders. By July, after several more invasive procedures, Jordan was diagnosed with gastroparesis.

Gastroparesis is a motility disorder of the stomach, resulting in a lack of normal peristalsis or movement of food out of the stomach and into the small intestine. The primary symptoms are nausea, followed by vomiting. The condition is not uncommon in diabetics or individuals ravaged by infectious stomach pathogens like the influenza virus. The difference amongst those afflicted however is the degree of severity as well as how long it persists. For some it fades away over a short period of time while others learn to live with it forever. There is no definitive cure.

Jordan ended up being tutored at home for the entire spring semester of 2010; his intense nausea and daily vomiting confined him to either the sofa or his bed. Through various medication adjustments and diet modification, over a year would pass before significant improvement would be seen. It was a long year for our family, yet once again a silver lining existed. My son's condition is not nor was it ever a death sentence. Rather, it is yet another important reminder regarding the fragility of life.

While learning to cope with Jordan's condition, I continued to work, traveling across the US and even abroad. Sometimes my trips allowed me to see my friends from the mountain. The first was Big Hot Gouda, aka Jim Holliday, at his home in Pittsburgh, Pennsylvania. Fortunately there was no battle for the bathroom like we engaged in during our Lukla Pukla event, yet we did share numerous laughs reminiscing about that night. Jim was a wonderful host and yes, he made sure there was plenty of hot sauce available to spice up the food.

During an August 2010 company sales meeting in Breckenridge, Colorado, Ellen Miller drove over from her home in Vail to have lunch with me. Catching up face to face, this time both clean and aroma free, was almost surreal. I will never forget the time we shared on top of Lobuche peak together and her kind words of encouragement. To say she was an inspiration to me during the trip would be an understatement.

Days later she flew back to Nepal to tackle Manaslu, another 8000 meter peak. She was once again climbing with Russell, along with Billi by her side. Team Didi may have been one person short yet to no surprise remained strong as ever, both of them reaching the summit in early October.

I did finally get back into the mountains. Blanca Peak, a 14,345-foot mountain located in the Sangre de Cristo mountain range in south central Colorado was the target. My Long's Peak partner and friend Dr. Mark Branine had traveled past that peak for the past thirty years, each time wondering what it would be like to stand on its summit. I suggested to Mark that there was no time like the present, so that same summer we set aside a weekend to give it a try.

We climbed over 6,000 vertical feet in two days and even battled a little bit of minor altitude sickness in the process. Just because a person has been to the top of Everest doesn't mean he or she is immune from altitude sickness, and I am no exception to that rule. As we pushed through the nausea and head pounding, after thirty years Mark saw his dream come true. Even though being able to tag the top of another fourteener was great, I was even more thrilled to have been part of Mark's accomplishment. I also couldn't have been more proud of him for having not given up on his dream.

Before Jordan's illness struck, we arranged a family vacation to England for the week preceding the start of the fall 2010 school semester. While my career has blessed me with the opportunity to travel abroad, being able to take my family on an international trip was a huge bonus. In addition to Kathy and the kids, my mother and stepfather would also accompany us across the Atlantic Ocean.

The plan was to do some sightseeing in London and Oxford. The trip would also reunite me with Christopher Macklin (aka Grizz) and Stuart Carder (aka Stuey), as well as introduce our families respectively. With Jordan's diagnosis in hand and summer rolling along we started to see improvement in his condition. We held out hope that the trip would continue as planned, yet just days before its start a relapse occurred.

After much deliberation, we realized that the long plane ride itself would pose the greatest struggle for Jordan, an added stress his body did not need. Rather than cancel the trip altogether, we made the tough decision that Jordan and Kathy would remain in Wisconsin to allow him the best chance possible to recover and hopefully get back in the classroom, the last time being almost eight months earlier. Before leaving, I promised my wife and son that I would take them to see England someday.

Upon landing at Heathrow International Airport, we were greeted by Grizz and his father Peter. Seeing Grizz standing outside of customs with a clean-shaven face and big smile brought back fond memories of when we first met in Kathmandu. I knew back then we had a special connection and now that bond was shining through.

There were hugs and handshakes all around. It was an honor to meet Peter, whom I had heard so much about during the expedition. Both of the gentlemen drove to the airport to accommodate transporting my family and luggage to the Macklin's flat in the wonderful neighborhood of Chelsea, part of greater London. Unfortunately Grizz's mum Pamela could not be at the airport, yet I knew that in just a couple days I would get to meet this terrific lady I had also heard so much about.

I actually spoke to Pamela while in base camp. One day after unsuccessfully reaching his mum on my satellite phone I failed to turn it off immediately after he returned it. Lying in my tent it startled me as it began to ring. Of course I answered only to hear Pamela's mixed American-English voice. She had been born and was raised for quite some time in the United States. It was only after meeting her beloved Peter that she moved to England, her home now for over forty years.

I felt extremely comfortable talking to her. She treated me like I was one of her own and thanked me for the blogs so that she could check in on her son from time to time. I knew how my own mother worried, so I completely empathized with Pamela's concerns over her son's safe return home. We conversed for several minutes after which I handed the phone back to Grizz.

After a couple wonderful days of sightseeing I was excited to finally meet Pamela at her home near Wimbledon. The Macklins had invited us for a barbeque, an invitation that would include Stuey and his wife, Jane. I was actually nervous about seeing Stuey, given our missed good-bye back in KTM and of course what we had gone through together high on the mountain.

After picking my family up at the train station, Grizz gave us a quick tour of the Wimbledon area before arriving at his parents' home. Forever the romantic, he cunningly mentioned that Stuey and Jane were running late in order to build my anticipation for the moment of our reunion. As I was greeted at the door with a warm hug and kiss by Pamela I looked over her shoulder to see Stuey standing in the living room.

It was another surreal moment for me. Almost fifteen months earlier his shoulder on the edge of the Death Zone helped release my inner demons. Now, standing in the thick air of England my appreciation for Stuey revolved full circle within me. It was pretty hard to hold back my tears, but unlike that night on the South Col, I managed to do so.

Of course Stuey's immediate teasing about that night helped to keep my floodgates securely closed. I figured since the fun-loving pecking started so quickly, I had to comment about his neatly pressed pink shirt, a color and style I had not seen on him before. It was like old times indeed, as if our adventure together had not ended. After the initial jabs Stuey introduced me to his beautiful wife. I was immediately impressed by Jane's elegance and warmth.

Reunited with Grizz and Stuey in the UK.
Photograph by Ira Giese.

Andrew Macklin, Grizz's brother, his wife, Justine, and their two beautiful children, George and Eloise, were also present. I was pleasantly surprised to hear Justine's accent, a good old American one, specifically of New York City descent. Listening to her amidst my English friends was a wonderful reminder of the ties shared between our two countries.

Andrew was the one who emailed me while on the mountain and as such proposed a toast at dinner for the blogs about Grizz. I also enjoyed learning about the details behind Whizz, Christopher's long-standing nickname given to him by his family. Perhaps ironic that Whizz and Grizz rhyme yet even more surprising is that the name does not relate to some young mischievous kid relieving himself in inappropriate places as I suspected. Rather, it represents his quick wit as a child, appropriate for sure.

Needless to say, the barbeque was incredible and the desserts Pamela conjured up were beyond even the top of the world. I was just glad I wasn't in training for Everest at the time! Many laughs and memories were shared around the table that night. I could not have been more pleased sitting there with my extended family from across the Atlantic Ocean.

Days later we headed to Oxford to visit Jane and Stuey for a couple nights. They live on a picturesque farm just outside of the city where Jane's brother raises beef cattle. The property is quite old, yet the Carder's have done an amazing job refurbishing and modernizing their home, a beautiful building which was once a loafing shed for cattle.

As a refined English lady, Jane delivered impeccable taste not only in the food she prepared during our stay but her choice in décor, which accentuated her superior class. With Stuey's uncanny gentleman-like qualities, the two complement each other quite well. Given his vocation, I couldn't help but tease Stuey about the shoddy plumbing throughout the house though! It was spectacular waking up to the sounds of cattle grazing in the fog-laden English countryside.

Stuey took some time off from work to show us around nearby Blenheim Palace, the boyhood tromping grounds of Sir Winston Churchill. He also took us into Oxford itself where we toured several of the colleges that make up greater Oxford University. A memorable moment for Stuey and I was our discovery of the memorial to Andrew (Sandy) Irvine at Merton College.

Irvine not only attended this school but also is best known as George Mallory's partner, both of whom died on Everest in 1924 while pursuing a dream to be the first to stand on top of the world. Unlike Mallory, whose body was discovered high on Everest in 1999, Irvine's has yet to be discovered. It is believed he carried the camera that may or may not reveal they actually made it to the summit before their unfortunate deaths. It was humbling to stand next to his memorial. It was also a strong reminder of just how fortunate we were to be alive.

With only a couple days left to our trip, it was time yet again to say good-bye to my friend, this time no excuses for not doing so appropriately. Stuey drove us to the train station where a quick embrace spoke volumes. In that moment I too did not want to think of it as a formal good-bye but rather a "see you soon" gesture. The convenience of email and the telephone have made the miles between us insignificant.

In fact, Stuey had surprised me back on May 21, 2010. My cell phone rang at precisely 8:45 in the morning. The caller id revealed a number much longer than a standard ten-digit domestic one. Still, I decided to answer it. The familiar jovial voice and initial fun-loving greeting choked me up something fierce. "Hello, honey, where were you a year ago?"

It had been a busy morning with many congratulatory emails between teammates from all over the world as well as phone calls from my family and friends. This included a heartfelt call from Big Hot Gouda, my polish brother, Jim Holliday. Despite the fact that he had to turn around on the mountain his call reinforced what I already knew. He is a genuinely sincere and unselfish man, someone I admire immensely.

However, it was Stuey's call from across the Atlantic that tugged at my inner emotions the most. He knew I was a softy, capitalizing on that by dialing my number at the time I was just about to step on Everest's summit one year earlier. I couldn't help but think about how much greater it would have been had he been there next to me at that moment.

In fact, during dinner at their home one night, Jane had asked if I thought Stuey should go back to try Everest again, to see what that last three-hundred feet was like. My answer was straightforward. Although he has every right to revisit the mountain, I was adamant that Stuey was just as successful as those of us who made it to the summit. Why?

His decision to head back down from the South Summit reinforced the importance of listening to our gut, that spiritual voice that resides within all of us. His courage, bravery, and ability to make such a decision epitomize what it means to be successful. It is what makes a person not only a great mountaineer but also a great person. In mountaineering, summit fever is a self-imposed disease that has taken the lives of numerous climbers.

There is no shame in turning around, no matter how close or far one is from the top. After all, the trip was not just about the summit, it was about the opportunity to pursue a dream. Stuey, Jim, Thomas, Eugene, Gilad, Osbjorn, Christophe, and Jon were all successful in that they chose to pursue their dream, regardless of its outcome. How many people simply talk about their dreams?

Our week in the United Kingdom flew by, and it was time for us to return home but not before saying good-bye to Pamela, Peter, and Chris. The Macklins had been gracious enough to allow us to use their spare flat in Chelsea, so at a minimum we wanted to take them out for a nice farewell dinner. A fitting choice, Grizz chose a traditional fish and chips restaurant in Nottinghill.

The meal was remarkable, and of course the company was even better. After toasting each one of them, hugs and handshakes followed. As for my young and enthusiastic English brother, I left Grizz knowing we would someday see each other again. We formed a special bond early in the expedition and will forever be bonded by our experience of climbing Everest together.

I couldn't return to the states, however, before trying to see one of my other Everest teammates. I jumped on the underground (i.e. subway) to London's downtown financial area where David Tait works. Although it was a short visit, I was lucky to catch up with him at his office.

We reminisced about Everest, shared a few laughs, and talked about the possibility of seeing each other again in the Khumbu the following spring. David was working on a plan to try Everest again without supplemental oxygen while I was in the process of working on another goal in Nepal, one that did not involve climbing per se. I left hoping I would see him again the following spring.

Back home it was back to work as usual. As the short-lived Wisconsin summer turned into fall, John Black from South Africa surprised me with an invite to his wedding, set for early February 2011. During our adventure on Everest together, I was fortunate enough to meet John's bride-to-be, Natalie. With the help of a guide, she did a solo trek to base camp to spend a couple days with John prior to his summit attempt. What a great story of love and commitment, so I immediately began looking at flight options to Johannesburg.

Just days after getting the invite I received an email from work that was too good to be true. One of my employer's distributors in Johannesburg requested my presence to visit some of their key customers. The irony was that they specifically requested I come in February. With the trip approved by upper management and the logistics in order, I was off to South Africa.

After a full week of work it was off to Cathedral Peak in the Drakensburg mountain region for the weekend festivities. Not only was I excited to be reunited with John and to visit more with Natalie, but I also knew Robby would be there serving as John's best man, literally and figuratively. I was hoping that Gilad and his wife Micky would be there too. I wasn't disappointed.

Natalie and John held a barbeque the night before the wedding so they could spend some extra time with all of us. Being reunited with Gilad, Robby, and John in the picturesque backdrop of the Drakensburg brought back so many memories of our time together on Everest. Seeing Natalie and Micky again was icing on the cake. Many stories and laughs were shared but an even greater blessing was standing among Natalie and John's closest friends and family witnessing their bond in holy matrimony.

As if the thrill of the wedding and camaraderie of my friends weren't enough, South Africa had one more surprise up its sleeve before I returned home. The morning after the wedding I woke to beautiful blue skies. I had a long drive back to Johannesburg, but I felt a little lazy upon waking up. Instead of a peaceful morning of packing up and saying my good-byes, an unexpected visitor stopped by my thatch-roofed chalet.

Resting in my bed looking out the patio door at the mountain landscape my peace of mind became distracted. I heard a strange rustling coming from what sounded like the bathroom. As I rounded the corner of the armoire separating the bedroom from the kitchenette area, I jumped back as my eyes locked onto the sight of a full-grown male baboon heading my way from the bathroom!

Luckily for me, the sight of the tall white guy standing in nothing but boxers was just as frightening for him. I spontaneously pointed my finger and yelled, "Hey, get out of here you son-of-a-bitch!" It wasn't the kindest greeting or the most poetic I know, but given my mouth hadn't had the time to register what my eyes clearly saw, the words could have been worse. As if standing on a miniature top, he spun around and with one enormous jump launched himself onto the toilet and out through the small bathroom window he had gained his unsolicited entry.

As I listened to his shrill bark of frustration on top of the chalet, I gained my composure to contemplate what just happened. After all, having a baboon come walking out of the bathroom isn't something I see every day in Wisconsin. I finished packing and made my way up to the main building to share my morning's surprise with Natalie, John, and the others.

It turns out that the day before, while getting her hair ready for the ceremony, Natalie and her bridesmaids had a similar encounter. Whether the same baboon or not, he got into Natalie's chalet the same way. But before they could chase him out he managed to grab a bag of potato chips from the kitchen counter. After trading baboon stories Natalie calmly said, "Welcome to South Africa."

South Africa was welcoming indeed, and I could not have been happier to be reunited with my Everest teammates. I was also grateful to have met their extended family and closest friends. The wedding was moving, and I am thankful each day to have witnessed the start of Natalie and John's new life together. With farewells complete, it was time to return home to make the final preparations for the return trip to Nepal.

At Cathedral Peak in South Africa with John Black,
Robby Kojetin and Gilad Stern.
Photograph by Natalie Black.

Chapter Fourteen

Yakety Yak Heading Back

The efforts of April 2009 to promote the health and well-being of the yaks and naks yielded results better than I expected. Less than two months after returning home, I received a promising email from Russell. Phurba Tashi's sister had made an astute observation. She noted that the naks we had dewormed at base camp were starting to produce more milk. Given the fact there is no automation in terms of milking or even how much milk is produced on a daily basis, I was thrilled to learn she could visibly see the difference.

The wheels in my head started turning almost immediately. Why not go back and work with more yaks and naks? With Russell's assistance, a new humanitarian project called *Healthy Yak* was set in motion through the Friends of Humanity (FOH) foundation he co-founded years earlier.

It would take a year and a half for me to save up my own money, collect donations in the FOH kitty, and line up additional cattle dewormer before a return trip to the Khumbu could take place. The logistics for the return were sorted out by Russell and Himex's sister company Mountain Experience Pvt. Ltd. based in Kathmandu. Two hard working gentlemen oversee the day-to-day operation of Mountain Experience, Chhuldim Temba Sherpa, and Tamding Sherpa.

I met both back in 2009 and was immediately impressed by their loyalty to Russell and to the clients. Even though they live in Kathmandu, both originated from the Khumbu near Namche Bazaar. In fact, Chhuldim is a two-time Everest summiteer with one of those successful visits while working for Himex. I knew the day-to-day planning for the yak project would be in good hands with them.

While I fell a little short of my fundraising goal, the FOH funds helped to see the project move forward in 2011. During the 2010 Everest climbing season I found out that some of the Sherpa had been asking, "Where is the yak doctor?" I wasn't going to let a shortage of funds let them down in 2011.

Thanks to several of my veterinary colleagues, I would have help in the project's inaugural year. Dr. Andrew Skidmore, a veterinarian from New York State and someone I have known for years in the dairy industry, asked if he could come along. He had a strong desire to help a people he had never met, while trekking amongst some of the largest mountains in the world.

The same is true of Dr. Claire Windeyer, a veterinarian from Canada who had also heard about the yak project. She was already going to be in Nepal working in the valley around Kathmandu through Canada's Veterinarians without Borders (VMB) program. VMB, based in other countries as well, is a charitable organization that sends veterinarians to remote and less fortunate parts of the world to promote animal health and well-being. Having only met her once at an industry meeting in 2010, Claire graciously extended her stay in Nepal to participate in the yak project.

Dr. Kristen Obbink rounded out the team. I first met Kristen in early 2010 while speaking at her alma mater, Iowa State University School of Veterinary Medicine. As a third-year veterinary student at the time, she was intrigued by my idea of going back to Nepal. With some of her professional interests lying in veterinary public health, she offered her time and assistance in the project. Our foursome was complete.

In early April 2011, we converged upon the glow of Kathmandu. It felt almost surreal being back in this bustling city. With a day and a half to enjoy the warmth and relaxation of the valley, we headed down to the Thamel district. Amidst dodging cars, rickshaws, and the masses of people, I made it a point to make two specific stops.

A return visit to the Rum Doodle Restaurant was in order. Instead of simply looking at the numerous yeti footprints of

Everest summiteers on the wall and ceiling, I presented my Everest climbing certificate from the Nepal government. In exchange I was given my own footprint to decorate and an official Everest Summiteers club card. Even more special is the fact that the restaurant custodian placed my footprint just steps away from the signatures of Sir Edmund Hillary, Ed Viesturs, and many other famous mountaineers.

The second stop was to YAQOOT, specifically to see the owner. I wasn't sure if Mansukh would be around, let alone remember me. Two years earlier he gave me that inspirational handwritten note which I carried to Everest, along with the good luck stone necklace I purchased for my wife. As I stepped over the store's threshold he called out, "My Everest brother!" I think Claire, Kristen, and Andrew were just as surprised as me.

He then went on to recite the handwritten note I had carried to Everest. It was icing on the cake for our reunion. With formal introductions in place we sat down to enjoy a cup of tea, graciously offered by our host. Mansukh was pleased to learn that we had come to help the Nepali people and their animals. Before heading back to the hotel, Mansukh grabbed his pen and paper one more time: *Life is like pleasure, greet it with a smile. Friendship is like treasure, keep it all the while.*

April 7, 2011. With an early start the next day, we headed to the airport for our flight to Lukla. Well before round two in Nepal started, my colleagues and I discussed the merits, or shall I say lack thereof, flying on a turboprop plane into one of the most dangerous airports in the world.

Digging into the wallet a bit deeper, my colleagues and I decided an upgrade was warranted. With the increasingly poor safety record on the props, Russell had proposed the use of helicopters months before arriving in Kathmandu. Rather than another jaw-dropping hundred mile per hour landing on the steeply pitched pavement, our chopper set down on the stone helicopter pad like a bee gracing the top of a flower's pedestal.

With feet firmly planted on the ground, we were immediately greeted by Ram Chandra Sunuwar, our Mountain Experience trekking guide. His short stature was immediately shadowed by his warm smile and happy spirit. Although home for him is Kathmandu, I found out Ram has climbed to Everest's South Col, as well as high on its north side as well. Alongside making a living as a trekking and climbing guide, it turns out he is a farmer too.

Ram's sidekick for our adventure was sixteen-year-old Nima Rita Sherpa. Initially quiet and reserved, Nima's strong work ethic and underlying interest in what we came to do for his culture opened the door to his exuberant personality. While visiting his family's home in the village of Pheriche, we learned that his father is one of Russell's climbing Sherpas. In fact, he was on the 2009 expedition as Ellen Miller's Sherpa on Lhotse. The picture of the two of them on the wall helped to facilitate fond memories.

With input from Phurba Tashi, Russell arranged for our nine to ten-day trek towards Everest base camp, along the way conducting several strategic yak clinics. Khumjung, home to Phurba and numerous other Sherpas, would provide the backdrop for our first clinic but not before an overnight stay in Namche Bazaar. As part of the standard acclimatization process, this miniature New York City of the Khumbu gave our veterinary team a chance to catch up on email, buy some souvenirs, and of course enjoy the incredible bakery at just over 11,000 feet above sea level.

I was pleased to find the same shop owner next to the Everest Bakery, tending his goods as if time had stood still. As you may recall, he was the one who helped fix the good luck bead necklace my daughter had made for me two years earlier. He had also graced me with a silk *khata* that I carried to the mountain.

On the trek out I placed it around his neck, in hopes of returning some of the goodwill it had surrounded me with while climbing Everest. Similar to Mansukh, I was amazed by his immediate recognition of me. With a smile on his face, he turned around and pointed at the back wall of his shop. As if I hadn't been surprised enough, there on the wall hung the *khata*.

Goodwill was replaced by irony as I asked him to fix another necklace. This time it was the string on one of the yak bone necklaces I had bought from him in 2009. After giving my son Jordan the one I wore to the summit, I ended up wearing out the string on the second one. Despite trying to fix it several times on my own, déjà vu brought me back here for his kind assistance once again.

The next day we trekked up and over the hill into Khumjung, along the way stopping at the Everest View Hotel for a hot tea. This time Everest did not hide behind the clouds but rather winked at me as if to say, "Good to see you again." Seeing both its beauty and magnitude reminded me once again how fortunate I was to have reached the top.

Shortly after arriving at Phurba Tashi's Friendship Lodge, I was reunited with Phurba's wife, their youngest daughter, and twin boys. All three had grown so much since I last saw them. Even though I didn't have the Nerf football along this time, the kids started playing a mock game of cricket. Soon, the entire veterinary team engaged in the breathtaking activity just outside the lodge.

After our fun, it was time to work. Phurba was already at base camp, so Ram called him on the cell phone. In 2009 cell phones were present but reception high in the valley was spotty at best. Since then a cell tower went up near Gorak Shep, allowing for more consistent communication all the way to the foot of Everest. It was sort of weird yet wonderful to talk to Phurba on the phone.

Phurba had been instrumental in working with the porters to have the dewormer strategically cached in several villages. I discussed with him where exactly the product was and how much had been left at each location so our team had an idea of how many yaks and naks we could treat at any one spot. By default, the number of naks would be greater down low as a lot of the male yaks were currently ferrying gear for the climbing season higher in the valley.

Phurba also arranged for an extra pair of hands to help with the yak project. Bhesh Bahadur Ghimire, the government's local agricultural and veterinary technician would be joining us during the rest of the trek up the valley. Bhesh lives just over the hill above Khumjung at a yak herding station. During the process of deworming the young yaks there, we taught Bhesh how to administer the product, something that proved to be invaluable for the rest of our trip.

*In Khumjung with (L to R) Dr. Claire Windeyer, Bhesh Ghimire, Dr.
Andrew Skidmore, and Dr. Kristen Obbink.
Photograph by Ram Sunuwar.*

Both Bhesh and young Nima took an immediate interest
in what we had come to do. I give them the largest chunk of
credit for the success we had while on the ground in the
Khumbu. In fact, during our last clinic in the village of
Pheriche my colleagues and I were able to set up a miniature
laboratory while Bhesh and Nima worked hard to treat a small
pen of over forty naks and a handful of yaks. Why the
laboratory? With the favorable response from the effort in 2009
I knew the yaks obviously harbored internal parasites, not
dissimilar to domesticated cattle around the world.

During this trip, documenting such parasitism would help
not only satisfy my curiosity but also support a reason for the
need to administer such products. One of my veterinary school
instructors, Dr. Garrett Oetzel, was kind enough to loan the
project a set of field parasitology microscopes that worked via
watch batteries. You are probably wondering what the purpose
of the microscopes was. Let's just say that in order for your
veterinarian to properly diagnose gastrointestinal (GI)
parasites, whether we are talking your pooch, your kitty, or

your barn critters, he or she utilizes a small amount of stool sample to do so.

You see, the life cycle of most GI parasites calls for their offspring, known as eggs to be passed into the environment by way of the animal's feces, only to be consumed by the next unwary victim that perpetuates the disease cycle from host to host. These eggs are microscopic, too small to be seen by the unaided eye. I am glad we brought the laboratory supplies along because we did identify a wide variety of parasites. Although it was a single snapshot in time, documenting such parasitism did satisfy my curiosity but more importantly validated the reason for launching the Healthy Yak campaign.

Working with the animals provided a deep sense of satisfaction for the veterinary team. A bonus, of course, was to be able to trek in a beautiful part of a country that hosts a large portion of the world's tallest mountains. Additionally, for me the icing on the cake for this return trip to the Khumbu was being reunited with several of my 2009 teammates, and a large portion of the Himalayan Experience staff.

Nine days after disembarking from the helicopter in Lukla, we approached Himex Everest base camp. Moments from camp itself I spotted Thomas, my Norwegian teammate from two years ago. He was heading back down the valley for the first of two acclimatization climbs on Lobuche. Wearing a big smile, he appeared eager for the challenge ahead. With a hug and a quick photo I wished him well for a safe and prosperous climb.

Knowing that all of the climbers were following suit, I wanted badly to see Jim Holliday, aka Big Hot Gouda. After careful consideration and commitment, he had come back to give Everest a second try. His goal was the same as in 2009, to get his late mother's picture to the top of the world.

Just meters outside of base camp I spotted those characteristic hat flaps protecting his ears. I yelled out, "Is that a Big Hot Gouda I see?" It was almost surreal, as if time had stood still since 2009. Yet Jim looked even more fit and with an elevated level of confidence. Although I had seen Jim since our time here together, not to mention kept in constant touch with him by phone, being able to put my arm around his shoulder to wish him God's speed was a blessing.

A few weeks before his return here I had mailed to him two wristbands. Blue with the white embossed phrase No Place but UP!, both would be with him throughout the adventure. One of the first things Jim did when he saw me was roll up his sleeve to show the bands off, proudly on display around his right wrist. I had asked him if he wouldn't mind taking one to the top for me while wearing the other as a positive daily reminder. I also sent along with him a copy of the story *The Little Engine That Could*. I wanted Jim to have a small part of me along on the journey beyond spirit, as well as some light, inspirational reading when times seemed tough.

I knew we couldn't visit long, so before he continued down the valley, I reached inside my pack to hand him one more item to carry. No, I didn't want to weigh him down, but this particular item had special meaning. Like my mother, Jim is a devout Catholic; she sent along for him a small St. Christopher medal to keep him safe while traveling up the flanks of the highest mountain in the world. I could see by the look in his eyes that Jim was touched by the gesture.

What I didn't show him was his small birthday gift. I knew his special day was coming up in about three weeks, so I left for him at base camp a bottle of Tabasco, some electrolyte tablets, and a card. I knew he would get a laugh out of the hot sauce, given his desire to put the stuff on just about everything he ate.

It was emotional seeing Jim as I could feel the positive energy around him and knew that, if the weather was right and the mountain was in a good mood, the next time I would see him would be as a fellow Everest summiteer. I hugged him, told him to be safe, to be confident, and that I loved him. With that he continued down the valley towards Lobuche. With emotions running high I turned towards the Himex tents.

As I weaved my way around the Sherpa and dining tents, the layout of camp much different than two years ago, I stumbled upon Russell in his communications tent. With a bit of a fun-loving expletive which I dare not repeat here, he looked up from his chair and asked, "What the [blank] are you doing here?"

With a firm handshake I sat down to visit with the man who not only helped make my dream come true but who now, once again, was donating his time and expertise to help my new vision become a success. Russell was quite busy readying some equipment for the Sherpas to ferry up the mountain early the next morning. We were scheduled to stay in base camp for only one night, so I was looking forward to catching up with him later that day. I excused myself to find David Tait before he too departed for acclimatization on Lobuche.

In the process of packing a few last items, I found him as he was zipping up his tent's vestibule door. Before he could turn around I yelled out, "See any yaks around here, mate?" After some small talk we headed down to the dining tent for a quick bite to eat. Head cook Tashi was back and just like 2009, organized a scrumptious meal.

After lunch I made my way around camp to visit with the base camp staff and Sherpas. Similar to Russell, Phurba was busy as ever overseeing the Sherpas' loads to be carried up the mountain. Still, he took the time to visit, curious about one of his yaks that we had examined two days ago. The female nak had been attacked by a snow leopard weeks ago. With injuries to the side of her face Phurba was concerned about the animal's vision.

Bhesh had actually already done a great job treating the animal's wounds, so by the time we looked at her there wasn't much we could do. Although her vision was altered in one eye, the lacerations inflicted during the attack were healing nicely. Several times Phurba thanked me for coming back to help the valley's animals. His gratitude provided such positive reinforcement for having come back to Nepal.

One by one the Sherpas left camp to ferry their loads. I recognized a number of them although I couldn't remember their names. One particular individual stood out and in fact, the moment he saw me he called out my name. It was Tashi Tshering Sherpa, my summit Sherpa! With slightly longer hair, he bore the look of a matured Everest climber. He seemed to have come out of his shell, taking the time to visit and have his photo taken with me, this time with a smile.

Back guiding for Russell was Adrian, Woody, and Shinji. Narly was responsible for overseeing the Lhotse climbing this year for Russell, all of whom were not set to arrive in base camp for well over a week yet. My hope was to run into him, along with Billi Bierling and Chris Jones somewhere on the trek out. Both had come back in hope of adding the fourth-highest mountain to their climbing curriculum vitae.

Dr. Monica was busy running back and forth between Himex base camp and traditional base camp, assisting with the last minute treatment of various patients before heading down to Lobuche base camp herself. I was able to catch up with her later, once again her medical expertise coming to my assistance. My cold-air induced asthma had started acting up over the past few days, my meds not quite keeping it under control. Two years ago it was a minor annoyance and never gave me grief high on the mountain. With a couple different inhalers from her I eased back into a more comfortable visit with my friends.

It was a pleasure visiting with all of them, albeit briefly. Although Dean Staples was not back with Himex I had received an email from him weeks earlier stating that he could be found with the Adventure Consultants expedition up at traditional base camp. After bidding the rest of the Himex team a safe training climb, I headed up the trail to find Deano.

Once again, I got lucky. After seeking permission to enter the AC base camp area and interrogating several team members as to his whereabouts, I heard the familiar Kiwi voice calling out my name. Just like Shaun Hutson, Deano had been on the summit at the same time as me. Although with a different outfit, Deano was actually back privately guiding a single climber up the mountain. Out of respect for his time, I stayed for just a few minutes before heading back down to the Himex area.

That night over yet another outstanding meal, the Healthy Yak team got a chance to visit with Russell. With a very quiet base camp, I enjoyed listening to Russell speak about the mountain, this year's team and life itself. Before retiring, knowing that I would once again walk away from Everest base camp not knowing when I would be back, I presented Russell a small token, or rather "wedge" of appreciation.

When I first walked into camp that day Russell jokingly stated he hoped I hadn't brought my cheese wedge along again. The highest cheese wedge in the world remained back in Wisconsin, yet I didn't come empty-handed. As dinner ended I thanked him for all he had done for me two years ago but also for his effort with the logistics of this year's project. I then reached into my coat pocket to pull out a key chain. It wasn't just any key chain, but one in the form of a miniature golden cheddar wedge attached to a carabiner. He graciously accepted my gift saying he would have to put the key to base camp on it.

The next morning Tashi and the cook staff got up early to make us one of my favorite breakfast meals from two years ago: eggs, bacon, and toast. With final pleasantries exchanged with Russell and the remaining base camp staff, it was time to start our trek back down the valley. Somehow I knew it wouldn't be the last time I would see Russell Brice.

We timed our departure to arrive back at Lobuche base camp in order to refuel over lunch before continuing the descent down to Pheriche, where we had plans for our final yak clinic the next day. As we neared camp, I saw another familiar face. It was Ellen Miller! I knew she was back in the valley leading trekkers up to Everest base camp, yet I didn't know for sure if our paths would cross.

From a distance I yelled out, "Is that Team Didi I see!" With a bright smile and a mock British accent she responded "Lance!" David Tait stepped out of a nearby dining tent too, his acclimatization schedule slightly different than the rest of the team who were now well on their way up Lobuche. Over lunch we shared a number of laughs as we reminisced over our time together here twenty-four months earlier.

With packs back on, I gave Ellen another hug and wished her the best. I shook David's hand one more time, asking him to be safe and wishing him a prosperous climb up Everest. With that Ram guided the veterinary team down towards Pheriche. The next morning we conducted our last clinic under a beautiful blue sky, the holy peak Ama Dablam watching over us.

On the trek up the hill towards Namche Bazaar, I looked up in between breaths to see Billi coming down the trail. Similar to greeting Ellen, I shouted out "Team Didi!" Billi had her MP3 player going yet heard the calling. I introduced her to the veterinary team as we caught up on life in the few minutes we had. She informed me she was ahead of the rest of the Lhotse team by a few days. As a writer on the side, Billi was also busy blogging for Himex this year, so I told her I would be checking the posts on a regular basis when I got back home. Crossing paths on the final summit ridge two years ago, only to be reunited in the trees of the lower Khumbu was definitely surreal. I hugged her and wished her success for a safe climb on Lhotse.

Back at Namche, Ram turned the guiding of our team over to Lakchu, Russell's Everest base camp manager and someone who always had a smile on back in 2009. This time was no different. Although all of us were sad to lose Ram, his job now required him to guide a trekker up Island Peak, having Lakchu's familiar laugh was a blessing. Coming down from Himex base camp, he was also going to lead the Lhotse climbing team back up the valley, their scheduled arrival into Lukla via helicopter the same day as our departure back to Kathmandu.

Two days later and another beautiful morning in the Himalayas, our helicopter approached the airport. Fate was once again at hand as both Narly and Chris Jones disembarked, ready for their adventure to Lhotse. With rotors off, we posed for a quick picture. It was a short yet sweet reunion as the pilot called for us to load up for the ride back to Kathmandu. The gentle lift off the helipad paled in excitement compared to the slingshot launch of the plane two years prior.

With a day to regroup and repack back at the hotel in KTM, déjà vu struck. During the overnight hours in advance of my flight home, the Lukla Pukla dance made an ugly return! Apparently Nepal did not want me to avoid a perfect gastrointestinal batting average. With a reminiscent gurgle in my stomach I said good-bye to my friends, thanking them for all their efforts.

Because of my colleagues' generous help, the enthusiasm and work ethic of Bhesh and Nima, Ram's guidance, our porters' strong backs, and the planning done by Russell, Phurba, Chhuldim, and Tamding, the inaugural year of the project was a success. We treated almost a thousand yaks and naks, close to two-dozen ponies, and a handful of canine companions in numerous Sherpa villages. The Sherpa people had been very welcoming and appreciative of our efforts.

I departed the country knowing that the remaining product strategically left behind in the villages would be in good hands with Bhesh. He offered to take charge of administering not only an initial dose to new patients as they arrived back down in the villages after weeks of portering high up in the mountain valleys, but was also excited about providing a follow-up dose to all of the animals we treated. At least 2,000 more doses of the dewormer were at his disposal.

As the plane sped down the runway, my stomach's churning started to ease, replaced by that of another type of tingling sensation. It was that of an overwhelming level of satisfaction settling deep within. The Sherpa people will never know the profound influence they have on my life. With nothing but air between the plane and the ground below, I gazed out the window wondering not if, but when I would revisit the highest mountains in the world. For now, all I could do was hope that the efforts of the past few weeks would set in motion a much larger and longer cascade of events to help promote the well-being of the animals, and the livelihood of a people, all nestled deep in the mighty Himalaya Mountains.

Afterword

Days, weeks, months, and even years have now passed since May 21, 2009 but the excitement of the Everest journey and life afterwards has not. While some things in life have changed dramatically, others have stayed the same. My children grow like weeds and amaze me every day. Jordan has made strides fighting his gastrointestinal condition, starting to come out of the shell that formed a thick circle of confinement around him.

Bailee has become an accomplished equestrian rider and continues her adventurous spirit. I am very blessed to have both of them in my life. Katherine continues her work as an equine veterinarian and has also resurrected her prior life of riding horses competitively. It's great that she and Bailee can share such a passion together.

I am excited to report that Jim Holliday made it to Everest's summit on May 20, 2011. He fulfilled his quest to leave a picture of his late mother while there. In the process he also wore the No Place but UP! wristbands I gave him, all the way to the top. Shortly after returning to the US, he mailed one back to me, which I now proudly display, every day.

Billi Bierling went on to become one of just a handful of women in the world to summit Lhotse. To say Ellen and her are my two illustrious Didi sisters would be an enormous understatement. I am humbled to have them in my life, not to mention having been able to climb side-by-side on the flanks of the world's highest peak.

Alec Turner was kind enough to mount a rock from the top of Everest onto Alaskan jade, hand carving into it my name and the date of my summit. He also polished two smaller stones from the top of the world, both of which I had made into tie and lapel pins. With Denali (Mount McKinley) sitting in his backyard, a peak that is as intriguing to me as Everest, we have talked about the possibility of climbing it together someday. In fact, the ever-present communication amongst Everest teammates has revealed a number of them who have expressed an interest in reuniting on North America's highest peak.

Megan Delehanty took over the management and resurrection of www.foxeverest.com, giving it a new and improved look. Aside from hosting several websites including her own (www.hitopimages.com) and keeping busy with her regular day job, she has gone on to become a member of the 7 Summits Club. In June of 2011, John Black stood on top of Mount McKinley, alongside Alec. At the time of this book's publication, one peak remained for him to join the ranks of Megan.

My buddy Moises Nava (aka Moses) of Mexico did accomplish this task. Robby is closing in on joining the elite club while also becoming a sought after motivational speaker (www.robby.co.za) and sponsored athlete. Only a handful of South Africans have summited Everest, and I am proud to call two of them my friends. Everest is indeed more than a mountain. It has created impenetrable bonds between friends that will last a lifetime.

I have been asked repeatedly if I will ever attempt Everest again. The short answer is no. The long answer is that I am content in that I fulfilled a dream and have no desire to put not only myself, but more importantly my family, through such a lengthy excursion again. Luck, health, good fortune, and the mountain were all on my side, not to mention the incredible team of friends under the Himalayan Experience umbrella.

I wish I could have retained Jon Hansen's friendship beyond Everest. Although I am disappointed, the loss has been replaced by having gained so many irreplaceable friends. The mountain's summit may have been the pinnacle of the trip, yet it was laughing, crying, agonizing, and celebrating with such wonderful people that really made the journey a success.

Following the 2011 Healthy Yak project, I have received multiple updates from Bhesh Ghimire, the agricultural technician near Khumjung. The yaks and naks continue to respond favorably to the deworming. My hope is to create a non-profit organization to be able to continue returning to the land of the Sherpa people to oversee the project's growth and success. There are many yaks and naks, along with horses, donkeys, and dogs that will benefit from our efforts, not to mention the Sherpa people as well.

Not long before the completion of this book, Alpharma was sold to another company, a trend not confined to the pharmaceutical industry in this ever-changing world of business. While the name no longer exists on paper, it will be forever etched in history as the company that supported the "Quest for Success," standing by me every step of the way not only to the mountain, but also up it, all the way to its top.

During the editorial process of this book the Green Bay Packers accepted my offer to enshrine within their hall of fame & museum the cheese wedge hat I carried to the top of the world. Plans have been set in motion for its display for all to see.

I have spoken in front of thousands of people in various venues, young to old, small to large, and will continue to do so. Through amazing photos and videos, I not only share what it was like to get to the top of the world, but also challenge my audience members to believe in their visions, to rise up in the face of adversity, and to live life to its fullest potential.

Simply put, I hope to inspire people to find the Everest within. Accomplishing one's goals may not always be easy. Challenges may seem insurmountable. If you truly believe, you can achieve. Just remember, there is No Place but UP!

Acknowledgements

In closing, I would again like to thank my mother for always believing in and supporting me; Ryan, for your heroism and sibling love; Katherine, for your understanding, support, love, and for the greatest gift of all: nurturing our children. Bailee and Jordan, I would not have had the courage to follow my dream. You were and always will be my inspiration. Barry, you've always stood by me, and for this I love you, brother. And, lastly, I am indebted to Russell Brice for helping me fulfill a dream and my Everest teammates, for their "top of the world" camaraderie.

Additional thanks to the following for offering valuable feedback on the manuscript: John McMonagle, Dr. Kristen Obbink, Bob Powers, Megan Delehanty, and Melissa West.

Special thanks to the contributors of the 2011 Healthy Yak project: John McMonagle, Antoine Boulanger, Lincoln High School, Charles City High School, Bob and Barb Fox, Chris Giese Family, Linda and Doug Meddaugh, Jim Holliday, Megan Delehanty, East DePere High School, Friends of Wautoma Library, Karen and Ira Giese, Land O' Lakes Animal Milk Products, Manawa School District, Mosquito Hill Nature Center, Hortonville Middle School, Jim Aron Family, Wildcat Booster Club, Mike Turba, Maritza Morales, Dr. Julie Gard, Eugène Constant, Bloomer Assembly of God, Travis Thomas, Paula Meyer, Southwest Rotary Oshkosh, Jennifer and Michael Bender, Bobbi Cunningham-Ortiz and Michael Ortiz, Karen and Ned Isaacson, Amy Van Ess, Professional Business Women of Plymouth, Marite Flodrops, Mr. and Mrs. Soland, Jay Bartel, Minnesota Milk Producers Association, Ann McDonald Family, LaGrange Fire and Rescue, Jenny and Ryan Fox Family, Ryan Dunn and Family, Hortonville Elementary School, Coloma PTO,

Dr. Andrew Skidmore, Dr. Claire Windeyer, Dr. Kristin Obbink, Bhesh Bahadur Ghimire, Nima Rita Sherpa, Ram Chandra Sunuwar, Russell Brice, Phurba Tashi Sherpa, Tamding Sherpa, Chhuldim Temba Sherpa, Intervet/Schering Plough Animal Health, and Dr. Garrett Oetzel.

Thank you to Pfizer Animal Health and Dr. Jim Metz of Animart for your 2012 donations of veterinary goods as well as Tim and Donna Prior for the financial contribution towards the future success of the Khumbu animal project. To see a complete list of current donors following the publication of this book, please visit my website at www.foxeverest.com.

23513811R00155

Made in the USA
Lexington, KY
15 June 2013